I'll Tell You Mine

I'll Tell You Mine

THIRTY YEARS OF
ESSAYS FROM
THE IOWA NONFICTION
WRITING PROGRAM

Edited by Hope Edelman and Robin Hemley
Prologue by Robert Atwan

THE UNIVERSITY OF CHICAGO PRESS
CHICAGO AND LONDON

HOPE EDELMAN is best known for her internationally best-selling book *Motherless Daughters*, which has been followed by two revised editions and two sequels, and her memoir *The Possibliity of Everything*. She teaches nonfiction writing at Antioch University in Los Angeles and returns every summer to teach in the Iowa Summer Writing Festival.

ROBIN HEMLEY is writer-in-residence and director of the writing program at Yale-NUS College in Singapore. He served as director of Iowa's Nonfiction Writing Program from 2004 to 2013. He has won many awards for his writing, including the Guggenheim and three Pushcart Prizes, and has published eleven books of prose.

The University of Chicago Press, Chicago 60637
The University of Chicago Press, Ltd., London
© 2015 by Hope Edelman and Robin Hemley
All rights reserved. Published 2015.

Printed in the United States of America

24 23 22 21 20 19 18 17 16 15   1 2 3 4 5

ISBN-13: 978-0-226-30633-9 (cloth)
ISBN-13: 978-0-226-30647-6 (paper)
ISBN-13: 978-0-226-30650-6 (e-book)
DOI: 10.7208/chicago/9780226306506.001.0001

Library of Congress Cataloging-in-Publication Data
I'll tell you mine : thirty years of essays from the Iowa Nonfiction Writing Program / edited by Hope Edelman and Robin Hemley ; prologue by Robert Atwan.
     pages ; cm
Collection of stories by graduates of the University of Iowa Nonfiction Writing Program.
ISBN 978-0-226-30633-9 (cloth : alk. paper)—ISBN 978-0-226-30647-6 (pbk. : alk. paper)—ISBN 978-0-226-30650-6 (ebook) 1. Creative nonfiction, American—20th century. 2. Creative nonfiction, American—21st century. 3. University of Iowa. Nonfiction Writing Program. I. Edelman, Hope, editor. II. Hemley, Robin, 1958– editor. III. Atwan, Robert, writer of introduction.
     PS688.145 2015
     814'.5408—dc23   2015017770

♾ This paper meets the requirements of ANSI/NISO Z39.48–1992 (Permanence of Paper).

*To the members of the University of Iowa's Expository
Writing Committee, whose vision in 1976 of what could be
became the Nonfiction Writing Program that exists today.*

Carol de Saint Victor
Paul Diehl
David Hamilton
Carl Klaus
Richard Lloyd-Jones
Susan Lohafer

"We must acquiesce to our experience and our gift to transform experience into meaning. You tell me your story, I'll tell you mine."

PATRICIA HAMPL, *I Could Tell You Stories*

Contents

Contents

(Chronological)

Introduction

Choosing essays for a collection such as this felt at times like composing a symphony. It began with an overall sense of emotion to convey, followed by the selection of individual components, and then the development of variations and themes. If we think of this collection as a literary orchestration, we were fortunate to work with a group of such skilled performers. The writers in this anthology are all highly adept practitioners of nonfiction, their essays the products of intensive (and in some cases, years of) crafting and thought.

Their works are even more remarkable when we consider that all of these pieces were conceived and begun while the authors were in graduate school. Specifically, they were all students in the same program, the Nonfiction Writing Program at the University of Iowa, at different points throughout the past thirty years. From Tom Montgomery Fate's "The Rain Makes the Roof Sing," written in the mid-1980s, to "The Last Days of the Baldock" by 2013 graduate Inara Verzemnieks, the works in this collection showcase the type of fine writing that can be produced in graduate nonfiction programs where students have the chance to immerse themselves in craft and study for two or three consecutive years with a community of like-minded peers. They also illustrate the practical and philosophical issues these writers engaged with to bring their essays to final-draft stage. And they reflect how the craft of nonfiction itself has evolved over the past three decades.

Most readers have heard of the Iowa Writers' Workshop, the eighty-year-old icon of fiction and poetry instruction. What many don't know is that the University of Iowa has a separate Nonfiction Writing Program, familiarly known as the NWP. It's the nation's oldest freestanding program devoted exclusively to the study and craft of nonfiction, a highly selective program that admits only about a dozen students per year.

The NWP, which consistently takes the number one spot among nonfiction MFA programs in the United States in *Poets and Writers*'s annual rankings, is a much younger program than the Writers' Workshop, which dates back to 1936. As Robert Atwan—founding editor of *The Best American Essays* series—notes in his prologue to this collection, nonfiction writing did not begin to gain literary prominence as a genre until the mid- to late 1960s. The popularity of college courses in the study and writing of nonfiction followed soon after.

A group of six English professors at the University of Iowa were particularly attuned to this shift, and founded the Iowa nonfiction program in 1976. Initially it was designed as an all-purpose expository writing program that students could shape to suit their individual professional needs. Some who received the early "Master of Arts in English/Expository Writing" degree, or MA/W, focused on literary criticism, others on personal essays; some wrote film reviews, and others created short works of memoir. Very little of the writing from this era saw publication, mainly because so few outlets published nonfiction at the time.

This changed in 1985, when Professor Carl Klaus assumed the role of director and transformed the program into an MA with an exclusive focus on literary nonfiction. Students studied the essay from a historical approach, reading Montaigne and Swift, Didion and Orwell, Nancy Mairs and E. B. White. They learned to write probing nonfiction and also to read, analyze, and teach the work of its pioneers.

Students during those early years produced mainly personal narratives grounded in the type of reflective, meditative prose that became the hallmark of the Iowa program. Klaus admired essays that revealed "the mind on paper," and many of his students aspired to achieve that sensibility in their own work. This is particularly evident in the earliest pieces in this collection, such as George Yatchisin's mid-1980s essay "Desperate for the Story," which, through a series of twenty "essayettes," seeks to capture a creative mind in flight.

The 1990s marked an explosive period for writing, publishing, and selling memoirs, as well as for publications devoted to nonfiction narratives. By the end of the 1990s, three journals had launched with an exclusive focus on high-quality nonfiction prose, *Creative Nonfiction* (1993), *Fourth Genre* (1999), and *River Teeth* (1999). The 1990s also saw a sharp upswing of interest in experimental forms of nonfiction. The lyric essay came to prominence at this time, led in large part by the work of John D'Agata, who graduated from the NWP in 1998, four years after the program began granting the terminal MFA degree. His essay "Round Trip" offers a mosaic of personal observations, interview transcripts, excerpts from original documents, and lists that abandon straightforward, linear narration in favor of a disjointed, associative, and collage-like form infused with beautifully lyrical prose.

When Robin Hemley took over as director of the NWP in 2004, he began expanding the program into one of international prominence. He founded the NonfictioNOW conference, a biennial gathering of 400 writers of nonfiction from around the world, and also created the Overseas Writing Workshop, which brought students in the program to such countries as Cuba, the Philippines, Greece, Croatia, Australia, and Hong Kong. These efforts helped attract talented students to the program, as did the hiring of new faculty, such as D'Agata (now the NWP's director) and Stephen Kuusisto. D'Agata, in turn, brought many prominent writers to the program through a reading series he curated, and a number of well-known visiting nonfiction writers have taught in Iowa City for a term, including Geoff Dyer, Mary Ruefle, Lia Purpura, and Bernard Cooper.

The idea for this anthology dates back to the summer of 2006, when Robin and Hope Edelman met for coffee in Iowa City and began discussing how much had changed—and yet how much remained the same—in the nonfiction arena since Hope's time as a student in the NWP in the early 1990s and Robin's tenure as its director, which ended in 2013. What would an overview of the past thirty years of literary nonfiction look like, we wondered, if we charted it through writing produced by students in a single program?

Starting with the first handfuls of MA/W theses from the late 1970s and working our way up to the most recent years, we paged through the bound, green volumes in the University of Iowa's Main Library, looking for representative and exemplary pieces by graduates from each decade. We also solicited work from dozens of alumni. The only criterion for submission was for the work to have been started while the writer was a student in the program. Started, but not necessarily finished, since very often a piece begun in a graduate program can take years to mature to publication quality. Graduate writing programs are, above all, places where young writers come to learn their craft, and bringing a piece to completion typically involves multiple revisions and even several total rehauls along the way.

To convey the intricacies of this process and enhance the usefulness of the collection for aspiring writers and instructors of writing, we asked the eighteen authors ultimately selected to contribute short addenda to their essays that explained a specific craft issue they'd grappled with while writing their pieces and how they'd resolved the problem to bring the essay to final-draft stage. Faith Adiele, for example, writes about how she structured her essay "Black Men," which introduces readers to the large cast of tragic, Finnish male ancestors who shaped her biracial identity. John T. Price writes about why it took more than a decade for him to understand the deeper meaning of "High Maintenance," an essay he began in Klaus's graduate nonfiction workshop in 1990 and published in *Orion* in 2006.

Price explains how an early draft of an essay sometimes must wait for additional life experiences to accrue before the work can achieve its thematic potential. While this is certainly one way an essay ripens, other writers in this collection share different methods for bringing their works to fruition. Ashley Butler, for example, explains how her quest to capture the bodily nature of loss and absence in "Anechoic" included time spent in the University of Iowa Medical and Music Libraries, a sensory deprivation chamber at the university Speech and Hearing Center, and flotation tanks in downtown Chicago, as well as a journey deep into the history of Harry Houdini's life. Similarly, Elena Passarello writes about finding the "entry point" to her portrait of Judy Garland through her research into the architecture of Carnegie Hall. As these writers' process pieces reveal, inspiration can come from unexpected sources, form and subject are often closely intertwined, and experimenting with multiple early, failed drafts can be a useful (and perhaps necessary) precursor to an essay's success.

Although the Iowa Nonfiction Writing Program technically began in the mid-1970s, we have started this anthology in the mid-1980s when the program, as we know it today, took shape. In addition, we chose to arrange the essays alphabetically in the spirit of other essay collections, including the well-known *Best American Essays* series. We believe this creates interesting dialogues and juxtapositions among the texts and also illustrates a consistency of talent over the decades, regardless of graduation year (indicated in parentheses beside each author's name within the collection). From the soaring arabesque of Marilyn Abildskov's "One Blue Note" to Yatchisin's affirmation of narrative's transcendent power in "Desperate for the Story," the pieces here offer a wide range of nonfiction, from personal essays and memoir to lyric essays, travel writing, and literary journalism. For those who wish to experience the pieces chronologically by the author's graduation year (though not necessarily by publication year), we have provided a secondary table of contents.

The authors in this collection range from those who are nationally known to those with just a few publications. Sixteen of the essays have been published in journals and magazines such as *Tin House, Creative Non-fiction, Bellingham Review*, and *Indiana Review*. Michele Morano's "Grammar Lessons: The Subjunctive Mood," a poignant tale of gaining mastery in a new language while exiting a troubled romantic relationship, appeared in *The Best American Essays 2006*, and David Torrey Peters's "The Bamenda Syndrome" was a featured essay in *The Best Travel Writing 2009*. "Slaughter," a deeply personal and surreal meditation on death by Bonnie Rough, was the recipient of the prestigious Annie Dillard Award for Creative Nonfiction. Two of the pieces (the emotionally charged "Borders" by Jon Anderson and the harrowing "O Wilderness" by Joe Blair) appear in print here for the first time, including one (Anderson's) that is published posthumously.

Yet by no means are the eighteen essays collected here meant to constitute a "Best of the NWP" collection. We would have needed to include dozens more worthy essays for the book to achieve that status. Many superb, and in some cases award-winning, submissions that were just as deserving as others had to be omitted for reasons of length, pacing, year of graduation, or repetition of material. To achieve breadth and balance, we were conscious about choosing essays that did not repeat the same general themes. An overabundance of coming-of-age memoirs would tip any scale, for example.

We did, however, deliberately choose essays to highlight some of the specific craft issues that have dominated nonfiction discussions over the decades. Some pieces in this collection—such as Jo Ann Beard's "Cousins" and Will Jennings's "How I Know Orion"—offer a narrator who is both observer and participant, functioning as the main character and the filter, while in others, such as Verzemnieks's "The Last Days of the Baldock," the author takes a clear secondary role in favor of the subjects whose lives she seeks to portray. Verzemnieks's process piece explains how, from draft to draft, she vacillated between narrative omniscience and narrative presence before realizing her choice needn't be quite so black or white.

Approaching the same issue from a different perspective, Peters writes about the difficulties he encountered by creating a narrator who was too reliable for the ethereal story he sought to tell. "How," he wonders, "do you deploy an unreliable 'narrator' in nonfiction while still maintaining some level of credibility for the 'author'?" To write his final draft of "The Bamenda Syndrome," a riveting journey into a witchdoctor's compound in Cameroon, he found inspiration in the work of cultural anthropologists of the 1980s and 1990s, whose ethnographic reports allowed for the inclusion of empathy and doubt.

The murky matter of "truth" in nonfiction has been vigorously debated at writing conferences for more than a decade. Morano touches on this issue in her process piece, when she explains why she chose to compress time and place in an early draft of "Grammar Lessons" and then changed the scene back to its original chronology. As she explains, sometimes "letting your imagination run off with real life" removes a vital authenticity from a story. Narrative persona has recently become a popular subject in nonfiction classrooms, and Hope Edelman writes about trying out different narrative personas on the page before landing on the one who could best tell her story, a persona that was still her but also not-quite-her anymore.

While reading eighty-plus submissions for this book, we were struck by how many of them involved authors thrust outside their comfort zones, requiring them to integrate unfamiliar surroundings and foreign cultural practices into their former belief systems. Travel as a vehicle for achieving new insights, particularly about the self, is a classic theme in nonfiction, and one that's still very much alive in graduate writing programs. As a result, this anthology invites readers to circumnavigate the globe, from Japan to the Philippines to Europe and Africa, and then back into the heart of the American Midwest. Similarly, quite a few of the essays (including Abildskov's breathless "One Blue Note" and Passarello's exultant "JUDY! JUDY! JUDY!") explore the influence of music on the individual psyche and also on the culture at large, and we were conscious of bringing that theme into the collection. And several other essays, including Ryan Van Meter's brutally honest "Things I Will Want to Tell You on Our First Date but Won't," reveal the painful longing that so often comes hand in hand with the search for and the demise of intimate relationships.

Van Meter is one of the most recent graduates in the collection, having received his MFA in 2008, the same graduating class that included Passarello and Butler. As editors, we initially sought an even representation of essays from each decade of the program's existence. Yet we discovered that as the popularity and legitimacy of nonfiction has increased over the past thirty years so too did the quality of work NWP students have produced. As a result, this anthology is inevitably weighted more toward the last ten years of the program than the first ten. This is precisely what a writing program seeks to achieve: to produce a growing number of talented graduates over the decades, whose work will reach wider audiences each year.

It is our hope that the scope and variety of the essays in this collection will entertain and educate readers and also serve as a contemporary teaching tool in nonfiction classrooms. We hope they reveal the kind of work young writers are capable of producing while immersed in an intensive nonfiction writing program and the detailed thought processes that go into bringing these works to completion. Above all, we hope this collection will inspire the next generation of writers to create thoughtful, provocative, moving essays of their own.

Hope Edelman and Robin Hemley
October 2015

Prologue

*How Nonfiction Finally
Achieved Literary Status*

ROBERT ATWAN[1]

When I invited Gay Talese to guest-edit *The Best American Essays 1987*, he hesitated because he didn't consider himself an essayist. I had just launched the essay series the year before with Elizabeth Hardwick, one of the nation's most prominent literary figures and an indisputable essayist, even though she opened her introduction to the inaugural volume with two words: "The Essay?" A perfectly justifiable puzzlement. I wanted the new series to showcase the essay as a literary genre, to call attention to the fact that essays, despite a seriously diminished publishing status, were still being written and had a claim to be considered creative writing that warranted a "best" anthology. I didn't know Philip Larkin had recently claimed that "the essay, as a literary form, is pretty well extinct." I did know my publishers thought a new series was risky (maybe they'd read Larkin?) and probably doomed to a brief existence; a large part of the problem involved the use of the dreaded E-word itself, but, though we tried, I found it difficult to come up with an agreeable alternative term. So, I had to make a case for "The Essay?" as literature and hope the annual collection would last two years and might even stimulate a renewed interest in the genre. My idea was that the first volume would feature someone associated with the traditional, literary essay and the second would feature one of the most prominent New Journalists. I realized that the series had to embrace both types of nonfiction or it would fail to reflect the variety of prose I considered most significant at the time.

In April 1966, Talese had contributed to *Esquire* one of the best nonfiction pieces I had encountered back then. The long profile "Frank Sinatra Has a Cold" was ostensibly a specimen of celebrity journalism, but I was impressed by how Talese could offer such a remarkable portrait of a celebrated entertainer and unique American personality without so much as an interview and with little direct quotation. Talese had spent weeks hanging around Sinatra, but never granted the interview promised at the outset, he made the best of the assignment by interviewing instead many of Sinatra's friends, family, and staff, while at the same time assiduously following Sinatra about at bars, casinos, recording sessions, and rehearsals, where he meticulously recorded the ways Sinatra made his presence felt everywhere he went. Talese's prose is modulated and precise, and though it depends almost entirely on fastidious reporting, it struck me as traditionally essayistic in its unhurried pace, concentration, and level of observation. Talese hoped to capture Sinatra's interiority and, in striving to give readers a sense of the man's complicated struggle between his brooding privacy and public personality, managed to imbue the profile with a pervasive atmosphere of melancholy, the same mood that lingered in much of Sinatra's music.

Although Talese's prose lacked the fireworks of his fellow New Journalists Norman Mailer or Tom Wolfe, it exemplified many of the characteristics of this genre that came into its own amid the tremendous social and cultural energy of the American 1960s. In the introduction to his influential 1973 anthology *The New Journalism*,[2] Wolfe dissected the techniques of a genre that was essentially a new way of composing what journalists had long called "features" as opposed to "hard news" stories. Hoping to explain to readers and aspiring writers the "extraordinary power" of the New Journalism, he broke down its elements into "four devices": (1) scene-by-scene construction ("telling the story by moving from scene to scene and resorting as little as possible to sheer historical narrative"); (2) full and realistic dialogue (which "involves the reader more completely than any other single device" while it "establishes and defines character more quickly and effectively than any other single device"); (3) the third-person point of view ("presenting every scene to the reader through the eyes of a particular character, giving the reader the feeling of being inside the character's mind and experiencing the emotional reality of the scene as he experiences it"); and (4) status details (recording "everyday gestures, habits, manners, customs, styles of furniture, clothing, decoration, styles of traveling, eating, keeping house. . . . and other symbolic details that might exist within a scene").

As Wolfe acknowledged, all of these techniques had been pioneered by the great realist novelists of the nineteenth century, especially Dickens, Trollope, Thackeray, and Balzac, who had perfected scenic movement, character-defining dialogue, point of view, and the realistic description of details signifying social and economic status. Writers closely connected to the world of newspapers and magazines—including outright reporters such as Walt Whitman, Mark Twain, Stephen Crane, Theodore Dreiser, H. L. Mencken, and Ernest Hemingway—had also long brought literary techniques to bear on their reporting and editorializing, so the idea of blending fact and fiction was nothing writers hadn't considered before. And the reportorial technique of immersion in a culture, subculture, or— to use a fancier term—*milieu* (whether of New York City street hustlers, baton twirlers on the Ole Miss campus, or Leonard Bernstein's elegant penthouse) in order to describe it so accurately and vividly that the reader felt wholly present had been practiced before by Twain (Mississippi riverboat culture), Crane (the slums and opium dens of Manhattan), Jack London (the East End slums of London), and more recently Dan Wakefield (Sumner, Mississippi, after the Emmett Till trial).[3] But despite these many notable precedents, something had erupted in nonfiction around 1960. Reporters had grown tired of conventional journalism and were eager to try out new forms of storytelling, with the support of magazines such as *Esquire* and *New York* that seemed hungry for new material, even as the novelists who (or so Wolfe claimed) stubbornly occupied the top of the literary ladder abandoned realism and the dynamic life buzzing around them for fabulism.

In many ways, what was truly new about the New Journalism could not be explained by Wolfe's four devices or by the need to re-energize a socially diminished and anemic novel. To a large extent, every literary characteristic associated with New Journalism can be found in the nonfiction of previous decades. What struck the reading public as new was its explosive, stupendous appeal. It took over the cultural landscape the way that the sonnet sequence had once become the rage in Elizabethan England or abstract expressionism in post–World War II America.

Never a cohesive literary movement, the New Journalism was really a flourishing of many talented new journalists, an assortment of diverse writers from many different literary and educational backgrounds, who suddenly recognized—along with some gifted editors—the creative opportunities of nonfiction.[4] And it was not without its critics, one of whom— Dwight Macdonald—may have inadvertently and dismissively given the form its name in a scathing attack in the August 1965 *New York Review of Books* that began: "A new kind of journalism is being born, or spawned." Macdonald referred to this new journalism as "parajournalism" and called it "a bastard form, having it both ways, exploiting the factual authority of journalism and the atmospheric license of fiction."[5] He put his finger on what would arguably become the central controversy surrounding contemporary nonfiction: its attempt to tell true stories in an imaginative, literary fashion. Although he would later acknowledge that parajournalism could be "a legitimate art form," singling out James Agee's *Let Us Now Praise Famous Men* and Mailer's *Armies of the Night*, he nevertheless considered most of the work coming out of the movement as subliterary. Similar criticism of the form and its descendants persists to this day: writing in 2013, Adam Kirsch would criticize recent forms of the essay by saying that the author's creation of a "fictional alter ego who shares the author's name . . . allows the essayist to claim the authenticity of non-fiction while indulging, with the reader's tacit permission, in the invention and shaping of fiction."[6]

Although Wolfe's flamboyant style was atypical of most of the New Journalism, Macdonald singled him out as the new genre's leading culprit and effectively turned him into its chief spokesperson, a role he fully assumed eight years later with the publication of *The New Journalism* anthology. By then, however, many of the selections he and coeditor E. W. Johnson included had already achieved "classic" status and practically all of the great work had been done, whether in the form of magazine pieces or books. In a five-year period alone, every serious reader had become familiar with Wolfe's *The Kandy-Kolored Tangerine-Flake Streamline Baby* (1965), Truman Capote's *In Cold Blood* (1966), George Plimpton's *Paper Lion* (1966), Hunter Thompson's *Hell's Angels* (1967), Terry Southern's *Red Dirt Marijuana and Other Tastes* (1967), Joan Didion's *Slouching Towards Bethlehem* (1968), Mailer's *Armies of the Night* (1968), and Talese's *Fame and Obscurity* (1970). Even before their publication as books, readers had amply sampled their contents in *Esquire, New York,* the *New Yorker,* the *Saturday Evening Post, Harper's,* and *Rolling Stone.*

When Talese published *Fame and Obscurity*—which opens with the Sinatra piece—he looked back in an "Author's Note" on his own work nostalgically, as though he were viewing it from another era. Yet for all of its undefinable characteristics and its lack of a unifying vision, the New Journalism had one indelible effect on our literature: it announced loudly and clearly that writing nonfiction was a respectable enterprise that could be just as creative and imaginative as any other literary genre. Since the early 1960s, readers, writers, critics, and especially book publishers have taken nonfiction seriously.

Yet even Wolfe, in his landmark anthology, was dismissive of another nonfiction genre—the old familiar essay. In his introduction, he characterizes it as an antiquated form composed by "men of letters" (*rolled eyes*), who concentrate on composing "polite" (*sneer*) and "genteel" (*gag*) literary constructions, and who are too diffident (*snigger*) to dirty their hands with actual reporting. He did include the work of Didion in the anthology—she's one of only two women whose work is featured[7]—and he considers her a reporter despite her protestations that journalism is not her strong suit. Of all the writers included in *The New Journalism*, Didion comes closest to a traditional essayist.

It is true that the traditional essay—personal, familiar, reflective—was largely the product of writers who followed Montaigne by retiring to their study (or "ivory tower") to muse about their lives, the follies and foibles of humanity, and share delectable and applicable tidbits of wisdom garnered from their wide reading. This style of essay irked the new magazine editors as far back as the Progressive Era, who wanted to see less "navel-gazing" and more hard-hitting reportage, especially of the "muckraking" sort. They shunned the old-fashioned belletristic product and paved the way for the new reporter-based essay that eventually came to be called "literary non-fiction." For decades, writers like Jane Addams, Mencken, Edmund Wilson, or Agee would endeavor to find new literary styles and structures as they labored in the "impolite" essay.

But the form needed no dismissal from Wolfe: it was already consigned to the lower branches of the literary hierarchy and in certain circles was not considered genuine literature.[8] Influential twentieth-century critics such as John Crowe Ransom, and later Rene Wellek and Austin Warren, defined literature as essentially poetry, plays, and novels; there was little room for nonimaginative works such as essays, which were compositions written about literature, not the real thing itself. (Of course such definitions usually accommodated a few great exceptions, say Thomas Burton or Ralph Waldo Emerson and his friend Henry David Thoreau.) Ransom in particular emphasized the primacy of poetry over prose. In a rather astonishing extended metaphor, he stated that prose is a "totalitarian state" whereas poetry is a democracy, and he suggested an entire range of dichotomies: if poetry is art, prose is argument; if poetry is iconic, prose is statement; if poetry is intuitive, prose is logical and rational . . . and so on. But the essential critical dichotomy (in his view) was not so much between poetry and prose as between poetics and rhetoric, between the aesthetic uses of language and the practical—or between literature and the essay.[9]

Norman Podhoretz noticed a similar attitude in a 1958 essay, "The Article as Art," an important antecedent to Wolfe's New Journalism manifesto. Writing about the superiority "creative" writers feel toward essays and reportage, he says, "Some novelists (and this applies to many poets too) tend to express their contempt or disdain for discursive prose in the very act of writing it. . . . You can hear a note of condescension toward the medium they happen to be working in at the moment; they seem to be announcing in the very construction of their sentences that they have no great use for the prosy requirements of the essay or the review, that they are only dropping in from Olympus for a brief, impatient visit." Yet, he concludes that their discursive writing often "turns out to be more interesting, more lively, more penetrating, more intelligent, more forceful, more original—in short *better*—than their fiction, which they and everyone else automatically treat with greater respect." Presciently, he names as examples James Baldwin and Mailer, two writers then well known for their fiction. Podhoretz's piece remains one of the earliest critical statements at that time in support of the essay—and its close relatives, the magazine article, literary reportage, and review—as a legitimate imaginative form that can rival fiction and poetry.[10]

But his was decidedly a minority view. Book and magazine publishers would soon begin avoiding the word "essay." In a 1977 foreword to a collection of his essays, E. B. White dismayingly wrote:

> I am not fooled about the place of the essay in twentieth-century American letters—it stands a short distance down the line. The essayist, unlike the novelist, the poet, and the playwright, must be content in his self-imposed role of second-class citizen. A writer who has his sights trained on the Nobel Prize or other earthly triumphs had best write a novel, a poem, or a play, and leave the essayist to ramble about, content with living a free life and enjoying the satisfactions of a somewhat undisciplined existence.[11]

A few years after White's remark, the National Book Award winner Paul Fussell said, "If you want to raise a laugh in a publisher's office, enter with a manuscript collection of essays on all sorts of subjects."[12] As late as 1990, Wilfred Sheed claimed in his collection, *Essays in Disguise*, that few books "actually have the nerve to call themselves collections of essays." As Sheed explains, "the form has been in virtual eclipse for most of my writing life, squeezed to a shadow by the adjoining landmasses of the Article and the Review, not to mention its own dwarf love child, the Column."[13]

By the time I launched *The Best American Essays* series in 1986, the essay had thus been languishing for many years. New Journalism was a quarter of a century old and, as Talese would later maintain, also in the process of declining, mainly because magazines could no longer afford the expenses associated with immersion journalism.[14] Many leading magazines had folded. Editors, now relying more on a limited staff than on a stable of freelancers, had also shifted their assignments more toward the informative and news-oriented article. I was on the lookout for traditional first-person and reflective essays (which hadn't completely disappeared) and superior literary journalism, but I had little interest in the standard article, no matter how topically compelling, since many articles still did not demonstrate the aesthetic possibilities Podhoretz thought they could possess.

Writing on Emerson in the *Yale Review* in 1982, William H. Gass offered an invidious comparison between the two nonfiction forms: "The essay is obviously the opposite of that awful object, 'the article,' which like items picked up in shops during one's lunch hour, represents itself as the latest cleverness, a novel consequence of thought, skill, labor, and free enterprise; but never as an activity—the process, the working, the wondering." Unlike the essay, the article "pretends everything is clear, that its argument is unassailable, that there are no soggy patches, no illicit inferences, no illegitimate connections . . ."[15] Yet even as Gass was writing, the essay clearly appeared to be retooling for the purpose of engaging in yet another period of generic competition. Essayists had begun absorbing some of the objectivity and factual material commonly associated with articles. (Or was it that article writers and the magazines had begun to grow more comfortable with a subjective stance?) Essays were being published that depended on reporting and research, while articles appeared that displayed a personal voice and perspective and demonstrated a process of thought. Although many editors still preferred articles to essays (or, as one editor told me in 1990, "factual reporting to 'thumbsucking'"), magazine prose was no longer behaving in the ways Gass described. Suddenly, distinguishing between the informative article and the personal essay became more difficult than I had imagined when I started the series.

The creative crossbreeding of personal essay, informative article, and New Journalism-style reportage proved to be fruitful for literary nonfiction. The New Journalism hadn't disappeared—its flourishing permanently transformed American nonfiction—but it grew *quieter* (or, as Richard Preston puts it, "more subdued"),[16] less Wolfean and closer to the reportorial practices of writers like Talese and John McPhee, who published seven books of nonfiction between 1965 and 1969 (and twenty-five more since). In his invaluable collection of commentary on New Journalism, Ronald Weber in 1974 reminded readers that despite the highly publicized attention Wolfe had given to the novelization of nonfiction, a key strain to New Journalism was rooted not so much "in the effort to turn reporting into art as to bend the stultifying conventions of traditional journalistic practice and to extend the range and power of nonfiction writing." Weber added in a footnote an observation that explains very sensibly and accurately the influence the New Journalism would eventually exert: the "more strictly journalistic" strain "has lacked a spokesman of Wolfe's zeal and stature and consequently tends to seem of less importance. . . . It could be that in the long run, the literary New Journalists having switched (or switched back) to writing old novels, the less publicized changes at work in newspaper and magazine journalism will have the more lasting effect."[17]

After the explosion of New Journalism in the 1960s, there would be no new revolutionary moment that would shape literary nonfiction in an equivalent fashion. Though very few write with the rhetorical flair of Wolfe, nearly all of the many talented nonfiction writers today—Michael Lewis, Ted Conover, Susan Orlean, and Malcolm Gladwell, to name a few—are the direct heirs of New Journalism. The continued significance of the New Journalism and the *absence* of any radically new movement is perfectly conveyed by the title of one of the best recent books available on the craft of contemporary nonfiction—*The New New Journalism*.

In June 1980, *Esquire* magazine ran on its cover the photo of a satisfied looking chimpanzee in a LaCoste shirt sitting at a cluttered desk and typing on an electric typewriter; the headline read: "Is Anyone in America Not Writing a Screenplay?" By 1995 that question could be asked of memoir. In 1989 Tobias Wolfe published *This Boy's Life*, a year later William Styron came out with *Darkness Visible: A Memoir of Madness*, and these were followed over the next few years by such bestsellers as Susanna Kaysen's *Girl, Interrupted* (1993), Mary Karr's *The Liar's Club* (1995), Frank McCourt's *Angela's Ashes* (1996), Caroline Knapp's *Drinking: A Love Story* (1996), and Kathryn Harrison's *The Kiss* (1997). By the late 1990s, forums, symposiums, and countless reviews focused on the memoir as the latest rage. In 1996, a *New York Times Magazine* item "The Age of the Literary Memoir Is Now" by James Atlas called the "triumph of memoir" a "revolution." Critical hyperbole aside, the genre has continued to be a very popular publishing commodity since the mid-1990s, with several bestselling memoirs published each year, such as Cheryl Strayed's enormously successful *Wild* in 2012.

Autobiographies and memoirs had, of course, been stock in trade for publishers for centuries, including such American masterpieces as Henry Adams's third-person autobiography *The Education of Henry Adams* (1907), Gertrude Stein's experimental *The Autobiography of Alice B. Toklas* (1933), Vladimir Nabokov's *Speak, Memory* (1966), Frank Conroy's *Stop-Time* (1967), and Russell Baker's award-winning *Growing Up* (1982). These usually, however, happened to be written by famous public figures, movie stars, or writers best known for their fiction.[18] The customary distinction was that someone's autobiography usually covered an entire life (ancestry, childhood, education, early career, etc.), while traditional memoirs covered some of those essentials but focused more on the author's public life and encounters with famous people. But the new memoir (now singular) differed in that it was often written by a relatively unknown person and it often dwelt on a single *aspect* of that person's life—poverty, a bad marriage, drinking problems, experiences of chemotherapy, the death or illness of a child, caring for elderly parents. One advantage of this type of memoir—what Suzanne Strempek Shea calls "the slice-of-life-memoir"—is that one can write multiple memoirs, each one focusing on a different theme or issue. One then becomes mainly known as a memoirist. Another advantage, given the economics of contemporary publishing, is that—aside from the actual writing—the memoir isn't very labor intensive. Though the writer may want to return to old neighborhoods or engage in a little fact-checking, the memoir normally doesn't require much reporting or research and can be accomplished on a small budget.

The memoirs that emerged in the 1990s had their roots in the confessional essay, that candid subgenre that portrayed troubled childhoods and family dysfunction and that frankly and unabashedly acknowledged personal flaws, obsessions, criminality, and, a popular affliction, addiction. Like the New Journalism, the contemporary memoir received much of its unfavorable criticism from its use of fictional devices. Memoirists were often brought to task for the employment of fictional techniques used to enhance the drama, shape the narrative, and sharpen the dialogue. After the 2003 publication and heavy promotion of *A Million Little Pieces* by James Frey, a highly publicized controversy ensued when the supposed work of nonfiction was shown to be full of lies and distortions. The controversy called attention to the significance of truth in autobiography (and nonfiction in general) as critics and writers weighed in on whether such common devices as composite characters, reconstructed dialogue, and condensed narrative are permissible. The controversy persists, with some insisting that memoirists adhere to the strict standards of news journalism and others believing that the memoir should avail itself of all the techniques of imaginative literature.[19]

A large part of the memoir's critical difficulties comes not necessarily from deceitful authors but from an apparently inescapable publishing reality: many editors still flinch when they see a collection of personal essays the author has gathered and assembled from a variety of literary periodicals. Should they decide the work is publishable, they invariably insist that the author rewrite the essays with an eye to what is called a "narrative arc." Although the restructuring may eliminate some overlapping details and topics, the editor's demand for narrating a "story" may also interfere with what made the work essayistic to begin with. Some of the greatest essayists—Francis Bacon, Montaigne, Emerson—had minimal narrative talent or interest. For these writers, a true essay demonstrates the art of surprising digression. And, of course, by emphasizing an overarching narrative some fabrications and distortions will be inevitable. As one psychoanalyst who learned to be suspicious of narrative's unconscious lure has argued, patients will often attempt to shape their stories and alter memories to achieve a satisfying narrative resolution.[20]

As a genre, the memoir has been insufficiently studied; we can find countless books on how to craft one but very few on how to read one critically and intelligently.[21] It is useful to remember that at the creative center of every memoir that hopes to be considered literature readers will find a conflict between the expression of the literal truth and a striving for literary effect. The act of composition itself distorts. The first-person singular is invariably a *persona* whose existence depends on literary performance. Narrated time is not lived time but a special imaginary time—four years can pass by in a dependent clause. We cannot describe every detail of everything; something is always being omitted. We often, especially in anxious or heightened moments, can't recall what exactly was said five minutes earlier; how much of what was said can be recorded twenty-five or fifty years later? Composition can also be relentlessly self-censoring. While writing his autobiography, Twain recalled, "I have thought of fifteen hundred or two thousand incidents in my life which I am ashamed of but I have not gotten one of them to consent to go on paper yet."

"Narcissism" is another term commonly thrown at the memoirist, often unfairly, as if writing about oneself automatically suggests an inflated ego and a self-indulgent personality. Yet, as Thoreau memorably writes at the start of *Walden*: "In most books, the I, or first person, is omitted; in this it will be retained; that, in respect to egotism, is the main difference. We commonly do not remember that it is, after all, always the first person that is speaking. I should not talk about myself if there were any body else whom I knew as well." Every critical problem is of course a creative opportunity in disguise. One challenge of memoir is clearly to find an aesthetic solution to the issue of repetitive self-preoccupation. Lately, many personal and confessional essayists have taken to composing from a second-person perspective, but we all know that "you" invariably equals "I," so the "you" can quickly grow tiresome and seem artificial, especially in a longer work.

One solution often used by the personal essayist (and recommended by Philip Lopate) involves the orchestration of researched information into the memoir so that the reader does not feel incessantly cornered by a self-absorbed narrator.[22] As readers will see, the present collection contains a number of remarkable memoir-essays showing how contemporary writers have found creative ways to reconfigure the conventions of first-person narration.

Since the 1980s, writers have found innovative ways to implement the lessons of New Journalism, revitalize the personal essay, and reinvent the traditional memoir. The outstanding writers collected in *I'll Tell You Mine* have clearly absorbed all the various strands of creative nonfiction—repertorial, scenic, experimental, meditative, informative, advocative. They entertain many different forms, often in the same work, braided, mosaic, montage; incorporate into personal nonlinear narratives factual data and research, at times arcane; and they recount stories in a poetic, figurative prose that results in a hybrid usually referred to as the "lyric essay." Though they might bear some similarities, such as a meditative style and enigmatic stance, the lyric essay shouldn't be confused with the traditional "prose poem." According to one of its foremost practitioners, John D'Agata, the lyric essay "inherits from the principal strands of nonfiction the makings of its own hybrid version of the form. It takes the subjectivity of the personal essay and the objectivity of the public essay, and conflates them into a literary form that relies on both art and fact, on imagination and observation, rumination and argumentation, human faith and human perception."[23]

I recommend that anyone interested in recent literary nonfiction read, as I did, *I'll Tell You Mine* twice. The first time I followed the main table of contents; the book is simply an outstandingly good read, featuring not only some of the finest nonfiction writers of our time but also a rich diversity of topics, perspectives, and voices. Then, the second time, pen in hand, following the chronological organization, I read as a writer, observing and documenting the inventive and assimilative forms of literary nonfiction as it has evolved over the past several decades. Though focused on only one well-established writing program, *I'll Tell You Mine* is a tribute to all the MFA programs throughout the country that now play a vital role in inspiring and generating the newest literary nonfiction—and helping solidify its literary status.

Notes

1. Much of what I recount in this short survey of contemporary literary nonfiction I lived through, having read the New Journalists as their work first began appearing in magazines in the 1960s and then monitoring essays for *The Best American Essays* series since 1985. So a large part of this introduction depends on my recollections of how literary nonfiction has developed since the New Journalism — the fluctuating status of various genres, the publishing trends, and the revival of the essay. Still, I am especially indebted to three excellent books on the subject, which I enthusiastically recommend to all interested readers: Ronald Weber's *The Reporter as Artist: A Look at the New Journalism Controversy* (New York: Hastings House, 1974), a collection that remarkably assembles at such an early date so much of the most important coverage of the literary phenomenon that permanently altered the course of American nonfiction; Marc Weingarten's *The Gang That Wouldn't Write Straight: Wolfe, Thompson, and the New Journalism Revolution* (New York: Crown, 2005), by far one of the best accounts of the movement, admirably researched and engagingly presented; and Robert S. Boynton's *The New New Journalism: Conversations with America's Best Nonfiction Writers on Their Craft* (New York: Vintage, 2005), an indispensable collection of incisive interviews that amply documents the various ways the new generation of journalists has appropriated and refashioned the old New Journalism.

2. The book's cover title reads *The New Journalism by Tom Wolfe with an Anthology Edited by Tom Wolfe and E. W. Johnson* (New York: Harper & Row, 1973). All subsequent quotations from Wolfe are from the book's introduction.

3. Dan Wakefield, "Justice in Sumner," *Nation*, October 1, 1955.

4. Like many creative movements in the arts, the New Journalism was largely a result of what might be called "competitive collaboration." Wolfe speaks directly of the sudden shock he experienced when in 1962 he picked up a copy of *Esquire* and found a piece by Talese: it "didn't open like an ordinary magazine article at all. It opened with the tone and mood of a short story." Wolfe would take it from there, placing his own spin on magazine nonfiction. The work of others mining similar material (in this case, profiles, interviews, articles, reportage) becomes an incentive not just to borrow techniques but to try to do so while at the same time striving to outperform the latest literary model.

5. "Parajournalism, or Tom Wolfe and His Magic Writing Machine," in Dwight Macdonald, *Discriminations: Essays & Afterthoughts* (1974; repr. New York: Da Capo Press, 1983). This was the first battle between Macdonald and Wolfe, who would tussle a few months later, after Wolfe published a long, unflattering two-part essay on the *New Yorker* magazine and its editor William Shawn. Macdonald countered with a second blistering attack on Wolfe, again in the *New York Review of Books* (February 3, 1966). Wolfe's *New Yorker* pieces upset a good number of the New York literati; E. B. White would write a letter to Wolfe's magazine publisher defending William Shawn and saying that Wolfe's piece "violated every rule of conduct I know anything about. It is sly, cruel and to a large extent undocumented . . . The piece is not merely brutal, it sets some sort of record for journalistic delinquency . . ." (from *Letters of E. B. White*).

6. Adam Kirsch, "The New Essayists," *New Republic*, February 25, 2013.

7. A glance at the contents of *The New Journalism* would make it seem that women didn't play much of a role in the movement. But the fact is it included a large number of talented women writers who simply were—for whatever reasons—omitted from the book. A few of them (though not all were in Wolfe's camp) are Lillian Ross (an especially notable precursor), Vivian Gornick, Gloria Steinem, Jill Johnson, Ellen Willis, Pauline Kael, Gail Sheehy, and Veronica Geng.

8. For a fuller discussion, see Robert Atwan, "The Essay—Is It Literature?" in Janis Forman, *What Do I Know? Reading, Writing, and Teaching the Essay* (Portsmouth, NH: Boynton/Cook, 1996). Recently reprinted in *Essaying the Essay*, ed. David Lazar (Gettysburg: Welcome Table Press, 2014).

9. Or, to put it another way: poetry is what gets taught in literature classes, prose in freshman composition. See John Crowe Ransom, *Topics for Freshman Writing: Twenty Topics for Writing with Appropriate Materials for Study* (New York: Henry Holt and Company, 1935).

10. Norman Podhoretz, *Doings and Undoings* (New York: Farrar, Straus & Giroux, 1964).

11. Foreword to E. B. White, *The Essays of E. B. White* (New York: Harper & Row, 1977).

12. Cited by Jeffrey Pepper Rodgers in his review of Paul Fussell's *Thank God for the Atom Bomb and Other Essays* in *Monthly* (San Francisco), October 1988.

13. Wilfred Sheed, *Essays in Disguise* (New York: Alfred A. Knopf, 1990).

14. Gay Talese, introduction to *The Best American Essays 1987* (New York: Ticknor & Fields, 1987).

15. In William H. Gass, *Habitations of the Word: Essays* (New York: Simon and Schuster, 1985). A novelist, Gass excelled in the novella-length meditative, philosophical essay, a type that today would be considered a "lyric essay." One of his most compelling, *On Being Blue: A Philosophical Inquiry*, appeared in 1976.

16. Interview in Boynton, *The New New Journalism: Conversations with America's Best Nonfiction Writers on Their Craft*.

17. Weber, ed., *The Reporter as Artist: A Look at the New Journalism Controversy*.

18. For an assessment of the celebrity autobiography, see my introduction to Robert Atwan and Bruce Forer, *Bedside Hollywood: Great Scenes from Movie Memoirs* (New York: Moyer Bell, 1985).

19. I've covered the issue of truth in memoir in my foreword to *The Best American Essays 2006*. My basic position is that imaginative writing depends largely on prose style, original tropes and figuration, narrative and expository complexity, construction, and numerous aesthetic decisions, none of which requires a disregard for facts. Nonfiction writers, to retain a sense of credibility, need mainly to worry about verifiable information. With unverifiable information—such as what you dreamed one night at the age of ten or fantasized about while struggling through high school algebra—there are no ground rules since, from a pragmatic point of view at least, the truth of unverifiable information is a nonissue. It only becomes an issue when someone points out the verifiability of what you considered unverifiable. For an excellent survey of the topic, see David Lazar, ed., *Truth in Nonfiction: Essays* (Iowa City: University of Iowa Press, 2008).

20. See Donald P. Spence, *Narrative Truth and Historical Truth* (New York: Norton, 1982).

21. Two excellent books on the subject are Vivian Gornick's *The Situation and the Story: The Art of Personal Narrative* (New York: Farrar, Straus & Giroux, 2001); and Carl H. Klaus's *The Made-Up Self: Impersonation in the Personal Essay* (Iowa City: University of Iowa Press, 2010).

22. See Phillip Lopate's very pertinent chapter on "Research and Personal Writing" in his *To Show and To Tell: The Craft of Literary Nonfiction* (New York: Free Press, 2013).

23. John D'Agata, ed., *The Next American Essay* (Minneapolis: Graywolf Press, 2003). The collection features such innovative, "poetic" essayists as Albert Goldbarth, Anne Carson, David Shields, Susan Mitchell, Wayne Koestenbaum, and Mary Ruefle. Not surprisingly, many "lyric essayists" are chiefly known for their poetry.

One Blue Note

MARILYN ABILDSKOV (1997)

(Originally published in *Black Warrior Review*)

I heard a trumpeter interviewed on the radio some years ago, a musician who said he believed you could tell a whole story in a single note. I remember thinking it was impossible, a reaction not unusual perhaps for those of us musically untrained. Then this man—I forget now who he was—proceeded to play one long note—I wish I could tell you now what note it was—and in the middle of a traffic jam just outside Portland, Oregon, where I was listening to this trumpeter on the radio, waiting for the traffic to move, I began to cry. The note *was* a story, as promised, and like all stories, it held me, starting off as most stories do, ordinary enough, then veering off into something inexplicably sad but also terribly, terribly beautiful.

He started out an ordinary salaryman, a *sad-da-dee-maan*, working at a company in Tokyo, a city filled with salarymen, all of them in navy blue suits, bloodshot eyes, all of them staggering toward the subway after work, drunk but not on pleasure, but then something happened—he caught someone cheating and decided to quit, *had* to quit, was too honest for such a company, and the others congratulated him, envied him, they said, for they always wanted to quit, too, and he was glad, of course, but unemployed, too, out of work until, on a whim, he decided to open up a jazz bar back in his hometown, a jazz bar in Matsumoto that served coffee and mixed drinks and small elegant appetizers, salmon sandwiches and cheese toast and pretty plates of brie and crackers, a place where customers could listen to jazz—for jazz is a cultural hybrid, is it not?—and the blues, too, which, on the simplest level consists of three chords and that's it—*The only music I knew I could listen to twelve hours a day*—and he gave the venture

three months at best—*I figured three months would be good*—but the shop
lasted three, then four, then five, then six months and one year turned into
two and two into ten and ten into twenty so by the time you walk into the
shop, a narrow, rectangular place that reminds you of a shoe box, the kind
of shoe box where you store your favorite secret things, you know you are
walking into an establishment, so to speak, a place where the proprietor—
for this is how you think of him at first: as a *proprietor*—will, after only a
few weeks recognize you, nod slightly when you walk in, then carefully fix
you a drink—cafe au lait in the afternoon, red wine late at night—*Chilled,
do you mind if it's chilled?*—and you will say no, you don't mind, chilled
is fine, in fact you prefer your red wine cold, and you will notice what an
elegant man he is, this proprietor with a well-trimmed goatee and clean
pressed jeans and white cotton shirts he buttons to the neck, so refined
that at first you feel shy, but then you can't help it, can't help but wonder
what his secrets are, what ruffles his shirts, and you start asking questions,
innocent ones at first—*What does Eonta mean?* and *Have you ever been to
New York?*—but he hasn't, he couldn't—his hours as a salaryman wouldn't
allow it, he says, and you know that he and his wife, a woman whose name
you do not know, are the only ones who work here at the shop—so he stays
put, does the next best thing, meaning stays in the music, brings the music
here—*Jazz is freedom*, he says—and he chooses the music with the same
care he uses to fix you a drink—Charlie Bird and John Coltrane and Charles
Mingus and Thelonious Monk, Joe Turner, Sonny Rollins, Billie Holiday
and Miles Davis—and all the others too, voices like Ella Fitzgerald's, voices
you would never hear anywhere else in this country, except at Eonta, a
place where you whisper because of the music, and where one night you
and a man who will leave for Brazil the next day, will sit quietly, the two of
you not talking, him just holding your hand and you trying not to cry because what's to say on the night before someone leaves? and where later,
in the cold months to come, you will write letters to the man in Brazil, and
the slim, elegant proprietor will ask *Are you writing a novel?* and you will say
no, no, just a letter, only you are not yet fluent, not even close, so you confuse *tamago* for *tegami*, the word "letter" for "egg," saying, "No, not a novel,
I am writing an egg," and he will nod discreetly, leave you alone to your coffee and egg, reminding you the way he moves what true elegance means,
how much beauty lies in restraint, which is why, when you are there with
another man, the one who doesn't hold your hand, the one you are going to
leave soon (because he long ago left you?), you restrain yourself for once,
hold back many things you have to say, just sit quietly and look at his face,
such a beautiful face, you think, wondering why he is always so tired, and

why you haven't noticed before all those flecks of gray in his black black hair, which is why, when you are gone, when you are back in America, surprised to see that even your cat turned gray while you were away, you will write notes to the proprietor of Eonta (but not to the other men) and he will write to you as well, thanking you for the glasses you gave him, telling you he drinks milk from them in the morning, wine from them at night, writing his note on a small card with the sun and moon and stars shining on a blue backdrop—*How have you been? Best wishes as you pursue your new career*—and you will wish yourself back, not to the country itself or to the man with the beautiful face but to a small place, a jazz bar whose name comes from a Greek composition, a word meaning *existence* he told you once, a place where you could drink cafe au lait in the afternoon and chilled red wine at night, write love letters as if they were portions of a novel, and eat small, elegant sandwiches, a place where you could listen to the music, to the jazz and to the blues, a place where you could watch the man behind the counter, who is a salaryman, after all, mix Kahlua and cream in a dusty silver shaker, dry glasses with a clean white towel, change CDs and nod when customers enter the dark narrow room, no one ever mentioning what you all know to be true: that there are three chords to play with—what you do, who you love, and where you live—and the best you can do is hope they come together for a moment, in a shoe box, in a letter, or in one blue note, one long note that sounds like a song.

FROM THE AUTHOR

Someone in my first year at Iowa gave the exercise that a lot of writers are probably familiar with: to write three to four pages in a single, sustained, grammatically correct sentence. I'd never heard of the exercise before and was stunned by how lovely others' results were. Mine, however, was flat as a burnt pancake and went straight into the garbage without much thought. The next year, however, while working on a deadline for a submission in Carol de Saint Victor's workshop—and I should pause here to say what a pleasure studying with Carol was, how much we all worshipped her, and how whatever I have gleaned over time about the intersections of travel, love, and memory can be traced back to Carol in one way or another—I took a break to go buy notebooks at Iowa Book & Supply. I used to buy these great black notebooks filled with lined paper. They were cheap and durable and I bought them in bundles of five at the time. And in the course of browsing a bin of sale books before checking out, I found a book on jazz and read what is probably old news to musical people but what was brand new information to me: that when you've got three chords, you've got jazz. I found this interesting, arresting, even, and while walking home, I could hear a new essay, something whose rhythms made sense. I knew exactly where I wanted to start and exactly who I wanted to focus on. I'd tried writing about Eonta, a little jazz cafe that I used to visit when I lived in Matsumoto, Japan, and the proprietor of Eonta, but each attempt had been flat until then, dull in a way that that shoebox of a place and that proprietor was not. This time, as I began "One Blue Note," I was aware of why: that I'd been trying to write about the proprietor as part of a demographic of other Japanese salarymen when who he was was an individual, someone whose passion for work—for wine and coffee and most importantly for jazz—was delicate and daring; that I'd been trying to write about the place in a journalistic way rather than how I had experienced it: impressionistically. I didn't know the proprietor very well but I admired him as I admired many Japanese salarymen, who at the time were characterized in the American media as soulless, suicides waiting to happen. I wanted to write a love letter of sorts to them, to the Japanese sense of work as central in a person's life, and I wanted to do justice to the beauty of that tiny space, which I loved, and that proprietor who had made it happen. And now— without even realizing it until the week of feverish writing was done—I'd found a way in: a single sentence to capture that sense of one person, one place, one life, his and mine running parallel. I tell my students that it doesn't matter if this exercise or that one yields something they like right now because who knows? Maybe later it will. Timing is everything, isn't it? And readiness. Sometimes what helps us helps us later, rather than sooner. Well, good. We're in no rush. "One Blue Note" was published in *Black Warrior Review* as a short story, my first literary publication, and for that reason, it holds a special place for me. It is also the piece that has helped me define the genre of writing I engage in, which I think of not as "essay" or "short story" so much as "love letter" or "egg." Finally it is the first piece where I glimpsed—or heard, rather, in a very particular way—what I think Richard Ford may mean when he says of voice on page, "Voice is the music of the story's intelligence."

Black Men

FAITH ADIELE (2002)

(Originally published in *Indiana Review*)

Falling

When I was five years old, I tripped on a throw rug in my babysitter's house and hurtled face forward onto the coffee table, an immense slab of petrified California redwood. Quick as it happened, each arc of my fall segmented itself, colors separating in a kaleidoscope, and crystallized in my memory: the rug sucking at my ankles, the giddy lurch across the floor, the crest through the air, weightless, my jangling heart, disbelief as I spied the waiting block—solid, glistening.

I was already screaming when my nose smacked the table. Over the noise, I heard a crack like the cut that severs the tree, saw the brown spine of a Douglas fir submitting to my grandfather's ax.

The babysitter, who'd been in the kitchen coating slices of Wonder Bread with thick swirls of margarine and dousing them with sugar (an after-school snack I adored, much to my mother's horror) came tearing down the hall.

"What happened?" she shouted, the sugar shaker still clutched in her fist.

I couldn't respond. Pain vibrated through cartilage into the roots of my teeth. I crumpled to the floor, clutching my face against my skull.

She yanked my quivering hands away to check for fracture, her fingers leaving a gritty trail of sugar across my cheeks. Then, though not a particularly demonstrative woman, she lifted me into the large recliner and locked her arms around me.

"Go 'way!" I shrieked at the other children who, wide-eyed and solemn, ringed the recliner, some wailing helpfully, others tugging the babysitter's apron, wanting to know, "Why she crying?"

I howled and howled. More than the pain itself, I remember the taste of sugar mixed with tears leaking into my mouth, salt and sweet, the flavor of amazement, amazement to learn that yes, life was this too. I don't remember the trip to the ER, the arrival of my mother, the painkillers, the days and nights of ice packs.

By some miracle, my nose wasn't broken. "I fell," I announced proudly to strangers, and in 1968, people believed me, could still believe in children, especially brown ones, falling. Over the next few days, a thick root of blood spread out beneath the golden surface of my cheeks, staining them the color of bruised plums. The bridge of my nose puffed and held. For nearly six months I resembled a raccoon—curious, slightly anxious, with crusty, purple skin ringing my eyes.

One of my favorite photographs was taken a few months later. Michael-Vaino, a.k.a. Uncle Mike, and a friend are dancing in my grandparents' living room in cowboy hats. Uncle Mike, his pale Finn eyes droopy, snaps the fingers of one hand, wobbles a bottle of gin in the other. His friend, a Swede like Old Pappa, my lumberman grandfather, balances me on his hip, beaming at my bruised face.

My mother had been playing Nigerian Highlife LPs on the stereo, and Uncle Mike's friend, drawn by the hypnotic twang of the talking drum speaking to the guitar, like someone calling your name underwater, popped his head into the room. "Hey, what's this music?"

"Yeah, cool." Uncle Mike followed behind, drawing the string of his flat-brimmed hat tight. Ever since childhood he'd dressed like a cowboy in an old black-and-white movie.

My mother stared pointedly at his hand and shook her head.

"I know, I know." He gave the bottle a fluid twist of the wrist, a cowboy spinning his pistols before re-holstering. "It's only for a second. We're on our way out."

The Highlife swelled, spurred by the singer's admonition that *Everybody dey party*, and my uncle's friend swept me into his arms, saying. "Hear that? Everybody party, something-something."

My mother hesitated a moment, then smiled. Extending her arms before her like a hula dancer, crooked at the elbows, she swiveled her hips to the slower under-beat, the way my Nigerian father had taught her before he left. Like a grass skirt, her brown ponytail swayed from side to side.

Uncle Mike snapped his fingers, shuffled his feet across the carpet, sang "something-something" in my ear, and despite the fact that it was his friend holding me, his friend who told me how pretty I was (something

Uncle Mike had never said, either before or after my raccoon rings), my uncle was the one I loved.

My mother ended it.

"Look goofy!" she called, framing us in the lens of her Brownie camera. "In other words, just be yourselves." The flash bleached the room, breaking the spell.

Uncle Mike checked his watch and jerked his head toward the door. Outside the crunch of gravel signaled that the others were assembling in the driveway. Whenever his pack of loud, good-natured friends came by in their well-ironed jeans, they left their bottles outside in fast cars with deep bucket seats and carried me on their shoulders, recounting their latest motorbike triumphs.

The friend spun me one last time and released. "Thank you, madam." He bowed.

"Don't go," I begged.

Uncle Mike doffed his hat and flattened it onto my head with two pats. "'Night, cowpoke." Then he was gone. I listened hard in his wake: gravel flying, welcome shouts, car doors opening to blasts of squealing electric guitar and shuddering bass, metallic slams and revved motors. The music of my disappeared-to-Africa father couldn't compete.

Most nights Uncle Mike came home after I was in bed. Most days he slept past noon. Awake, he was often grumpy. His jovial moments were brief, always halfway out the door.

Baby Vaino, the One Left Behind

I come from a long line of unlucky men, men who disappeared to unsettled countries, to civil-war-torn countries, to mental institutions, to the barn with a bottle of vodka. Men in our family couldn't quite manage to stay home. They wandered—restless, driven by gold, war, emotion—and rarely returned, despite the best intentions. Growing up in their wake on the family farm, I inherited the understanding that men were fragile, prone to leaving us behind.

Who's to blame? Let's start with country—Finland, with its brooding soundtrack by Sibelius and tight-lipped, hard-drinking citizens. A Finnish friend once told me that she had never really heard her father speak. Occasionally he would grunt if asked a direct question. When, in his late seventies, he retired from the fields, she and her sisters were amazed to find that he had plenty to say. The family sat together at the kitchen table, drinking tiny cups of Finnish *kahvi* and peeling potatoes for *kalavuoka*, the women's mouths ajar as their father chatted about God, the annual moose hunt, the mid-summer strawberry harvest. That was the odd thing—not the seventy-year silence—but the decision finally to speak.

I blame the flat, icy landscape with its meager sunlight and long winter days. I blame history—Sweden and Russia leaning like the long shadow of death, recurring conquests interspersed with ill-fated stoic resistance. Or shall I blame hunger and displacement, the generic lot of the immigrant?

But why is it each generation assumed that history and landscape were things only women could survive? For that I blame twin legacies—names and lies: All the men in the family are named after Baby Vaino, the One Left Behind. His abandonment was the original lie.

In 1889 my great-grandfather the Cursed was born in Finland, the second of three sons. When he was still young, his father snatched him and his older brother out of the shade of Russia and fled to the United States. His mother remained behind with Vaino the baby. Father and sons settled in Ashtabula, Ohio, a bustling port city on Lake Erie, where the father found work as a carpenter.

When I was nine and much enamored of slave narratives, I thrilled to learn that fifty years before my ancestor's arrival, the Ashtabula River had been a stop on the Underground Railroad for slaves fleeing to Canada. I studied how runaways walked for miles in the dark, running their blistered hands up the sides of trees to feel where the north-facing moss was growing, how conductors placed burning candles in station windows, much like the ones we lit in December for the *tonttu*, farm sprites. My heart throbbed with justice and injustice. Despite a Nigerian and Scandinavian heritage, I longed to claim Black Americans like John Park, who ferried hundreds of fellow slaves across the Ohio River.

I had to settle for the Hubbards, a white family who owned a successful lumberyard and belonged to Ashtabula's anti-slavery society. William Hubbard built a large, white-pillared house near the lake, where nearly every night passengers slipped into cubbyholes in the cellar and hayloft, their last stop before freedom. The white man who likely employed my Finnish ancestors was as close as I came to slave resistance.

I imagined my great-grandfather the Cursed in his dark woolens and heavy boots clomping in late from Hubbard's lumberyard, unaware of the legacy of black slaves above his head, beneath his feet.

When his mother and Baby Vaino, the One Left Behind, died back in Finland, his father remarried and fathered three more children.

Handicaps

Michael-Vaino, a.k.a. Uncle Mike, is handicapped.

I am six, and we have moved to my grandparents' farm. This means two things: one, my mother and Old Pappa have reconciled, and two, my interest in family gossip is born. The sound of dropping voices, as my mother and Mummi start to whisper, is my sign to creep into hiding.

Handicapped! I freeze in the hallway. It sounds bad, like being retarded. Like giant Mark Kludas two doors down, who smells and weeps like an angry baby whenever the neighborhood kids rile him. Uncle Mike, who wears tight jeans and races motocross, is nothing like Mark.

Nonetheless, Handicapped is why he isn't able to go to Vietnam. This is also confusing. I've been in more protests than I can count, bearded graduate students passing me from shoulder to shoulder and singing folksongs Mom taught me on her Autoharp, so that he and his friends don't have to go. Uncle Mike will be the one who didn't disappear. Why, then, should he be disappointed?

"*Sssh*," my grandmother warns my mother. Uncle Mike is self-consciousness about his handicap.

When Uncle Mike finally awakens at three, I am stationed outside his door, trying not to stare. He grunts and staggers to the bathroom. Hearing the door, Mummi darts into his bedroom with a stack of freshly ironed clothes and grabs as many things as she can carry off the floor.

When Uncle Mike emerges in his white terrycloth robe, the bathroom mirror steamed up and his shaggy blond hair combed wet over his ears, I am waiting. He gives me a puzzled glance. I tilt my chin and pretend to study the embroidered hanging above the laundry hamper. Shaking his head, he saunters to the kitchen. I follow, close on his heels.

When he lifts me onto a stool, I scan his face, searching for handicap. I see Uncle Mike: Round ruddy face. My mother's blue, hound-dog eyes. Dashing blond mustache that droops a bit on the left beneath a slightly flattened nose.

Disappointed at the handicap's reluctance to show itself, I frown and demand to know what he's making.

He ignores me, his head burrowed in the refrigerator. Seconds later he emerges, arms loaded. Movements smooth and sure, no evidence of handicap, he builds a giant sandwich out of leftovers, cottage cheese, fried eggs and catsup.

"What next?" I ask of every step, trembling with horror.

He snorts an occasional answer: Meatloaf. Pickles. He loads the finished sandwich onto a baking sheet and shoves it into the oven. My stomach recoils.

"You know," he says, looking up from sawing at the bubbling sandwich, suddenly talkative. "I heard that President Nixon puts catsup on his cottage cheese." He grins. "He must be the only other person besides me!"

And though I know we aren't supposed to like President Nixon, I giggle.

Great-Grandpa the Cursed

Some time in the immigrant wave of the 1890s, my great-great-grandfather and his two elder sons came to Ohio. As was customary in chain immigration, his wife and newborn remained in Finland. When they died, my great-great-grandfather remarried and fathered three more children.

"Actually," my grandmother confesses, "they didn't die. My grandmother and Baby Vaino lived on in Finland for years."

Stunned, I watch her hands smelling of yeast and rye as she kneads the *limpa*. At ten I'm obsessed with family stories and photos. I can't imagine what compelled a father to tell his sons that their mother and brother had died. Was it his plan from the start to abandon his wife and construct a new life on the blank page of America?

Mummi shakes her head, working the brown dough with strong fingers. She doesn't know. Her father, my cursed great-grandfather, died of stomach ulcers when she was a baby. The story came second-hand to her.

I wonder if the two brothers knew what their father had done. In my experience, Finnish men are hardly forthcoming. Did they believe his terse story?

I imagine that this event—the loss of his mother and baby brother, his father's lie—is the moment my great-grandfather became cursed. I know how he feels. We two are alike, caught in between, with one foot, one parent in the New World, one still in the Old. Two years after my birth, without ever having seen me, my father disappeared to deepest, darkest Africa, never to be seen again. Like so many of those who invented America, my great-grandfather emerged from the dream of migration only partly intact. Half of himself he carried never waking, forever out of reach.

I study Mummi's face, her nose like a soft, drooping beak, and try to imagine her cursed father as a boy. I see a sleepwalker. A dark boy with light eyes, he stumbles though a house with hidden rooms beneath the stairs, behind the fireplace, blind to his American stepmother and new siblings. He tries to recall his mother's face, tries to imagine Baby Vaino, the One Left Behind, now grown to a boy. He lies awake nights, troubled by the voices of former slaves praying beneath the floorboards. Like they, he will rest in this place only momentarily. He wonders if he'll ever see his mother and brother again, fears they await a summons that will never come.

Bad Habits

Michael-Vaino, a.k.a. Uncle Mike, is in trouble.

From my hiding place in the hall linen closet, I hear Mummi stirring her tea, teaspoon tinkling. She says she fears he may take after Great-Uncle Vaino-Johan, her brother, and begins to cry.

"No, Mom," my mother says. "He just has Bad Habits."

Like not taking out the trash? Or watching too much TV, which rots your noodle?

Uncle Mike didn't come home last night. Wherever he was, Old Pappa wanted him to stay there overnight "to learn his lesson." So of course Tati Rauha's husband went to get him out, "just to spite Old Pappa."

My mother chuckles. "Dinner tonight should be fun." A metal chair leg scrapes across the linoleum. "Let me call the Funks to see if Faith can eat there."

Foiled, I steam in the closet. I am the only child among adults. If I am six, Uncle Mike is twenty-two, the family member closest to me in age.

I insist on taking my naps in his room. Except for the same heavy Scandinavian furniture that looks as if it's been shellacked in honey, his bedroom differs from the rest of the house. His shelves are crammed with tall, sparkly racing trophies. Two doors in the bed's golden headboard slide back to reveal tiny packets of tissue-thin paper called *zigzag* and tall glass tubes of stinky water. I am convinced these have something to do with Uncle Mike's Bad Habits. Back issues of *Playboy* and *Penthouse* rise in the closet. Fending off sleep, I read voraciously, dazed by mounds of breasts like the pale mountains surrounding our valley home.

Rivers

In the 1890s, one adult male and two male children, all named Hautajoki, left Finland for America. My great-great-grandmother nodded grimly from the misty banks of the Hauta River, their namesake (*joki* means river). The newborn balanced on her hip, she watched her husband and sons go. This was their agreement. He would take the two elder sons; she would remain behind with Baby Vaino. The Lutheran church banned divorce but couldn't control for the vicissitudes of immigration.

Father and sons settled in Ashtabula, where there was carpentry work and a thriving Finnish community. After some time, Great-great-grandpa Hautajoki took a wife. The Hautajoki thus cleaved in two, one stream on the motherland, the other a tributary transplanted to America. In time it split again. The branch from which I am descended turned out to be perpetually sickly, as if we never quite recovered from the wound.

On November 11, 1908, the cursed middle son left his father's house to marry another Finnish immigrant. He was nineteen. Like his father, he became a carpenter and fathered three children: Tati Rauha, the eldest; my grandmother, the baby; and a son. He named the son Vaino-Johan, after his younger and older brothers.

Even as a child, I knew that he had erred in naming. For a time, however, things were good. Husband and wife lived in a comfortable house that he built, and food was plentiful.

There is only one photograph of my great-grandfather the Cursed. In 1911 the family sat for a formal studio portrait: Husband, wife and the two elder children; my grandmother was not yet born.

Tati Rauha, large bow atop her pale curls, stands on a table, her hand pressed for leverage to her mother's breast. Holding her bottom lip between her teeth, she clutches her brother's hand.

Great-grandpa the Cursed, well groomed in a dark suit, also holds Vaino-Johan. The two of them, with their wide, angular jaws and olive skin, couldn't be more different from the women.

An odd distortion breaks the sharp sepia images, a smear or blur in the upper right-hand corner throwing Great-grandpa's head out of focus. Already, three or four years before his death at age twenty-six to stomach ulcers, he is receding from his family, becoming indistinct.

As if she senses this, Tati Rauha clenches her brother's hand, seemingly determined to wrest Vaino-Johan from their cursed father's grasp and keep him safe in the world with her—a role she and my grandmother played, with only limited success, all his life.

Gifts

Presents from Michael-Vaino, a.k.a. Uncle Mike, are always worth the wait. Despite this, as each birthday and *Joulu* approach, I see my mother watching him, worried, wondering if he will make it on time, or even remember.

There is the Frosty the Snowman Snowcone Maker, which though it requires hours of hard scraping to make a single snow cone, is exactly like the one I admired on television. There is a battery-powered pottery wheel that sprays mud everywhere.

One *Joulu* he builds a three-story dollhouse from my mother's design with real tile and Formica floors from factory remnants at work. He is so exhausted from all the late nights that he snores through Christmas dinner.

The *Joulu* I enter junior high, he hands me a heavy tan-and-brown envelope. Having recently discovered clothes, I instantly recognize the logo for Nordstrom, a department store in Seattle, and do a little prayer, *please let it be a lot, like twenty-five dollars*, before ripping it open.

A certificate for fifty dollars—more money than I have ever seen—slips into my trembling fingers. After he drags my arms from around his neck, I spend the rest of the evening glowing and shy.

"Half that amount would've been generous," my mother marvels later as they sit in the darkened living room sipping *glögi*. From my perch in the laundry room, I can see the colored lights blinking on the tree.

Uncle Mike chuckles. "Well, in fact, I only intended to spend twenty-five, but . . ." His voice drops, conspiratorial. "The guy in front of me spent forty dollars, and the saleswoman was uh, you know, pretty foxy."

My mother laughs. "Praise God for the male ego!"

I slump against the cold washing machine, careful not to make any noise. Junior high will be full of moments like this, the adult in me recognizing humor and the child wanting to cry. For one entire evening, I'd thought that his love finally matched mine. That I was worth twice as much.

Three decades after her father's death, some time between the end of World War II and 1958, when she started keeping a diary, my grandmother discovered that her father the Cursed had not died of stomach ulcers in 1915. In fact, he had not died at all.

She tells me the story when I'm eleven, sitting on my kitchen stool watching the *limpa* turn dark brown through the little yellowed window in the oven door.

One day by some miracle of mail forwarding, a letter arrived all the way from Ohio from the director of a sanitarium who regretted to inform the Hautajoki family that he had just expired.

Like milk left on the shelf too long.

Mummi pulls the *limpa* from the oven, heavy and dark. An acrid wave of rye floods the kitchen. Thirty years later, her dead father had died again, his life flickering across her cornea for only an instant.

I'm full of questions. How did her mother carry so many secrets to her

grave? That her husband had been alive all this time, insane, institutionalized for more than half his life. That all this time, his children had been
carrying this gene unawares. What, who, where?

When Mummi learned the truth she was in her thirties, the only one of
her siblings to have children, approximately the age her mother had been
when she surrendered her husband to the State.

She cuts the *limpa*, holding the sharp knife in soft hands, her voice low.
She doesn't say how it felt to learn the news about her father once it was
too late to do anything. I imagine she simply transferred those dark buds
of emotion to her brother, Great-Uncle Vaino-Johan, who was becoming
increasingly antisocial. I know she worried about her son, Michael-Vaino,
a.k.a. Uncle Mike.

Whatever her feelings, she does not voice them, does not commit them
to her diary, does not change the family register at the back of the album.
Great-grandpa the Cursed remains dead at age twenty-six of stomach
ulcers. This is an oral story, passed from her to my mother and me.

Rivers

After my great-grandfather the Cursed's institutionalization, the family
was always poor. For the next ten years wife and three children lived like
nomads, moving from state to state on the immigrant circuit, chasing
rumors of work. There is no family account of what happened to the other
Hautajoki men, father and older brother to the Cursed. Supposedly the
new American stepmother discouraged close relations. There is no explanation for the older brother's disappearance, another split in the river.

Bad Genes

Later I lug the encyclopedia up to the roof and pore over entries on schizo-
phrenia and depression, studying them as carefully as photos in the family
album. I'm convinced that I too am insane. I wonder how to break the news
to my mother. I am prone to fits of disordered thinking. Extreme sadness.
Exaggerated gaiety. Blame Finland.

Looking out on fields of mint, I weep a bit for Great-grandpa the Cursed,
my oft abandoned, lied to and lied about forebear. First taken from his
childhood home, and then replaced by an American stepmother and three
half-siblings, until haunted by the voices beneath his bed, he was finally
abandoned in the middle of a strange and unfriendly country by his young
wife.

Then I mist for his wife, left like my mother to raise her children alone. How in the world had she, who never learned to speak English, negotiated the American mental health system of 1915? Now I understand why she fled Ohio, taking her children west. And once the family got as far west as you can go, enter my mother, disowned at nineteen by Old Pappa for "going black," then abandoned for Africa, now trying to be both (white) mother and (black) father to the American child.

"More stories!" I demand, and my grandmother explains that Uncle Mike's mustache droops to hide the white veins where his face is sewn together, where there used to be an open cavity.

I follow her lead, punching the puffy *limpa*, watching it collapse.

Born with a cleft palate, ruptured left eardrum, and fused nasal cavity, Michael-Vaino, a.k.a. Uncle Mike, spent his babyhood in hospitals, arms sheathed in cardboard restraints. Mummi holds up her arms, articulating them stiffly at the elbows. So he couldn't pick at his face.

By the time he got out of the hospital, he was timid and cross. He hated speech therapy. He hated change. Every winter he cried at having to wear long sleeves, and then when summer rolled around, he cried to see his short-sleeved shirts again. Even now he refuses a hearing aid, despite my mother's claim that he can't hear "half of what's said." He would rather appear stuck-up than weak.

Mummi works the dough methodically, sniffling because *limpa* makes her cry.

"She blames herself," my mother explains later as we cut paper-dolls at the kitchen table. "She blames herself for Bad Genes."

My mother arranges a fan of American Revolution costumes across the sunny Formica. "And she's never forgiven herself for leaving him alone in the hospital. The doctors made her go home, but Mike was terrified. He sobbed all night. By morning the restraints were shredded."

Over the years, a series of operations were performed on Uncle Mike's face and ear. Every time he screamed, my grandmother screamed too. One, when he was an adult, entailed systematically shattering his nose and then reconstructing it like an ancient artifact, shard by shard. The procedure was so excruciating that he could only endure it partway and refused to return for the second installment. The left half of his nose remains smashed.

Great-Uncle Vaino-Johan the Depressed

During the Great Depression, the family split, for the first time since their father the Cursed's disappearance. Over his sister's objections, Great-Uncle

Vaino-Johan headed to Alaska. By 1934 he had panned enough gold to buy his mother and sisters a house in Portland, Oregon. He then embarked on a series of business ventures with his brothers-in-law and for the next two decades lived with or near the two couples. When my grandparents bought their farm, they built a bunkhouse especially for him, and when in 1945, my perpetually stoned Uncle Mike was born, a sickly, scarred creature who required a series of violent operations to repair a cleft palate and punctured eardrum, they named him Michael-Vaino, yet another ill-advised naming decision.

Soon after the truth about Great-grandpa the Cursed was revealed, his legacy began to manifest itself in Vaino-Johan, his son.

When my mother was a teenager, her uncle Vaino-Johan began to disappear for days at a time. The only hint a "spell" was coming was that he spoke even less than usual—if such a thing were possible. Though she knew her uncle's drinking binges involved hard liquor, she never saw him pick up anything harder than beer and never witnessed him drunk.

"What was he like?" I once asked.

She furrowed her brow, cocked her head, and finally shrugged. "I don't know."

"What do you mean you don't know? He lived with you your entire life!"

"I know." Her pouty lips rippled with concentration. "He was quiet. Very sweet. He would smile at you, but he never really talked."

She shrugged again, like my Finnish friend before her father's seventy-year-old decision to speak. "I don't know what he was like."

According to Mummi's diaries, Great-Uncle Vaino-Johan the Depressed was industrious and easy-going. He worked around the house and farm, babysat my mother and Uncle Mike, built and fixed and painted things for both sisters. In turn, his sisters fed him, washed his plastic bachelor's dishes when he wasn't living with them, and drove him to jobs and each other's houses in their pale, large-fender cars.

On the weekends he fished and hunted with my grandfather; in the evenings he worked puzzles and word games with my grandmother. One day in 1960, he and my grandmother spent seven hours driving to farms looking for harvest work.

As far as I can tell from Mummi's restrained wording, Vaino-Johan had a breakdown in 1958, the year she began keeping a diary. Like the family album, her diary maintains the official fiction of their father's death. And though she faithfully records driving Vaino-Johan to the doctor week after week, my mother along for company, she neglects to mention that the doctor is administering Electro-shock therapy.

According to my encyclopedia, shock therapy is exactly what it sounds like: currents of electricity zapping through the patient's head until he loses consciousness or convulses. It was, in 1958, a common treatment for depression.

My grandmother's diary reads like a catalogue of Vaino-Johan's disappearances, hospital sessions, more disappearances. Her February 26, 1959 entry stuns me: *Thursday, after having my regular argument with Vaino about keeping on going to the Dr., he left for his appt.* Amusing as it is to try to imagine either of my soft-spoken relatives arguing with anyone—let alone each other, regularly—it hurts to know that Vaino-Johan resisted. That same night, after the argument and treatment, he drank himself into oblivion.

Five years later, in February 1964, he and a friend went gold prospecting in California. There was no warning in the diary of the intended trip, and after his departure, he virtually disappears from its pages. As far as I can tell, he never returned.

Handicaps

Occasionally my mother and Michael-Vaino, a.k.a. Uncle Mike, slip into the comfort of childhood. These moments she is once again his sister, not The One Who Got Herself Knocked Up By A Black African, and he is just her brother, not The One Who Is At Best An Unreliable And At Worst A Bad Influence on her child.

One evening she follows him into the bathroom and perches on the edge of the bathtub. She's been prattling about Borlaug winning the Nobel Peace Prize, *yay for farmers!*, but falls silent, watching him shave.

He laughs uneasily. "It's hard to get it even," he apologizes, "with the deformity."

"What're you talking about?"

He shrugs, the blade flashing up the tender flesh of his neck.

She joins him at the mirror, standing on tiptoe, tan cowlicks sprouting like weeds over the hill of his shoulder. "Describe yourself!"

"Go away," he says, resting his elbow atop her head. "You're short, and I'm late."

"I may be short, but I'm tougher than you." She ducks and jabs his ribs. When he doubles over, she grabs his ears. "There," she turns him back to the mirror. "Tell me what you see."

He describes a face split like a mask, a huge, jagged scar and flattened, misshapen nose cleaving the landscape in two. Under the spell of his words, he transforms into an ogre straight out of Norse mythology, the Goddess Hel who haunts me too. In my grandmother's tales, Hel appears vertically split, half white–half black, the black half a putrefying corpse. Though not perhaps the healthiest biracial model for me, she is satisfyingly literal.

My mother gasps. "Sweetie, are you crazy?"

Years later she will find me weeping before a mirror after my first junior high dance: *Big Lips*, the only black girl in school, left to hold up the gymnasium walls for two excruciating hours, and ask the same of me.

It seems that leaving the house is a dangerous proposition. Difference announces itself out there, worms its way in. Strangers for whom familiarity doesn't hide handicap see clearly, instantly, who is half-rebuilt and who is half-black. *Hey man, why is your moustache so weird? What are you, deaf? Hey little girl, that white lady can't be your mom; where's your real mom? And why are your lips so big?*

In the unforgiving fluorescence of the bathroom, my mother tries to explain to her brother that his scar and nose are virtually unnoticeable, much as she will try to convince me after the dance that *Black is Beautiful, fuck junior high*. She speaks desperately, her hands, her cowlicks waving, but it is years too late.

"Yeah, whatever," he says, slapping on Brut cologne like punishment, slipping a flask of something clear into his rear jeans pocket.

Genes

I am pilfering again. Searching for someone who looks like me. Anyone.

Wedging myself into the back of my grandparents' closet among board games and jigsaw puzzles, I sift through shoeboxes of photographs: Monochrome snapshots of white relatives in black clothes. Hand-tinted portraits with my grandmother's whimsical colors. These are the ones who didn't make the cut; I've already looted the official family album.

It takes a while, the trick of comparing color to black-and-white distracting me, but I finally see the connection. Michael-Vaino, a.k.a. Uncle Mike, looks like his uncle, Vaino-Johan the Depressed, only paler. And Great-Uncle Vaino-Johan looks like his father, Great-grandpa the Cursed. Only Baby Vaino, the One Left Behind, who started it all, is missing.

The few times Great-Uncle Vaino-Johan eyes the camera directly, he still seems somehow at a distance, the forehead beneath his dark, slicked-back hair perpetually wrinkled from squinting. His broad, swarthy face with cleft chin and hooked nose (the only trait shared with the rest of the family) evokes the unknown origins of the Finns. In his face lies the possibility of Turkey and Hungary. He looks more Inuit than Nordic, and when he laughs, the dark slits of his eyes disappear completely.

In he goes to the box beneath my bed. He doesn't look like me, but at least he is different and dark.

Now I'm back for more. Snapshots soar through the air, piling up on the closet floor.

The aroma of *limpa* blooms at the mouth of the hallway, persistently faint as the cancer eating away at Mummi's insides, but at twelve I'm pushing my way out of childhood, wondering what I will become. After this golden skin and dark eyes my mother rhapsodizes over, these curls my grandmother twists around her fingers, this round nose my grandfather tugs before hanging me upside down, then what?

Gifts

My mother always knew the truth about her grandfather, Great-grandpa the Cursed, but can't recall what her mother did upon learning the news. What was the name of the Ohio sanitarium? How had it located the family after so many moves west? What was his official diagnosis? What happened to the letter? The body?

The details are forgotten, and who can tell whether it was Finnish closed-mouthedness, immigrant confusion, or newly acquired middle-class shame that allowed Great-grandpa the Cursed to be lost in America yet again?

This is the crossroads between the official family history that exists on paper, a more authentic history that was passed orally, and a third, more potent history that couldn't be spoken and is fading.

After Mummi's death, I combed her journal for clues, convinced that Great-Uncle Vaino-Johan the Depressed held the key to his father's mysterious madness. I remember once getting a birthday card from Great-Uncle Vaino-Johan as a very young child. Inside was an entire five-dollar bill. Perhaps because of this, or perhaps because I grew up hearing my grandmother missing him, I missed him too, just as I missed the African father I had never seen. Like my scarred, stoned Uncle Mike, like me, Great-Uncle Vaino-Johan was half in, half out. I imagined him as the key to all the family men who disappeared.

No Tragic Mulattos in our tree, only tragic Finns.

I question medicine. Michael-Vaino's, a.k.a. Uncle Mike's, ear and nose surgery. Great-Uncle Vaino-Johan's Electro-shock treatments. Great-Grandpa the Cursed's institutionalization.

I'm an adult, at the kitchen table with my mother, wondering how necessary shock treatments were for a man who disappeared quietly, sweetly, to the barn with a bottle of vodka. Certainly Vaino-Johan's benders wouldn't have caused alarm back in Finland. And what of his cursed father, institutionalized three decades?

My mother jokes. "They're Finns, for God's sake," she says. "How on earth did anyone even notice there was anything wrong?"

We imagine that Great-Grandpa the Cursed was like his son, Great-Uncle Vaino-Johan—quiet, prone to depression, at worst a drunk. Was it any more than standard Finnish dourness? Besides, what did 1915 America know about the mental health of a non-English-speaking immigrant who'd been ripped from mother and home?

Surely he couldn't have been violent, destructive, threatening. Not if his son is any indication. "Perhaps he just stopped functioning," my mother suggests. One day he didn't leave his room, content instead to listen to the faint voices in the walls, pleas from home.

Despite our shared genes, I pray that he was completely mad, better off forgotten by the few who knew where he was, hidden from those who might have saved him in more enlightened times. I pray that, at age twenty-six, his was an illness more profound than what afflicted his morose son Vaino-Johan, that it was something able to weather the vast medical improvements from 1915 to 1945. I pray to God there was no mistake.

Falling

After Mummi's death, my mother and I move to town. Michael-Vaino, a.k.a. Uncle Mike, who still lives at home, visits late in the evenings. I creep out in my nightgown to sit on his lap.

One night when I am full in the throes of adolescence, he points to the floor.

I look down.

He runs his finger up my chest and flicks my bottom lip. My lip, loose and jutting out, bobs up and down. An old trick, a child's trick.

"Got-cha!" he crows. He roars with laughter, much more so than the trick seems to warrant.

Smiling weakly, I look to my mother for direction. She is staring at Uncle Mike, her mouth tight, eyes slitted. None of the usual gentle pity or wary tolerance.

I know he can't be drunk or high, or she wouldn't have let him in. Those are the rules. So this is something else.

Each time my half-built uncle looks at me, he bursts into renewed, help-less gales.

Years later I recall the incident, the pain as sharp and stunning as the lesson of the coffee table against my nose when I was five, its taste as salty-sweet. I am grown before I finally realize, my stomach falling in disbelief the way it had that night, what he had been reacting to—the fullness of my lip. My difference, not ours.

FROM THE AUTHOR

"Black Men," the first piece I wrote in the NWP in the fall of 1998, repre-sents one of my toughest challenges ever. As I embarked on a book proj-ect about traveling to Nigeria to meet my father for the first time, I was haunted by the family men I did know—Finnish immigrants caught in a cycle of tragedy. Researching history showed me these characters em-bodied universal themes (e.g., the immigrant and Americanization pro-cess, the politics of medicine and race), and I became fascinated with the relationship between history and family. Investigating family secrets re-vealed a traumatic trigger three generations back, so I opened the essay with my own trauma, a childhood accident. The instant I finished the essay, I titled it "Black Men" and typed a note to my classmates: *This is a mess! My main question concerns structure. Is it too crazy to think I can ever possibly order all these historic relatives with odd names into a single work that moves back and forth through time, showing my connection to them all?*

I don't remember the discussion about structure, but I do remember being told I needed to change the title. "Black Men" was misleading; they'd expected to read about men who were actually *black*, not Finnish! I, the only black person in the room, sat silent as NWP instructor Sara Levine stepped in. She suggested that I'd intentionally subverted reader expec-tations and that the title symbolized how, in the absence of any blacks in the narrator's life, these men who were Other had become her longed-for "black" men. For the first time I heard my work analyzed from a literary perspective. Not someone saying *this* is working, fix *that*, but ascribing lit-erary strategy to what I, someone who'd majored in social sciences, did intuitively without having the language to articulate why.

Regarding my second concern—was it possible to organize characters with foreign names from different historical times?—the answer was a re-sounding no. Readers couldn't keep Veeti, Vaino, Johan, and Mike straight, nor their relationships to each other and me. The advice around the table fell into two camps: junk the historical characters completely or filter each through me, i.e., more narrator! I resisted both suggestions (out of stubbornness, I like to think, not arrogance). I would soon start a second book project (*Meeting Faith*, my NWP thesis) with an even more challenging structure inspired by the Talmud: memoir in the middle, journal entries in the margins. What I learned through "Black Men" and *Meeting Faith*—probably my biggest lesson from the NWP—was that when readers object to nontraditional structures and complicated storylines, *you're not doing it right*. If you get it right, no one even notices. I knew all the material fit together; I just had to figure how to do it right.

I was concurrently enrolled in the Writers' Workshop, so three semesters later (Spring 2000), I tested the revision on my fiction workshop. This version had subheadings, clearer parallels between the men's names (Baby Vaino, Vaino-Johan, Michael-Vaino), and a new ending, a traumatic incident with my uncle that brought the story full-circle, back to me. Classmates were touched but still hopelessly befuddled. I shelved "Black Men" as an ambitious failure.

A year or so after graduation, I traveled to an artists' residency for Christmas. I had only two weeks, so after thumbing through folders of annotated manuscripts from Iowa, I committed to a single task: to sit at my desk until "Black Men" worked. And if it didn't, we were through for good. Despite the gentle, rolling Virginia farmland, I felt razor-sharp, a sculptor carving away anything that got in clarity's way, ruthlessly shanking my darlings left and right. My NWP thesis director, Patricia A. Foster, had stressed the importance of establishing patterns to teach readers how to read my structure. So each character got his own tagline that repeated every time he came on-stage: *Great-Grandpa Veeti the Cursed*; *Baby Vaino, the One Left Behind*; *Michael-Vaino, a.k.a. Uncle Mike*. I told each one's story multiple times, with minor shifts in perspective. Subheadings identified recurring motifs and characters. The through-line became my grandmother's bread-baking.

The revised ending, however, felt heavy handed and accusatory: *I am grown before I realize what [my uncle] had been reacting to—the size of my lip. My blackness. His racism.* I needed readers to share my slow, reluctant realization, to feel my hurt and disbelief, not anger. The solution lay in the opening incident and peer feedback. I realized I could invoke the pain and confusion of that first accident though sense-memory, the taste of sugar and tears. Finally, I replaced my last four words with four penned in the margin during workshop by classmate Sarah Shun-lien Bynum (*Madeline is Sleeping*). The final (stolen) line became: *what he had been reacting to—the size of my lip. My difference, not ours.*

Indiana Review published "Black Men," which was then shortlisted for *Best American Essays 2005*. It was reprinted in an anthology on girls and race and in my anthology, *Coming of Age Around the World*, where commentary by my coeditor, who selected it, provided yet more insight: *By retelling different versions of her family's history, always subverting reader expectations of black and white, Adiele critiques the limitations of language to express identity and emotional reality.* Nearly a decade later, I finally learned why I'd resisted the easy fix.

Borders

JON ANDERSON (1990)

Mother raised African violets. She smuggled leaf slips into the US in the trunk of the car. We were a family of four, but we never talked much, especially near the border. On the run down from Montreal, bound for Cape Cod, my brother and I were told to be quiet. They had listening devices, Mother said, which could pick up conversations a long way away. At the border, we inched up in the line of cars, stopping under the overhanging roof at US CUSTOMS & IMMIGRATION.

"Fruits? Vegetables?" asked the guard, his hand on his gun, peering in, checking the front, staring into the back.

"No," Father said.

"Tobacco? Alcohol? Guns?"

"No," Father said.

". . . (African violets?)"

"No," Father said.

Borders are an illusion. So is fear. So is anger. So is future. So is past. They exist in the mind. There is no difference, for example, between the land of northern Vermont and of southern Quebec: it is all one valley, pressed flat over thousands of years of silence by glaciers scouring down from the north. It stretches a hundred miles from the Laurentians to the Green Mountains that once, long before the European settlers, formed the shoreline of a giant inland sea. One plain: indivisible, seamless, until French fur traders and Yankee farmers sent cartographers trudging across fields to draw lines and set up markers. Not a bad border, but an illusion nonetheless; Canadians and Americans, "we" split into "us" and "them."

I always felt bad about borders. On one side: me; on the other: some/

thing, some/place, some/one. Perhaps, people like me need to ferret into journalism. "I go berserk when I see a closed door," a writer said as we wandered the corridors of TIME after midnight, deep in stories, wrestling with transitions. He felt shut out, abandoned, lost, until he got inside. I said yes, aware of addictions, to secrets, the perfume of fame, the shimmer of opening nights, the right table at a sharp restaurant.

I was never clear what the penalty would be if Mother were caught smuggling her African violets. Prison for the adults in the car, certainly; foster homes for my brother and me. We would grow up as sullen wards of the state, chained to beds at night, sharing scraps at a table with bigger rougher kids in some dreary house, tolerated because we were income, as long as we were alive. I felt something dangerous about borders, about poking behind, reaching for the intimacy that comes with stripping off masks, tearing down walls. We send women sportswriters into locker rooms, but we want to be in there ourselves, showering, dressing with the stars slapping towels, sharing how they feel. We want to be at the center.

I went out with a woman in Washington who gave me, late at night after dinner, after brandy on the sofa in her apartment in front of a fire, the most precious thing she had: an insider's tip that President Carter would announce on the following Tuesday that he was canceling research on the neutron bomb. I didn't know what to make of it. It wasn't my beat. All I could think to do was kiss her on the mouth, whisper "thanks" and go back to my hotel.

My quest for intimacy led me to "support groups." I could tell how I got there, but that story involves my children, and people who sat around those tables, talking. Maybe it's better not to. Articles about such groups never get the flavor right. They can't, because they are based on print sound bites, quick specifics, logic. A support group is made up of slow drips of affection.

You can tell at a group when you're onto something. The room gets pin drop quiet, like theater. Murmuring stops. No one reaches for coffee, or passes the basket. People hang on every word. Often, the room is filled with smoke. The table looks like a wharf stretching out into the Atlantic. The talk has to do with buried memories that your father thought he was a wolf, or the devil, and ran around the living room howling at six kids? A woman said her father once came into a room naked, with an erection, and demanded that her mother, a former nun, have sex with him. "I am Satan," he said. "Well, I'm the Holy Father. Now go to your room," her mother replied. The children, on a sofa like teddy bears, watched their father's manhood fade.

"What do you do at your meetings?" Mother asks.

"We talk about feelings," I say. "You learn at your own pace. There are no judgments. No tests. You take what you need, leave the rest. It's safe intimacy. Like browsing at an art gallery, a sense that wonders are possible, that people can actually open up and connect."

"Oh, I couldn't possibly do that," Mother says. "Not in front of strangers."

I brought a candelabra into the bedroom and put it on top of the TV set. Anthony, my younger son, and I prepare to watch a video and eat spaghetti off trays on my bed.

"OK to light the candles?" I ask.

"No, Dad," Anthony says.

"Don't you like romantic dinners?" I say.

"Not with my Dad," he says.

Isaac Bashevis Singer says to begin a story with an address. Okay: 215 South Dodge, Iowa City, a brick coach house next to Delta Zeta, a stone mansion where the sisters walk around in their night gowns. Like Sam Spade, I lived by myself, within walking distance of my work. Last fall, during football season, I took a seminar on Jung on Saturday afternoons. Seven of us spent three hours at a stretch in Toma's attic near the stadium, sitting on pillows. I told of my dream where I was the insides of a baseball, a hairy core floating above the mall outside the TruValue. "This is significant," Toma said. "The TruValue is in a basement. So is the subconscious."

A woman in the class claimed that her dead brother lived in her ear canal disguised as waxy buildup.

All fiction is a movement from the familiar to the unfamiliar. What about the facts?

My daughter, Abra, a muscled girl, studied ballet and tacked a poster of Mikhail Baryshnikov to her bedroom wall. At the Treasure Island supermarket, amid the heaps of fresh produce, I whispered, "First position." Up she went on her toes, arching her hands over her head and pirouetting past the scales. She walked flat-footed, her feet splayed in that way dancers have, her brown hair in a bun, hunting for seedless grapes, which she put in my freezer and ate frozen. For eight years, her ballet teacher, Maria Tall-chief, reminded her to keep her back straight and to dance as if she carried, for all to see, a sparkling diamond on the top of her rib cage.

In 1986, on a Friday night, in early September, I drove my red Honda to the Drake Tower. My kids lived in the penthouse with their mother, Big Abra, who was redecorating, as always, tearing down walls, trying to get comfortable in what had once been her parents' apartment. She had re-married the week before, to the carpenter who rebuilt another of her par-ents' homes, in Lake Geneva, also tearing down walls, ripping up floors, adding onto the kitchen. He built a tree house for the kids with bunks, win-dows and a telephone. They rarely used it.

"I call 'front,'" Abra said, as I pushed open the passenger door for three of my kids. It was a big deal, who had the front seat, next to me. Ashley, a second behind, and Anthony, a second behind her, looked at me for a ruling. Abra pressed her case. "I said it first," she said and then I saw her forehead. A mound the size of a small egg, a hard embryo growing out of her head, colored blue and black, pushed out the skin above her eyebrows.

"Tell me again," I said to Abra in the morning, after I had taken the kids to my apartment, boiled them spaghetti, heated the meat sauce, put them to bed and sat up through the night in the bathroom, wondering. "Tell me again exactly what happened."

Like a court reporter, Abra sat up straight on the day bed in my living room, where she had slept. She talked as if she were reading from short-hand. There was no doubt.

"I came in from school," she said. "It was the first day and Anthony and I were arguing. We went upstairs to see Mom. She'd been up all night talking to a lot of people, but she was sitting in bed with a lot of pillows.

"Mom said, 'Well! What bus did you take?'

"And I said, 'The 36. It goes right past Latin School.'

"And Mom said, 'Don't contradict me, young lady. You'll take the 151, if you know what's good for you.'

"And I said, 'But Mom, the 151 doesn't go past school.'

"And Mom said, 'Oh, yes, it does, young lady.'

"And I raised my eyebrow and left and Mom followed me."

In my mind, I saw the dancers. I saw the moves: the big one rose from the canopied bed as the little one walked out of the bedroom and down the corridor toward the back stairs, the narrow twisting stairs with sharp cor-ners that stuck out around the iron water pipes. The little one at the top of the stairs, one foot in the air to take a step, the big one's hand, from behind, out of vision, pushing at the cashmere sweater that covered the little one's shoulders. The little one, the ballerina, shoved out of "first position," off balance, falling, hands moving up to protect the face, the middle of her forehead catching the edge, chipping the paint, brown bun snapping back as she banged down the rest of the stairwell, coming to rest in "last position," on the bottom step, sitting there, stunned.

If I do nothing, I thought, that in itself will be something. My kids will know that nothing can be done. If I do not crash the border between my business and their mother's business, I will lose these children, forever.

It was the start of the Wolf Network, the villagers against the wolf. I called Burt, my lawyer, a dozen friends, two pediatricians, a minister, a psychiatrist, a family counselor, Al-Anon, A.A., ACA, two of Abra's teachers and put Abra and Anthony in the Honda and took them to the Degerberg Academy of Martial Arts and Physical Fitness on North Lincoln Avenue. Abra said the mats were smelly, but she never took her eyes off the kid who was throwing an instructor over her shoulder.

I rented a beeper from an answering service that said they could track me down anywhere in Chicago, except under bridges. I typed out the codes and I dropped off the kids at the Drake Tower. Abra slipped the numbers in back of her wallet. I held her shoulders, kissed her egg.

"Be brave," I said. "Page me if anything happens."

"Sure, Dad," she shrugged, "if I survive."

FROM THE AUTHOR

"Borders" was part of my master's thesis ("And I Met the King of Siam"). Much of it came together while I was taking classes from Carl Klaus and William Cotter Murray. Both were important elements of what I might call "my ripening process," and I got to know both of them well enough to call them by their first names. Carl encouraged me to take not only courses in the English department but whatever might tickle my fancy. I opted for "The Art of the Japanese Cinema" and a multimedia course taught by Hans Breder that demolished a number of emotional walls that I had erected. For example, when I first started, another writer and I found it tremendously daring to read our works aloud while music played. By the end of the course, I was constructing novel forms of drama. I remember one scene where I, sitting on a dimly lit stool, displayed nonverbal reactions while a series of messages from my telephone answering machine played overhead on stereo speakers. It drew applause. Bill Murray, in turn, taught a course called "The Literary Journalists," which was aimed squarely at my problem. That was how to move beyond the flatness of contemporary feature writing and shape facts into a form that would, in the words of Tom Wolfe, look at experience through "the eye sockets" of the people involved, speaking in their own voices, as if the narrator knew their thoughts and feelings.

This is not easy to do. First off, you have to find the right situation to describe. Before I went to Iowa City, I had a wonderful writing teacher at the University of Chicago, Molly Daniels. One of her favorite sayings, as we gathered for classes near the bar where Saul Bellow hung out, was "Look for the moments after which everything is different." Another favorite was "Don't explain all the mysteries." What you want, she said, is for the reader to have a full grasp of the questions.

A second mandate is to read up on what others before you have done. You can't borrow other people's words. (That's plagiarism.) But you can study their style, see how they begin a story, introduce new people and bring the work to a conclusion. That's what I did, constantly refining "Borders" to eliminate unnecessary words, to make each facet of the story straightforward and plain. I spent a lot of time following up on tips from my various teachers. Once, on the phone with a friend in Chicago, I mentioned that the library at the university was open some nights until 1 a.m. "Wow. And is there a lot of rowdiness when the library lets out?" she asked, teasing, recalling our days in the journalism bars of Chicago's Old Town. Well, no, I admitted, but there was a lot of reading goin' on.

Finally, a writer, especially a writer of nonfiction, needs to be brave. What I was after in this essay was some sort of larger truth, an understanding of a difficult situation. The writer of nonfiction has to work around two piles of rocks. One is built on "the temptation to embellish." The other has to do with "the temptation to soften." Truth is the truth. Truth shall set you free. My adventures in Iowa taught me a lot about that.

Cousins

JO ANN BEARD (1994)

(Originally published in *The Boys of My Youth*)

Here is a scene. Two sisters are fishing together in a flat-bottomed boat on an olive green lake. They sit slumped like men, facing in opposite directions, drinking coffee out of a metal-sided thermos, smoking intently. Without their lipstick they look strangely weary, and passive, like pale replicas of their real selves. They both have a touch of morning sickness but neither is admitting it. Instead, they watch their bobbers and argue about worms versus minnows.

My cousin and I are floating in separate, saline oceans. I'm the size of a cocktail shrimp and she's the size of a man's thumb. My mother is the one on the left, wearing baggy gabardine trousers and a man's shirt. My cousin's mother is wearing blue jeans, cuffed at the bottom, and a cotton blouse printed with wild cowboys roping steers. Their voices carry, as usual, but at this point we can't hear them.

It is five a.m. A duck stands up, shakes out its feathers, and peers above the still grass at the edge of the water. The skin of the lake twitches suddenly and a fish springs loose into the air, drops back down with a flat splash. Ripples move across the surface like radio waves. The sun hoists itself up and gets busy, laying a sparkling rug across the water, burning the beads of dew off the reeds, baking the tops of our mothers' heads. One puts on sunglasses and the other a plaid fishing cap with a wide brim.

In the cold dark underwater, a long fish with a tattered tail discovers something interesting. He circles once and then has his breakfast before becoming theirs. As he breaks from the water to the air he twists hard, sending out a cold spray, sparks of green light. My aunt reels him in, triumphant, and grins at her sister, big teeth in a friendly mouth.

"Why you dirty rotten so-and-so," my mother says admiringly.

It is nine o'clock on Saturday night, the sky is black and glittering with pin-holes, old trees are bent down over the highway. In the dark field behind, the corn gathers its strength, grows an inch in the silence, then stops to rest. Next to the highway, screened in vegetation, a deer with muscular ears and glamorous eyes stands waiting to spring out from the wings into the next moving spotlight. The asphalt sighs in anticipation.

The car is a late-model Firebird, black on black with a T-roof and a tape deck that pelts out anguish, Fleetwood Mac. My cousin looks just like me except she has coarse hair and the jawline of an angel. She's driving and I'm shotgun, talking to her profile. The story I'm recounting to her is full of what I said back to people when they said things to me. She can sing and listen at the same time, so she does that, nodding and grimacing when necessary.

She interrupts me once. "What's my hair doing?"

"Laying down. I'll tell you if it tries anything." Her hair is short but so dense it has a tendency to stay wherever the wind pushes it. When she wakes up in the morning her head is like a landscape, with cliffs and valleys, spectacular pinnacles.

"Okay, go ahead," she says. I finish my story before my favorite song comes on so I can devote myself to it.

We sing along to a tune about a woman who rings like a bell through the night. Neither of us knows what that means, but we're in favor of it. We want to ring like bells, we want our hair to act right, we want to go out with guys who wear boots with turned-up toes and worn-down heels. We're out in the country, on my cousin's turf. My car is stalled in the city some-where on four low tires, a blue-and-rust Volkswagen with the door coat-hangered shut. Her car is this streamlined, dark-eyed Firebird with its back end hiked up like a skirt. We are hurtling through the night, as they say, on our way to a bar where the guys own speedboats, snowmobiles, what-ever else is current. I sing full-throttle: *You can take me to paradise, but then again you can be cold as ice, I'm over my head, but it sure feels nice.* I turn the rearview mirror around, check to see what's happening with the face.

Nothing good. But there you have it. It's yours at least, and your hair isn't liable to thrust itself upward into stray pointing fingers. It doesn't sound like corn husks when you brush it.

My cousin, beautiful in the dashboard light, glances over at me. She has a first name but I've always called her Wendell. She pushes it up to eighty and the song ends, a less wonderful one comes on. We're coming to the spot on the highway where the giant trees dangle their wrists over the ground. In the crotch of an elm, during daylight hours, a gnarled car is visible, wedged among the branches.

Up ahead, the cornfields are dark and rustling. The deer shifts nervously behind the curtain of weeds, waiting for its cue. The car in the tree's crotch is a warning to fast drivers, careening kids. Hidden beneath the driver's seat, way up in the branches, is a silver pocketwatch with a broken face. It had been someone's great-grandfather's, handed down and handed down, until it reached the boy who drove his car into the side of a tree. Below the drifting branches, the ground is black and loamy, moving with bugs. In the silence, stalks of corn stretch their thin, thready feet and gather in the moisture. The pocketwatch is stopped at precisely 11:47, as was the boy. Fleetwood Mac rolls around the bend and the deer springs full-blown out of the brocade trees. In the white pool of headlights, in front of a swerving audience, it does a short, stark, modern dance, and exits to the right. We recover and slow it down, shaking.

"He could have wrecked my whole front end," Wendell says. This is the farm-kid mentality. Her idea of a gorgeous deer is one that hangs upside down on the wall of the shed, a rib cage, a pair of antlers, a gamy hunk of dinner. She feels the same way about cows and pigs.

We're in the sticks. Way out here things are measured in shitloads, and every third guy you meet is named Junior. I've decided I don't even like this bar we're going to, that howling three-man band and the bathroom with no stalls, just stools. Now I'm slumped and surly, an old post for me. That deer had legs like canes, feet like Dixie cups.

Wendell pats my knee, grinning. "Settle down," she says. "It didn't *hit* us. We're safe." She likes excitement as long as her car doesn't get hurt. I light a cigarette, begin dirtying up her ashtray, and mess with the tape until our favorite song comes on again. We're back up to eighty on the narrow highway, daring the ignorant to take a step onto the asphalt. This is Illinois, a land of lumbering raccoons, snake-tailed possums, and flat-out running bunnies, all trying to cross the road. The interior of the car smells like leather and evergreen trees, the moon peers through the roof, and Wendell drives with one finger.

"Hey, how's my hair?" she asks suddenly. Her eyes are clear brown, her cheekbones are high and delicate, brushed with pink, her lips aren't too big or too little. She's wearing my shirt. A clump of hair has pushed itself forward in the excitement. It looks like a small, startled hand rising from the back of her head.

I make an okay sign, thumb and forefinger. The music is deafening.

Back in the cluster of trees, the deer moves into position again and the willows run their fingers along the ground. The corn whispers encouragement to itself. In the bar up ahead waitresses slam Sloe Gin Fizzes down on wet tables and men point pool cues at each other in the early stages of drunkenness. The singer in the three-man band whispers *test* into the microphone and rolls his eyes at the feedback. The sound guy jumps up from a table full of ladies and heads over to turn knobs.

We crunch over the parking lot gravel and wait for our song to finish. *I'm over my head, but it sure feels nice.* The bar is low and windowless, with patched siding and a kicked-in door; the lot is full of muscle cars and pickups. A man and a woman burst through the door and stand negotiating who will drive. He's got the keys but she looks fiercer. In the blinking neon our faces are malarial and buttery. As the song winds down, the drama in front of us ends. He throws the keys at her as hard as he can but she jumps nimbly out of the way and picks them up with a handful of gravel, begins pelting his back as he weaves into the darkness.

Wendell turns to me with a grin, a question on her lips. Before she can ask I reach over and press her excited hair back down.

Their house has a face on it, two windows with the shades half down, a brown slot of a door, and a glaring mouthful of railing with a few pickets missing. Pink geraniums grow like earrings on either side of the porch. It's August and the grass is golden and spiky against our ankles, the geraniums smell like dust. A row of hollyhocks stands out by the road, the flowers are upside-down ladies, red, maroon, and dried-up brown. An exploded raccoon is abuzz over on the far side of the highway and crows are dropping down from time to time to sort among the pieces. On either side of the house, fields fall away, rolling and baking in the heat.

The sisters are sitting on the stoop shelling peas, talking overtop of each other. My mother says mayonnaise goes bad in two hours in the hot sun and my aunt says bullshit. They've just driven out to the fields and left the lunches for the hired men. They argue energetically about this, until the rooster walks up and my aunt carries her bowl in the house to finish the discussion through the screen door. She and the rooster hate each other.

"He thinks you're a chicken," my mother explains. "You have to show him you won't put up with it." She picks up a stick, threatens the rooster with it, and he backs off, pretends to peck the yard. My aunt comes back out.

The front of her head is in curlers, the brush kind that hurt, and she keeps testing her hair to see if it's done. She has on a smock with big pockets and pedal pushers. Her feet are bare, one reason why the rooster is scaring her so much. My mother doesn't wear curlers because her hair is short but she has two clips crisscrossed on either side of her head, making spit curls in front of her ears. Every time a car drives by she reaches up automatically, ready to yank them out. She has on Bermuda shorts and a wide-bottomed plaid blouse with a bow at the neck. They are both pregnant again.

We're going to be in a parade at four o'clock, Wendell and I, riding bikes without training wheels, our dolls in the baskets. We asked to have the training wheels put back on for the parade but they said no. Our older sisters are upstairs somewhere, dumping perfume on one another and trying on bracelets. They'll be in the parade, too, walking behind us and throwing their batons in the air, trying to drop them on our heads.

Wendell jumps at the rooster suddenly and he rushes us, we go off screaming in different direction while he stands there furious, shifting from one scaly foot to another, slim and tall with greasy black feathers and a yellow ruff like a collie. He can make the dirty feathers around his neck stand up and fall back down whenever he gets mad, just like flexing a muscle. Even his wives give him a wide berth, rolling their seedy eyes and murmuring. They get no rest. I haven't yet connected the chickens walking around out here with what we had for lunch, chopped up and mixed with mayonnaise.

The mothers give up and go in the house to smoke cigarettes at the kitchen table and yell at us through the windows. Wendell and I work on decorating our bikes and complaining about no training wheels.

"What about if there's a *corner*?" I say.

"I know," says Wendell. "Or if there's *dog* poop?" I don't know exactly how this relates but I shudder anyway. We shake our heads and try twisting the crepe paper into the spokes the way our mothers showed us but it doesn't work. We end up with gnarled messes and flounce into the house to discipline our dolls.

Here is the parade. Boys in cowboy getups with cap guns and rubber spurs, hats that hang from shoestrings around their necks. The girls squint against the sun and press their stiff dresses down. This is the year of the can-can slips so we all have on good underpants without holes. Some kids have their ponies there, ornery things with rolling eyes and bared teeth, all decorated up. Two older boys with painted-on moustaches beat wildly on drums until they are stopped. Mothers spit on Kleenexes and go at the boys' faces while fathers stand around comparing what their watches say to what the sun is doing.

Two little girls wear matching dresses made from a big linen tablecloth, a white background with blue and red fruit clusters. One has a bushy stand of hair and the other a smooth pixie. Both have large bows, one crunched into the mass and the other practically taped on. The scalloped collars on their dresses are made from the border of the tablecloth, bright red with tiny blue grapes, little green stems. There are sashes tied in perfect bows, and pop-bead bracelets. Our shoes don't match.

The dolls rode over to the parade in the trunk of the car so we wouldn't wreck their outfits. They have the ability to drink water and pee it back out but they're dry now, our mothers put a stop to that. They have on dresses to match ours, with tiny scalloped collars and ribbon sashes. We set them carefully in our bike baskets with their skirts in full view. Mine's hair is messed up on one side where I put hairspray on it once. Wendell's has a chewed-up hand and nobody knows how it got that way. We stand next to our crepe-papered bikes in the sunlight, waiting for them to tell us what to do.

Our sisters have been forbidden to throw their batons until the parade stars and so they twirl them around and pretend to hurl them up in the air, give a little hop, and pretend to catch them again. They are wearing perfume and fingernail polish with their cowboy boots and shorts. They don't like us very much but we don't care.

My mother tells me to stand up straight and Wendell's mother tells her to push her hair back down. The baton twirlers get a last minute talking-to with threats. The parade moves out ragged and wobbly, someone immediately starts crying, a pony wanders out of line and looks for some grass to chew. The main street is crowded with bystanders and parked automobiles. It is never clear what this parade is for, except to dress up the children and show them off, get the men to come in from the fields for a while.

As the parade pulls itself slowly down the street, the mothers stand with wry, proud faces and folded arms while fathers stand smoking, lifting the one-finger farmer's salute as their sons go by. Wendell and I steer carefully and watch our mothers as they move along the sidewalk, following. Tall, lanky frames and watermelon stomachs, the gray eyes and beautiful hands of the Patterson side of the family. Our dolls are behaving perfectly, staring straight ahead, slumped forward in their baskets. My sash has come untied and Wendell's underpants are showing. We don't care. They won't bother fixing us now. We're in the parade and they have to stay on the sidewalk.

The street is brilliant in the sun, and the children move in slow motion, dresses, cowboy hats, tap shoes, the long yellow teeth of the mean ponies.

At the count of four, one of our sisters loses control, throws her baton high in the air and stops, one hand out to catch it when it comes back down.

For a long, gleaming moment it hangs there, a silver hyphen against the hot sky. Over the hectic heads of the children and the smooth blue-and-white blur of crepe-papered spokes and handlebar streamers, above the squinting smiles and upturned eyes, a silver baton rises miraculously, lingers for a moment against the sun, and then drops back down, into the waiting hand.

Back at the bar, someone has hold of me and I'm on the dance floor. Wendell's standing just inside the door. I'm going backward swiftly, in a fast two-step, there's an arm slung across my shoulder. It's good old Ted, trying to make a girl feel welcome. The bar is as dark as a pocket and my eyes haven't adjusted yet. Ted runs me into a couple of people and I tell him his arm weighs a ton. He grins but doesn't move it. He has long legs and a drinking problem. Two ex-wives follow him everywhere, stirring up trouble.

When the song finally ends, I untangle from Ted and look for Wendell. She's got us a table back by the wall, beneath the bored head of a deer. As I pass the bar several guys in turn swivel their stools around and catch me. Blue-jeaned legs are parted, I'm pulled in, pressed against a chest, clamped. Hello, hello. I bum a cigarette from the first one and blow smoke in the face of the second when his hand crawls like a bull snake up the back of my shirt. Even way out here I'm known for being not that easy to get along with.

Wendell takes her feet off my chair and pushes a rum and Pepsi my way. She tries to tell me something over the din.

"What?" I holler back and turn my ear to her.

"I *said*, your *buddy's* here," she yells into my hair. I pull back and look at her. She jerks a thumb upward, to the passive, suspended face of the deer. Someone has stuck a cigarette butt in one of its nostrils. I show her my middle finger and she sits back again, satisfied. Side by side at the spindly table, we drink our drinks for a while and watch the dancers go around.

Ida's out there, going to town, seventy-five if she's a day, with dyed black hair and tall, permanently arched eyebrows. From nine to midnight, even when it's just the jukebox, she takes herself around the dance floor—fox-trot, swing shuffle, two-step. She comes here every Saturday night to dance by herself while her grandson drinks Mountain Dew and plays pool in the back room. Her tennis shoes look like they're disconnected from the rest of her body. Every once in a while, she presses one hand against her waist and closes her eyes for an instant, keeping time with her shoulders, all part of some interior dancing-drama, some memory of Pete and her, before they got old, before she up and got widowed. Apparently, they were quite a deal on the dance floor. Nobody ever bumps into her out there, even the drunkest of the drunk make a space for those shoes and that head of hair. She's dancing with a memory, putting all the rest of us to shame.

Here comes our darling Nick. Everyone's in love with him, blond hair in a ponytail and wire-rims, drives a muddy jeep. Too bad he's related to us. He sets us up with two more drinks, takes a joint out of his shirt pocket, puts it in my cigarette pack, and lays a big kiss on Wendell, flat on the lips. Right as he leaves, he zooms in on me unexpectedly. I give him one hand to shake and put the other one over my mouth. Wendell takes a drink and leans over.

"Gross," she shouts into my ear. I nod. Cousin cooties.

"I'm telling Aunt Bernie," I shout back. Aunt Bernie is his mom.

We've been sitting too long. Wendell carries her drink, I light a cigarette, and we move out into the revelers, and lose each other. The rum is a warm, dark curtain in my chest. I suddenly look better than I have in weeks, I can feel geraniums blooming in my cheeks, my mouth is genuinely smiling for once, my hair, fresh from the ironing board, falls like a smooth plank down my back. It's Saturday night and I'm three rum and Pepsis to the wind. I love this bar. The floor is a velvet trampoline, a mirrored ball revolves above the dance floor, stars move across faces and hands, everyone encountered is a close personal friend. I'm in line for the bathroom, chatting with strangers.

"I like your shirt." This from the woman behind me, she may be trying to negotiate her way up the line.

"Thanks," I tell her. She's pretty. "I like yours, too."

"Your cousin's really drunk," she says, rolling her eyes. I guess she knows me. She means Nick, not Wendell. Women are always striking up conversations about Nick.

"I know" is what I tell her. I smile when I say it and shrug, trying to indicate that she can come to family dinner with Nick as far as I'm concerned. We lapse back into silence until the door bursts open and three women come out, reeking of reefer and perfume.

I look at the woman who struck up the conversation with me. We raise our eyebrows.

"Nice perfume," she says, wrinkling her nose.

"Nice reefer," I say. I let her come in while I go and she checks her makeup and examines her teeth in the mirror. I wait for her, too, bending over at the waist, shaking the hair out, and then flipping it back. It makes it fluffier for a few minutes, before it settles into the plank again. The bending and the flipping sends the room careening for a moment, I'm in a centrifugal tube, then it halts. She wants to know who Nick's going out with.

"His dog, I think," I tell her. I'm politely not noticing her peeing. "He's got the nicest golden retriever you ever saw." I love that dog; it refuses to hunt, just walks along and stirs up ducks and pheasants, watches with surprise when they go flapping off. "That's one thing about Nick. His dog's nice." I don't think Nick ever shoots anything anyway, he just looks good in the boots and the vest.

Actually, I think Cousin Nick's going out with everyone, but I don't tell her that. She looks hopeful and sparkly and she's not nearly as drunk as me. I give her a swimmy smile on the way out and we part company forever.

The band rolls into a slow one, with a creaky metallic guitar hook and a lone warbling voice. Someone asks me to dance and we stroll around the floor, amid the stars and the elbows. I close my eyes for a moment and it's night inside my head, there are strange arms moving me around, this way and that, feet bumping into mine. The steel guitar comes overtop of it all, climbing and dropping, locating everyone's sadness and yanking on it. In the shuffling crowd the dark curtain of rum parts for an instant, and reveals nothing. I open my eyes and look up at my partner. He's leading away, a grinning stranger, his hand strolls down and finds my back pocket, warms itself. Christ Almighty.

Ida swims through, and past, eyes blank as nickels, disembodied feet, arms like floating strings. One song ends and a new one starts up, I shake my head at my partner and he backs off with a sullen shrug. Apparently he likes this song because he begins fast-dancing by himself, looking hopefully around at the other dancers, trying to rope a stray.

This is Wendell's favorite song, *She's a good-hearted wo-man, in love with a two-timing man.* Here she is, ready to dance. I move with her back into the lumbering crowd on the dance floor, and we carve out a little spot in front of the band. *She loves him in spite of his wicked ways she don't understand.* The bar has gone friendly again while I wasn't looking, the faces of the other dancers are pink with exertion and alcohol. Nick's dancing with the bathroom girl, Ted's twirling an ex-wife, the singer in the band knocks the spit out of his harmonica and attaches it to his neck again. Look at Wendell's face. She's twenty-one and single; her hair has a story to tell. In the small sticky space in front of the band, we twirl a few times, knuckles and lifted elbows, under and over, until I get stomped on. We're singing now, recklessly, it's almost closing time and us girls are getting prettier by the moment. *Through teardrops and laughter we pass through this world hand in hand.* Of course, both Wendell and I would like to be good-hearted women but we're from the Patterson clan, and just don't have the temperament for it.

The sisters are making deviled eggs. They have on dark blue dresses with aprons and are walking around in nyloned feet. No one can find the red stuff that gets sprinkled on top of the eggs. They're tearing the cupboards apart right now, swearing to each other and shaking their heads. We all know enough to stay out of the kitchen.

We're at my grandma's house in our best dresses with towels pinned to the collars. Our older sisters are walking around with theatrical, mournful faces, bossing us like crazy, in loud disgusted whispers. They have their pockets loaded with Kleenex in preparation for making a scene. We're all going to our grandfather's funeral in fifteen minutes, as soon as the paprika gets found.

Wendell and I get to go only because we promised to act decent. No more running and sliding on the funeral-home rug. Someone has *died*, and there's a time and a place for everything. We'll both get spanked in front of everyone and put in chairs if we're not careful. And if we can't keep our gum in our mouths then we don't need it: both pieces are deposited in a held-out Kleenex on the ride over. Wendell and I are in disgrace from our behavior last night at the visitation.

"It wasn't our fault he moved," Wendell had explained, right before being swatted in the funeral-home foyer. Our grandfather had looked like a big, dead doll in a satin doll bed. We couldn't stop staring, and then suddenly, simultaneously, got spooked and ran out of the room, squealing and holding on to each other. We stayed in the foyer for the rest of the night, greeting people and taking turns sliding the rug across the glossy floor. We were a mess by the end of the evening.

Our dads have to sit in a special row of men. They're going to carry the casket to the graveyard. We file past them without looking, and the music gets louder. The casket sits like an open suitcase up front. After we sit down in our wooden folding chairs all we can see is a nose and some glasses. That's our grandpa up there, he won't be hollering at us ever again for chewing on the collars of our dresses or for throwing hangers out the upstairs window. He won't be calling us giggleboxes anymore. He doesn't even know we're all sitting here, listening to the music and the whispers. He is in our hearts now, which makes us feel uncomfortable. Wendell and

I were separated as a precautionary measure; I can just see the tips of her black shoes. They have bows on them and mine have buckles. She is swinging hers a little bit so I start to swing mine a little bit too. This is how you get into trouble, so I quit after a minute and so does she.

Pretty soon the music stops and my mother starts crying into her Kleenex. My aunt's chin turns into a walnut, and then she's crying too. Their dad is dead. Wendell puts her shoe on the back of the chair in front of her and slides it slowly down until it's resting on the floor again. I do the same thing. We're not being ornery, though. A lady starts singing a song and you can hear her breath. I can see only one inch of her face because she's standing in front of the dads. It's a song from Sunday school but she's singing it slower than we do and she's not making the hand motions. I do the hand motions myself, very small, barely moving, while she sings.

Wendell's mom leans over and tells me something. She wants me to sit on her lap. She has a nickname for me that nobody else calls me. She calls me Jody and everyone else calls me Jo. She's not crying anymore, and her arms are holding me on her lap, against her good blue dress. It's too tight in the armpits but you can't tell from looking. My mom's got Wendell.

After a while everyone starts crying, except Uncle Evan, my grandma's brother who always spits into a coffee cup and leaves it on the table for someone else to clean up. My aunt rests her chin on my head and rearranges her Kleenex so there's a dry spot. I sit very still while the preacher talks and the mothers cry, not moving an inch, even though my arms don't have anywhere to go. Wendell keeps moving around but I don't. Actually, I don't feel very good, my stomach hurts. I'm too big to sit on a lap, my legs are stiff, and now my heart has a grandpa in it.

The fairgrounds are huge and hot, an expanse of baking bodies and an empty stage. There are guys monkeying around on the lighting scaffold, high in the air. Mostly they're fat, stoned, and intent on their tasks, but Wendell's spied one that might be okay. Ponytailed and lean, he has his T-shirt off and stuck in the waistband of his jeans. I can't look at him because he's too high up, hanging off of things that don't look reliable. Wendell trains her binoculars on him, focuses, and then sets them down. "Yuck," she reports.

We will see God this afternoon—this is an Eric Clapton concert. We're sitting on one of our grandmother's worn quilts, spread out on the ground twenty feet from the stage. "Hey, look." I show Wendell a scrap of fabric. It's blue-and-red plaid with dark green lines running through. She and I used to have short-sleeved shirts with embroidered pockets made out of that material. On the ride over here we each took a small blue pill, a mild hallucinogen, and now Wendell has to put her face about an inch away from the quilt in order to get a sense of the scrap I'm talking about.

"It used to be seersucker," she says sadly. "And now it isn't." We think that over for a few minutes, how things change, how nothing can be counted on, and then Wendell remembers something. "My shirt had a pony on the pocket and yours had a *schnauzer*." She snickers.

For some reason that irritates me no end. I hadn't thought of that schnauzer in years, and she has to bring it up today. Thanks a whole hell of a lot. It did used to be seersucker, too, which is very strange, because now it's not. What could have happened to it? How can something go from being puckered to being unpuckered? You could see if it was the other way around, but this just doesn't make sense. My halter top keeps feeling like it's coming undone.

We put the cooler over the unsucked seersucker so we can quit thinking about it. Wendell stretches out on her back and stares at the sky. I stretch out on my stomach and stare at some grass. We are boiling hot but we don't know it; my hair is stuck to my back and Wendell's is standing straight up in a beautiful manner.

"Your hair is standing straight up in a beautiful manner," I tell her. She nods peacefully. She holds her arms up in the air and makes a *c* with each hand.

"I'm cupping clouds," she says. I try to pay closer attention to my grass, which is pretty short and worn down. It looks like it's been grazed. I read somewhere once that hysterical fans used to eat the grass where the Beatles had walked.

"Do you think Eric Clapton walked on this grass?" I ask Wendell. She looks over at me and considers. She thinks for so long that I forget the question and have to remember it again.

"No," she says finally. I feel relieved.

"Well then, I'm not eating it," I tell her flatly.

"Okay," she replies. I wish she had said, "Okey-dokey" but she didn't. She said, "Okay," which has an entirely different meaning.

I sit up and my halter top sags alarmingly. All I can do is hold it in place. There's nothing else to be done, I wouldn't have any idea how to retie it. Wendell is curled up in a ball next to me with her eyes shut.

"My top is falling off," I tell her. She doesn't open her eyes. I can feel sweat running down my back like ball bearings. Wendell groans.

"The clouds are cupping *me* now," she says. "Get them off." She's still got her eyes shut, making a whimpering sound. I don't know exactly what to do because I can't see any clouds on her and my shirt is falling off. I have to think for a moment. If I had just taken one bite of grass this wouldn't have happened.

A guy on the blanket next to us tries to hand me a joint. I can't take it because I'm holding my chest. He looks at me, looks at Wendell balled up on the ground, and nods knowingly. "Bummer," he proclaims.

I can't stand to have Eric Clapton see me like this. I let go of my shirt for one second and wave my arms over Wendell. My halter top miraculously stays in place. In fact, it suddenly feels too tight. "I just got the clouds off you," I inform her. She opens one eye, then the other, and sits up.

"You look cute," she tells me. She's turning pink from the afternoon sun and her hair is hectic and alive. We open beers from our cooler and start having fun.

By the time old Eric comes out, we've completely forgotten about him, so it's a pleasant surprise. We climb up on our cooler and dance around, waving our arms in the air. We're so close to the stage he is almost life-size. This is amazing. We dance and mouth the words while Eric sings tender love songs about George Harrison's wife and plays his guitar in a godlike manner.

The sky has turned navy blue. Eric stands in a spotlight on the stage. I pick him up once, like a pencil, and write my name in the air, then put him back down so he can play his guitar again. My halter top stays stationary while I dance around inside it naked. *Darling*, we sing to Eric, *you look wond-der-ful tonight*. The air is full of the gyrations of six thousand people. My cousin is covered with clouds again but she doesn't seem to notice. Although it's still five months until Christmas, tiny lights wink on and off in her hair.

The tablecloth is covered with pie crumbs and empty coffee cups, a space has been cleared for the cribbage board and ashtrays. The sisters are smoking, staring at their cards, and talking about relatives. Neither of them can believe that Bernice is putting indoor-outdoor carpeting in her kitchen.

"You can't tell her a thing," my mother says. She lays down a card and moves her red peg ahead on the board.

"Shit," my aunt says softly. She stares at her cards. One of the husbands comes in for more pie. "What do I do here?" she asks him. He looks at her hand for a moment and then walks around the table to look at my mother's hand. He points to a card, which she removes and lays down. "Try that on for size," she tells my mother.

The back door flies open and two daughters enter. There is a hullabaloo.

Barbie's little sister, Skipper, was sitting on the fence and accidentally fell off and got stepped on by a pig. "She's wrecked," Wendell reports. "We had to get her out with a stick." I show them the stick and Wendell shows them Skipper.

"Stay away from the pigs," my aunt says. She's looking at her cards.

"We *were* staying away from the pigs," I answer, holding up the muddy stick as evidence. "Tell them to stay away from *us*, why don't you?" My mother looks us. "Well," I say to her.

"You might find out *well*, if you're not careful," she tells me.

Wendell takes a whiff of Skipper, who is wearing what used to be a pair of pink flowered pajamas. A small bit of satin ribbon is still visible around her neck, but the rest, including her smiling face, is wet brown mud and something else. "Part of this is *poop*," Wendell hollers.

My aunt turns around finally. "Take that goddamn doll outside." She means business so we go upstairs, put Skipper in a shoe box, and find our Barbies.

"Mine's going to a pizza party," I say. My Barbie has a bubble haircut, red, and Wendell's has a black ponytail.

"Let's just say they're sitting home and then Ken comes over and makes them go to a nightclub," Wendell suggests. Hers doesn't have a pizza-party outfit so she never wants mine to get to wear one either.

"Mine's going to sing at the nightclub then," I warn her.

"Well, mine doesn't care," Wendell offers generously. She's eyeballing a white fur coat hanging prominently in my carrying case. Her Barbie walks over to mine. "Can I wear your fur tonight?" she asks in a falsetto.

"If I can wear your bola," my Barbie replies.

"It's boa, stupid," Wendell tells me. She digs out a pink feathered scrap, puts it in her Barbie's hand, and makes her Barbie throw it at mine.

"Let's say it's really hot out and they don't know Ken is coming over and they're just sitting around naked for a while," I suggest.

"Because they can't decide what to wear," Wendell clarifies. "All their clothes are in the dryer." She wads up all the outfits lying around and throws them under the bed.

"Oh God, it's so hot," my Barbie tells hers. "I'm going to sit at the kitchen table." Naked, she sits down in a cardboard chair at a cardboard table. Her hair is a smooth auburn circle, her eyes are covered with small black awnings, her legs are stuck straight out like broomsticks.

Black-haired, ponytailed Barbie stands on tiptoe at the cardboard sink. "I'm making us some pink squirrels," she announces. "But we better not get drunk, because Ken might come over."

Both Barbies do get drunk, and Ken does come over. He arrives in an ill-fitting suit, and the heat in the Barbie house is so overwhelming that he has to remove it almost immediately.

"Hey baby," Ken says to no one in particular. The Barbies sit motionless and naked in their cardboard kitchen, waiting for orders. This is where Dirty Barbies gets murky—we aren't sure what's supposed to happen next. Whatever happens, it's Ken's fault, that's all we know.

The Barbies get tired and go lie down on their canopied bed. Ken follows them in and leans at a forty-degree angle against their cardboard dresser. He's trying to tell them he's tired, too.

"You're going to prison, buddy," Wendell finally says, exasperated. She heaves him under her bed and we get our Barbies up and dress them.

"Ken better not try anything like *that* again," ponytailed Barbie says. She's wearing a blue brocade evening gown with the white fur coat, and one cracked high-heeled shoe.

"He thinks he's funny but he's not," my Barbie replies ominously. "He's in jail and *we're* the only ones who can bail him out." She's got on a yellow satin-and-net dress with a big rip up the back, and the boa is wrapped tightly around her neck. By the time they get Ken out of jail and into his tuxedo, the whole evening is shot. The judge has to be bribed with a giant nickel that ponytailed Barbie holds in her outstretched hand.

"Crap," Wendell says when they holler at us from downstairs. I pack up my carrying case, drag it down the steps and out to the car. I keep sitting down the whole way because I'm tired.

"Get moving," my mother tells me. My aunt calls me Jody and gives me a little whack on the behind, but she doesn't mean anything by it. I climb in beside my sister and roll down the window.

"Whaaa," Wendell says to me. This is the sound her Betsy-Wetsy makes when it gets swatted for peeing.

The car pulls out onto the highway and turns toward town. I left my Barbie's pizza-party outfit under Wendell's pillow so she could use it until next time. Too bad, I miss it already. Red tights and a striped corduroy shirt with tassels that hang down. It goes better with a bubble cut than a ponytail, really. I should never have left it.

August, early evening. We're crammed into Uncle Fred's yellow Caddie, driven by Little Freddy, our cousin. I have on a low-backed, peach-colored dress with spaghetti straps and a giant, wrist-itching corsage made of greenery and tipped carnations. Wendell is wearing an ivory wedding gown with a scoop neck and a hundred buttons down the back. It's the dress our grandmother married our grandfather in and it makes Wendell look like an angel. There are guys present—my boyfriend, a sweet, quiet type named Eric, and Wendell's brand-new husband, Mitch, a mild-mannered, blue-eyed farmer who is gazing at the cornfields streaking by.

Cousin Freddy is in control at this point, possibly a big mistake. One misplaced elbow and all the windows go down at once, causing hot air to whirl around inside the Caddie, stirring up everyone's hair and causing a commotion. "Okay, okay," Freddie says in a rattled voice. He pushes another button and all the windows go back up, the commotion stops, the air conditioning comes back into play.

Wendell has a wreath of baby's breath perched on top of her head like a crown of thorns. A slight crevice has appeared in the front of her hair, the baby's breath has lifted with the landscape and sits balanced on two distinct formations. The back is untouched. She wrestles herself over to the rearview mirror and gets a glimpse.

"Oh my God, it's the Red Sea," she says. "You parted my *hair*, Freddy."

There is an audible combing noise inside the car for a moment as she tries to impose some discipline on it. Freddy looks at her in the rearview mirror. He's got Uncle Fred's five-o'clock shadow and Aunt Velma's tiny teeth, he's wearing a powder blue short-sleeved shirt and a flowery necktie, fashionably wide. "We can borrow you a rake at one of these farmhouses," he says, braking. The Caddie, dumb and obedient as a Clydesdale, slows down, makes a left and then a right, pulls onto a dirt track leading into a cornfield. Freddy gets his wedding present from under the seat, lights it, and passes it back. We pile out into the evening and stand, smoking, next to the car.

The sky is way up there, a lavender dome. There's a gorgeous glow of radiation in the spot the sun just vacated, a pale peach burst of pollution that matches my dress. The corn is waxy and dark green and goes on forever. We're standing in a postcard.

"This is my big day," Wendell mentions. The crown of thorns is resting peacefully, swifts are swooping back and forth, drinking bugs out of the sky. We're trying to keep the hems of our dresses from dragging in the dirt.

"This corn is *ready*," Mitch says quietly, to no one in particular. The stalks are taller than us by a foot, a quiet crowd of ten million, all of them watching us get high and wreck our outfits.

"Don't lean on the car," I tell Wendell. She stands in her usual slouch, one arm wrapped around her own waist, the other bringing the joint to her lips. She squints and breathes in, breathes out. "You look like Lauren Bacall only with different hair," I say.

She considers that. "You look like Barbara Hershey only with a different face," she says kindly. We beam at one another. This is Wendell's big day.

"Hey, bats," Eric says suddenly. He's looking up into the air where the swifts are plunging around. I'm very fond of him for a moment, and then I feel a yawn coming on. A breeze has picked up and the corn is rustling, a low hiss from the crowd. We're making Wendell late to her own party.

The Caddie takes us out of the cornfield, haunch-first. Freddy steers it up to the highway, sets the cruise, and we all lean back, stare out the side windows, and watch the landscape go from corn to soybeans to cows to corn. Next thing you know we're getting out again, this time at Wendell's old house, the farm.

The wedding cake is a tiered affair with peach-colored roses and two very short people standing on top. Our mothers made the mints. This is a big outdoor reception, with a striped awning and a skinned pig. The awning is over a rented dance floor, the pig is over a bed of coals. There are as many relatives as you'd want to see in one place: the men standing around the revolving pig, the women putting serving spoons in bowls of baked beans, potato salad, things made with Jell-O, things made with whipped cream, things made with bacon bits.

Two uncles are tapping the beer keg. They keep drawing up tall glasses of foam and dumping it on the ground.

"I need a beer bad," Wendell says. She touches her head. "How's the crown?"

"Firm," I tell her. We get ourselves two glasses of foam to carry around and wander over to the food tables.

"This has prunes in it, if you can believe that," an aunt tells us, uncovering a bowl full of something pink that just came from the trunk of her car. Our mothers are standing at a long table where more women are unwrapping gifts and logging them in a book. Wendell's mother is wearing a long dress, gray silk with big peach-colored roses and green leaves down the front. My mother has on a pantsuit that everyone keeps admiring. They're both wearing corsages. "Ooh," my aunt says. A box has just been opened containing an enormous macramé plant hanger, with big red beads and two feet of thick fringe.

"Holy shit," Wendell says, taking a drink of foam.

The guests eat salads and chips and pig, the sky turns pewter, deep cobalt, then black. The band strikes up; four guys, two of them relatives. They play a fast number and everyone under the age of ten gets out there to dance. The littlest kids concentrate on trying to get it exactly right, swinging their hips and whirling their arms around. After about two songs all of them are out of control and sweating, hair stuck to their head, girls seeing who can slide the farthest on patent-leather shoes, boys taking aim and shooting each other with their index fingers without mercy. The parents have to step in, remove a few examples, and put them in chairs. One gets spanked first for calling his mother a dipshit in front of the whole crowd.

A waltz begins to play and the older couples move out onto the floor, husbands and wives, various uncles with various aunts. My own dad dances me around a few times, tells me my dress is pretty, and delivers me in front of Eric, who looks stupendously bored and not quite stoned enough. "Hey, lotta fun," he says insincerely. I make him dance with my mom.

Wendell takes a break from talking to people and we pull up lawn chairs next to the dance floor. Her ivory dress shines in the darkness. "I keep losing my drink," she says. We share a full, warm beer that's sitting on the ground between our chairs, passing it back and forth, watching the fox-trotters.

"I wish I could do the fox-trot," I say wistfully.

She nods. "We can't do anything good," she says wearily.

"We can two-step," I answer, in our defense.

"Yeah," she says through a yawn. "But big whoop, the two-step." Two short great-aunts glide by at a smart clip and wave at us, the bride and the bridesmaid. Wendell waves back like a beauty queen on a float, I smile and twinkle my fingers. "Yee-haw," I say quietly. On the other side of the dance floor Mitch stands listening intently to one of our distant, female relatives. He winks at us when she isn't looking and we wink back hugely. "That's my first husband, Mitch," Wendell says fondly.

The night air is damp and black against my arms, like mossy sleeves. There are stars by the millions up above our heads. Wendell and I are sitting directly under Gemini, my birth sign, the oddball twins, the split personality. Part of me wants to get up and dance, the other part wants to sit with my head tipped back. All of me wants to take off my wrist corsage.

"Nice ragweed corsage," I tell Wendell. My arm itches like fire, long red hives are marching up to my elbows. I take it off and put it under my chair.

"Give it a heave," she suggests, and I do. It lands within twenty feet of our lawn chairs. A giant calico farm cat steps out from nowhere, sniffs it, then picks it up delicately and fades back into blackness. Under the awning the air is stained yellow, the band is playing a disco song. Our mothers are in the midst of a line dance, doing their own version of the Hustle, out of sync with everyone else. Their work is done, they've mingled, they've been fairly polite. Now they've got about twenty minutes of careening before they collapse in lawn chairs and ask people to wait on them. They're out there trying to kick and clap at the same time, without putting their drinks down. I decide I'd better join them.

My mother's cheeks are in bloom, from sloe gin and exertion, her lipstick has worn off but her corsage is still going strong, a flower the size of a punch bowl. She tries for the relaxed shuffle-kick-pause-clap of all the other line dancers but can't do it. She sets her drink down at the edge of the dance floor where it's sure to get knocked over and comes back to the line, full steam ahead. She starts doing the Bump with Wendell's mom and another aunt. Before they can get me involved, I dance myself over to the edge of the floor and step out into the darkness.

"The moms need to be spanked and put in chairs," I tell Eric, who hands over his beer without being asked. He looks peaceful and affectionate; his hair is sticking straight up in front and there's something pink and crusty all over the front of his shirt.

"One of those kids threw a piece of cake at me," he says placidly. He's been smoking pot out in the corn with Freddy, I can tell. The band pauses between numbers and the mothers keep dancing. In the distance, two uncles stand talking, using the blue glow of a bug zapper to compare their mangled thumbnails. Up by the band, the bride is getting ready to throw the bouquet. I'm being summoned to come stand in the group of girl cousins clustered around Wendell. I walk backward until I'm past the first row of corn, Eric following amiably, pink-eyed and slap-happy. He's using a swizzle stick for a toothpick.

Inside the corn it is completely dark, the stalks stand silent, the sounds of the party are indistinct. We can hear each other breathing. There is a muffled cheering as the bouquet gets thrown, and then someone talks loud and long into the microphone, offering a toast. Eric begins nuzzling my ear and talking baby talk.

"Hey," I whisper to him.

"Mmmm?" he says.

"Have you ever seen a corn snake?"

He refuses to be intimidated. A waltz begins and we absently take up the one-two-three, one-two-three. Around us the dark stalks ripple like water, the waves of the blue Danube wash over us. "I can show *you* a corn snake," he says softly, into my hair.

Here is a scene. Two sisters talk together in low voices, one knits and the other picks lint carefully off a blanket. Their eyes meet infrequently but the conversation is the same as always.

"He's too young to retire," my mother says. "He'll be stuck to her like a burr, and then that's all you'll hear, how she can't stand having him under-foot." One of my uncles wants to retire from selling Motorola televisions and spend the rest of his years doing woodworking.

"How many pig-shaped cutting boards does anybody need?" my aunt says. She holds her knitting up to the window. "God*damn* it. I did it again." She begins unraveling the last few rows, the yarn falling into a snarl around her feet.

"Here," my mother says, holding out a hand, "give me that." She takes the ball of pale yellow yarn and slowly, patiently winds the kinked part back up. While they work, a nurse enters and reads a chart, takes a needle from a cart in the hall, and injects it into the tube leading into my mother's arm. When the door snicks shut behind her, my aunt quits unraveling long enough to get a cigarette from her purse.

"They better not catch me doing this," she says, lighting up. She's using an old pop can for an ashtray. The cigarette trembles slightly in her long fingers and her eyes find the ceiling, then the floor, then the window. She adjusts the belt on her suit, a soft green knit tunic over pants, with silver buttons and a patterned scarf at the neck. She's sitting in an orange plas-tic chair.

My mother is wearing a dark blue negligee with a bed jacket and thick cotton socks. She takes a puff from my aunt's cigarette and exhales slowly, making professional smoke rings. "Now I'm corrupted," she says dryly.

"If any of them walked in right now, they'd have a fit," my aunt replies uneasily. She's worried about stern daughters, crabby nurses.

"Do I give a good goddamn?" my mother asks peacefully. She's staring at the ceiling. "I don't think I do." She's drifting now, floating upward, her shot is taking effect. She gets a glimpse of something and then loses it, like a fish swimming in and out of view in the darkness under water. She struggles to the surface. "I hope you get a girl," she says.

My aunt is knitting again, the long needles moving against each other, tying knots, casting off, creating small rosettes. Wendell is ready to have a baby any day now. "Well, she's carrying it low," my aunt answers skepti-cally. The room is dimming, she turns her chair more toward the window. There is a long pause, with only the needles and the tedious breath, the sterile landscape of cancer country.

"That doesn't mean anything," my mother finally replies. Her father bends over her head to kiss her, as substantial as air; he's a ghost, they won't leave her alone. She moves slowly through the fluid and brings a thought to the surface. "We carried all of ours low, and look what we got."

They swim through her lake, gray-eyed sisters, thin-legged and mouthy. They fight and hold hands, trade shoes and dresses, marry beautiful tall men, and have daughters together, two dark-eyed cousins, thin-legged and mouthy. A fish splashes, a silver arc against the blue sky, its scales like sequins. She startles awake.

"I hope you get a girl," she says again. This is all she can think to say. Her sister, in the dimness, sets down her work and comes to the bed. She bends over and pulls the blanket up, straightens it out. She can't think of what to say either. The face on the pillow is foreign to her suddenly, distant, and the weight of the long afternoon bends her in half. She leans forward wearily, and lets herself grimace.

"We got our girls we wanted so bad, didn't we?" my mother whispers to her, eyes still shut. My aunt straightens and fingers a silver button at her throat.

"Those damn brats," she comments. She presses both hands against the small of her back and shuts her eyes briefly. For an instant she sees the two original brats—wearing their droopy calico dresses, sassing their mother, carrying water up from the pump at the home place, knocking into each other. "You were always my sister," she says softly.

My mother is completely without pain now, the lake is dark, the fish move easily out of her way. Her sister swims by and makes a statement. "I know it," she answers. She tries to think of a way to express something. Sequins fall through the water, fish scales, and a baby floats past, turned upside-down with a thumb corked in its mouth. The morphine is a thin vapor in her veins. She rouses herself.

"He did do a nice job on those Christmas trees," she says. My aunt nods. She's talking about the woodworking uncle now, who made Christmas trees for all the sisters to put in the middle of their dining-room tables.

"I told him to make me a couple more for next year," my aunt says. "My card club went nuts over it." She lights another cigarette, hating herself for it. My mother is silent, her hands cut the water smoothly, like two long knives. The little gray-eyed girls paddle and laugh. She pushes a spray of water into her sister's face and her sister pushes one back. Their hair is shining against their heads.

In the dimness of the hospital room, my aunt smokes and thinks. She doesn't see their father next to the bed, or old Aunt Grace piddling around with the flower arrangements. She sees only the still form on the bed, the half-open mouth, the coppery wig. She yawns. Wendell's stomach is out to here, she remembers—any day now. That's one piece of good news.

My mother sleeps silently while my aunt thinks. As the invisible hands tend to her, she dives and comes up, breaks free of the water. A few feet over a fish leaps again, high in the air. Her arms move lazily back and forth, holding her up, and as she watches, the fish is transformed. High above the water, it rises like a silver baton, presses itself against the blue August sky, and refuses to drop back down.

FROM THE AUTHOR

Summer of 1991, Utah, at a writing conference, me in a cotton dress that I got at a clothing-exchange back in Iowa, all those great women in some- one's little leaning living room, and heaps of various no longer wanted things that we were politely pawing through. And I claimed Sue Futrell's blue seersucker jumper-dress, really smart and really Sue, and it fit me and I liked it. So there I was, suddenly out of the shadows of my regular life, carrying with me an essay written in Carl Klaus's workshop, about a coyote I once saw in Arizona. The Utah workshop really went for that essay, mainly because of the setting—the southwest, with its low buttes and rock forma- tions, everyone at the conference wearing the early version of turtle-fur and Tevas, except for Jane, a woman like me who was getting attention unex- pectedly, and she wore M. C. Hammer harem pants and east coast jewelry and we would drink beers together. She told me about her recent divorce, in great Jane-detail—explaining how she was alone one weekend, her hus- band away at a conference, and she felt just fucking terrible. Terrible, she said, but nothing new. She had felt terrible for a long time. And then she felt even worse, and then ended up at the hospital. Rippling world, agony, and then fading into darkness, waking up in a white room. Where some- one asked her gently if she hadn't felt *really awful*, and why she didn't get help earlier, and she had to admit to herself that she had been so miser- able for so long that she didn't even notice that her own appendix was bursting. The frog while the water boiled, etc. So she and I, and the feel- ing of being noticed, which was good and bad at the same time. Good be- cause it was about writing and bad because it was about people seeing me. But nevertheless, good overall, and I had a private conference with Terry Tempest Williams, who had read my submission and in talking to me dis- covered that I hadn't published it. She liked it very much, being a western- minded and western-landed woman who wrote about nature and animals in a personal-essay style, and ended up having but one thing to say to me about it: "Why aren't you willing to claim your power?"

Leave it to a prominent writer to think that it's as easy for everyone to get published as it is for her. And I hated the velvet shawl she was wearing, the mane-style hair, and the general air of writing privilege. But I was also grateful, and admiring, and wished I too had a velvet shawl and an Indian-bead necklace and all those rings. But the idea that I wasn't published, or successful, because I wasn't willing to claim my power irked me, and I told her so. We stared each other down and then she invited me to attend one of the faculty parties with her that night, which I declined out of shyness.

But I have thought of that moment a thousand times over the last twenty-something years, and how someone said to me in that bold and New Age way that I needed to claim my power. Not by accident was it a woman saying that — no man would bother thinking that way, of whether to claim power or not claim it. It was June, and I drove my silver Toyota all the way home, through the blinding shimmering heat on an endless highway, keeping a Styrofoam cooler next to me filled with melting ice that I would thrust an arm into while driving. Daydreaming the "Cousins" essay and letting it propel me through Moab and all its little hippie streets, through the different palisades, through Arches, with its, well, arches, and vivid blue sky, through the long stretches of endlessness and heat like a furnace coming through all the open windows, the years before car air conditioning was universal, the years when it cost too much to run it even if you had it (I didn't), and thinking about my favorite girl cousin, and my mother and my aunt, and putting together, loosely inside my brain, the story of how we all connected, of our dolls and our drinking, of our little home-made dresses and the homespun mothers who made them. And I felt . . . not power exactly, driving in that car through the burning furnace of Utah, right arm benumbed to the elbow, but I felt profound engagement. With my own process of thinking and of imagination and of construction — the story telling itself to me in anecdotes, one after another, and the anecdotes arriving in images. Of scalloped collars and mothers with long cigarette fingers and geraniums growing on either side of a front porch, of my cousin's bristling hair and her green eyes and my mother being lost to me forever and lost to herself. Hospital rooms and the sound of a rubber-hinged door swinging shut, a nurse's shoes, the pale endless breathing of someone who isn't conscious. Or is and can't tell you so.

Terry Tempest wanted me to claim my power, and she might as well have been speaking to me in Aramaic. But on the way home, my seersucker dress in its suitcase, the sun berating me through the windshield, the wind buffeting my fenders, I began to feel my power as it bloomed around me, sweeping in and out of the car through the two open windows. My cousin and me, all those years before, in love with each other and with life and sharing clothes and a DNA history that neither of us could have given a rat's ass for. Mothers, sisters, brothers, all those picnics and all the dolls whose faces I remember as well as our own. All of it went sweeping in and out of the car as I drove through the Terry Tempest landscape, writing power, stronger than a black Camaro on a starry night.

O Wilderness

JOE BLAIR (1995)

I'm sitting in the lobby of the Park Hotel, hardhat between my knees, steel-toed boots on my feet, Carhartt coat on my lap, complimentary cup of bad coffee in my hand. The place is set up to look like someone's living room: a couch, a comfy chair, a throw rug and a coffee table with six or eight magazines all neat and displayed the way they never would be if they actually were in someone's living room. Before I came down from my room, I listened at Chuck's door to make sure he was up and I heard water running which I took as a good sign.

The digital clock behind the front desk reads 4:43. Chocolate chip cookies are displayed in a little clear plastic set of drawers. The woman behind the desk looks tired.

"You should stop looking at them and take one," she says.

"No," I say. "I'm good."

The wallpaper is purple and pink with wide stripes.

I feel I should say something more. To be polite.

"Much snow last night?" I say.

"Oh, we got a little less than a foot," she says. "So, that's not too bad."

"Yeah," I say.

"So," she says, "where you off to this morning?"

"I Falls," I say.

"Oh," she says.

To break the awkwardness, I leave my hardhat and coat on the chair and walk to the front entrance. Fine flakes are being pushed this way and that by the wind. A GMC Crew Cab is parked under the carport and inside the cab, the imposing shape of Warren Anderson, Cooper Mechanical's rep in Northern Minnesota. I shove my way through the doors. Warren looks my way and pushes a button that opens the passenger window.

"Hey, kid," he says.

"Hey Warren," I say. "You're early."

"It's pretty bad," he says. "Don't know how long it's gonna take this morning."

"Chuck's not down yet," I say. "You want me to go get him?"

Warren looks out the windshield for a beat and then back at me.

"Why don't you go get him," he says.

Warren is a large man. He used to be a big-time college wrestler. Got a full boat to the University of Minnesota. Everything about him gives me confidence. He sells supplies and equipment to industries in the area—power plants and taconite plants and paper mills like the one in I Falls, where we have a service call today. The wind is strong and, glancing at the lights across the street, I notice that the snow is still coming down hard. The truck is a three-quarter ton four-wheel-drive pickup—three tons of steel and plastic. A much safer vehicle to drive in a blizzard than the shitty little KIA Soul we'd rented for the trip up, which Chuck described as a roller skate with an engine.

I hustle back to the lobby where it's warm and cozy and there are free cookies, grab my coat and hardhat and carry them out to the pickup where I stuff them in the backseat. By the time I'm entering the hotel lobby again, I see Chuck. Chuck, as he told me last night while we were leaning on the bar with our 22 oz. glasses of Guinness, goes about 250 pounds. He has strong legs and broad shoulders and a good-sized belly. In high school, he was a football player. A running back. Now he's a salesman for Cooper Mechanical, carrying his winter coat and steel-toed boots along with his briefcase. We toss everything in the back and soon we're on the road. Normally, Warren says, the drive would take about two hours, but we've given ourselves an extra half-hour due to the storm. I'm in the back—Chuck and Warren up front. I think about the possibility of a car crash. I consider the big truck we're in. And I consider how lucky I am to be positioned in a place with plenty of padding in case we do crash. Chuck and Warren immediately fall into conversation about hunting and fishing and trapping and the habitat for pheasant and how the deer population was really under control now, they think, because of the wolf population, which is on the rise.

"I never got a wolf," says Chuck, wistfully. "I've seen 'em, but I never got one."

"If you want to get a timber wolf," says Warren, "we're going to be passing by a natural crossing right on the way here. I'll show you. You see the tracks there all the time. You won't seem 'em today because of the snow, but usually, they're all over."

They go on and on. And on. About croppies and muskies and lakes with what they called "structure" and lakes with zebra mussels and the diminishing habitat for pheasant. Luckily, I have my outmoded Walkman CD player and am in the middle of a pretty good detective novel about a guy named Jack Reacher. Jack Reacher's big things are coffee and time. He always wants coffee and he always knows what time it is even though he never wears a watch. His other big thing is, he always kills all the bad guys. And there are always bad guys.

Warren has the habit of driving his truck in the very center of the road and then switching lanes only when he sees approaching headlights. This unnerves me a bit, but then I consider Warren, born and raised in northern Minnesota, a man who knows a thing or two about driving in the snow, and I think of the four-wheel-drive GMC loaded down with, among other things, almost 800 pounds of Warren and Chuck and me.

The roads between Hibbing and International Falls are, for the most part, perfectly straight and wide, two-lane with no divider. People say the logging industry is in trouble partly due to the downturn in the paper business, but every five minutes or so a fully loaded logging truck rumbles by on its way to a lumber mill or wood-burning power plant or paper mill.

We're about an hour into the trip when I need to change CDs. It's still dark and there seems to be nothing but pine trees, all muffled by new snow, lining the road. We haven't seen a city light since we left Hibbing. Deep in the wilderness now. I think of the timber wolves roaming around in that silent forest of snow-covered pines, absolutely at home. Another logging truck is approaching. I can tell by the high, widely spaced headlights as well as the orange marker lights on top of the cab. Warren cuts the wheel to position the truck safely in our own lane, over the ridge of snow directly in the center of the highway. I have the old disc in the audio-book box and am digging for the next one when I feel the rear of the pickup lose its grip and slide toward the ditch to the right. There's a high bank where the plows have pushed the snow and beyond that about twenty yards of luminescence and beyond that the black pine forest. Warren shifts in his seat, his huge body twisting strangely so all his weight is on his left side and says, matter-of-factly, "We're in trouble, boys."

He's spinning the wheel madly to the left rather than, as they teach you on the very first day of driver's education class, in the direction of the skid. The truck responds by fishtailing and slowly changing direction. Now we're drifting sideways at a diagonal toward the unstopping, unstoppable logging truck headed south, fully loaded, as all the southbound trucks have been thus far. My mind is lagging a bit. I'm disappointed. Wishing that Warren had taken us into the ditch. Trying to believe that we have some chance of changing direction again. Away from the crushing weight and steady velocity of the logging truck. My mind can't seem to catch up to the fact that there is no way we'll be changing directions again. Not soon enough. I'm still thinking lovingly of that safe, beautiful, white, soft ditch, even as Warren whips the wheel all the way to the right now and we begin, almost leisurely, our first 360 degree spin. I know how the steering wheel must feel right now. Like a toy. It matters not at all. I know what it's like to begin that uncontrollable spin. I've done it before in parking lots for fun. And once when I was a kid in my mother's Volkswagen beetle when I tried to corner too sharply during a rainstorm. I know we are dead men. I know it just now, my mind having finally caught up and I'm deeply disappointed. The pickup spins once. The broad headlights of the forty-ton logging truck come and go. The pickup spins again. Headlights again. This time much more widely spaced. We are fully in the oncoming lane now. There is no stopping the collision. Another half spin and our truck, bumping up against the far snow bank, ceases its rotation, our tailgate squarely facing the logging truck. Nothing but a few pieces of sheet metal and soft steel between me and the cab of the oncoming behemoth. And there is a moment. They say you have an extended moment before you die. Before you are flattened like a nickel on the train tracks. And all sorts of miraculous thoughts are supposed to come.

I knew we were dead men before the steel bumper of that logging truck crumpled the bed of the GMC, pushing it down rather than lifting it up and pushing it aside the way a smaller vehicle would do. The truck will be pushed down beneath the forty-ton load traveling in the opposite direction, making our combined speed somewhere in the vicinity of ninety miles-per-hour. There was never any hope. And there was never one thought that flashed through my mind. I simply closed my eyes and flinched, like the doomed Vietcong prisoner in the Eddy Adams photo, just before the terrible impact. I wasn't afraid. I had no time. I was simply disappointed. And apprehensive. I did have, at least, time to close my eyes and think, "Okay." Just that one word. "Okay." Which, I suppose, isn't too bad as final thoughts go.

But there is no blinding light. No impact at all, other than the impact of air, clapping loudly with the sound of the passing semi which, somehow, has maneuvered itself to the right of our truck through the deep snow on the edge of the ditch, ever so slightly changing direction, never slowing down, passing very close to the passenger's side of our tiny little pickup truck. There is a clap, like I said. A thunderclap. When I open my eyes, I see the tail lights flitting by. And they're gone. We are, the three of us, surrounded—sixty miles in any direction—by snow-laden forest and silence. Then the two in the front seat are laughing. Warren looking left then right. Now he's turning the wheel and accelerating. Doing a U turn in middle of the two-lane highway. Moving again. Just the same as before, only more slowly. Chuck and Warren hooting and laughing. Moving through that holy place. Our piddly little headlights forcing themselves upon the darkness of the road. The darkness of the surrounding world. The first snowstorm of the year. The wolves, somewhere, moving the way I imagine them doing. The way I've seen them do in so many photographs and paintings. One. Two. Three. Four. One after the other. All in a row. Heads low. Pads on the snow. All in unison. Leaving their tracks on the forest floor. An unreadable message for all mankind.

FROM THE AUTHOR

After we got to International Falls, I learned that the tires on Warren's pickup truck were original. They had over one hundred thousand miles on them and the treads were nonexistent. I was pissed off. I called Warren an idiot. I told him I wasn't riding back with him on those tires. "There's plenty of tire places in I Falls," I said. "We can drive it over there and get a cab to the meeting." But Warren shook his head, smiling sadly. "That ain't the way things work," he said. And Chuck agreed with him. That ain't the way things work. You don't buy new tires when there's been a snowstorm and you're riding on slicks and you just did a few 360s directly in the path of an oncoming lumber truck. You don't buy new tires. What kind of a fool does that?!

At the paper mill, I sat in the guard shack glaring at my steel-toed boots. Chuck and Warren tried to make me laugh, but I wasn't in the mood. A guy in an orange vest and a hardhat came out and led us over a railroad crossing and through the grimy, hand-stained rear door of the plant, up a galvanized steel stairway and into a meeting room where there was a Bunn coffee machine. We had our meeting. Then Warren and Chuck drove back to Hibbing in that same pickup truck on those same bald tires. And I went with them.

We were all fools—all of us pursuing the sale of a product we really didn't know a hell of a lot about. Chuck claimed that within a year we'd own our own private jet. And I, somehow clinging to the idea that I was, in fact, a writer and I didn't care about money and I didn't want my own private jet, went along with him, in the backseat of his deathmobile.

It's not a small thing, to have a gun pointed at your head. To hear the click of hammer on empty chamber. Not for the person it happens to, at any rate, and it had an effect on me. It wouldn't be a stretch to say it changed my life, which is a clichéd statement and, at the same time, true. I wrote the essay quickly on the evening of my return to Iowa City the following day. It took me an hour or so to get the words down. Something about those wolves. Just the thought of them, wedged up against the thought of the three of us big, foolish, circus clowns stuffed into that tiny little three-quarter-ton pickup truck. Has there ever been a foolish wolf? I don't think it's possible. A wolf cannot be foolish because it is impossible for a wolf to have a false view of himself, to believe he is something other than himself when he is so obviously and entirely lupine.

The wolves were the force behind this essay. The wolves and the forest, so silent and final. I never went back and edited this essay even though I should have because even now, after I sent it off for publication, I find two ridiculously obvious errors—the lack of a conjunction in one spot and an extra article in another—but I didn't want to touch it because I was fond of it and afraid I might kill it. They are so fragile sometimes. Sometimes they live and sometimes they die. And often we don't know why. That's the way I look at essays.

The week after I wrote this one, I quit my job as a salesman. I told Chuck I didn't care about the jet. We had a few beers while sitting at the wet bar in his basement. He told me he'd make the business work. He said he'd take it all on his back. "I'll take it all on my back," he said. Then I left.

Anechoic

ASHLEY BUTLER (2008)

(Originally published in *Creative Nonfiction*)

Houdini leans to rise from the sofa on which he has been reclining and, in rising, receives a succession of punches to the lower abdomen. Although the magician endured a similar blow before a small crowd days before, it is backstage in the dressing room at the Princess Theatre that the story of his death often begins. Here, Houdini has been talking with one young man while another uses pen and paper in an attempt to capture his likeness. The magician says he can predict the outcome of any detective story given a few excerpts from the book, and the soon-to-be assailant pulls a mystery from his bag to test this claim. After a few selections are read, Houdini recounts the rest. Then, the young man, Mr. J. Gordon Whitehead, asks Houdini if he might demonstrate the incredible strength of his "iron stomach," and the magician, tired and enduring what may be a case of appendicitis, tries to direct attention to his equally impressive back and forearm muscles, against which he invites the 28-year-old theology student to lay a hand.

Escape relies on a rejection of pain and fear, Houdini had said three days earlier in a lecture at McGill University. To demonstrate, he stuck a needle through his cheek without drawing blood. He added that the imagination inflates suffering; if we could really see, we'd see through so-called miracles. These sorts of claims had gotten him in trouble with the Spiritualists, who believed the living could communicate with the dead through mediums. Houdini considered Spiritualism a manipulation of those who mourned the departed. Although he had devoted more than 30 years of his life to exposing fraudulent mediums, he continued to hold out hope that some communication might be made with his dead mother. He created secret code words, shared with at least 20 individuals; whoever died first would send the message back to him, thereby bridging the inexplicable terrain between life and death and providing proof of the hereafter.

The punches Houdini took to the abdomen backstage on October 22, 1926, would later be considered murder. Or maybe it was the "experimental serum" administered by the doctor in Detroit days later that killed him. Houdini didn't know. And neither of his biographers has been able to determine the exact cause of his death. Several Spiritualists wanted him dead and had sent him letters to this effect, though mediums often attributed these predictions or threats to a spirit. Sir Arthur Conan Doyle, a Spiritualist and former friend of Houdini, claimed to hear his spirit guide say, "Houdini is doomed, doomed!"

Spiritualism is a movement, a philosophy, a religion and a science of continuous life that started in 1848, in Hydesville, NY, where sisters Kate and Maggie Fox had devised ways to scare their mother by threading a string through an apple, directing it down the stairs and claiming the noises were those of a ghost in the dark. They started making sounds by cracking their toes, knees and ankles, and they answered these "calls from beyond" by rapping their knuckles on a table: "Mr. Split-foot, do as I do." Soon their mother, who believed her daughters, was inviting the neighbors over to bear witness to these occurrences. Their older sister, Leah, returned from Rochester then to form a local "society of spiritualists," which she gathered at the house. This is how the Fox sisters came to be called the first modern mediums. Scientist William Crookes, following an investigation of Kate's abilities, later said of Ms. Fox:

> [I]t seems only necessary for her to place her hand on any substance for loud thuds to be heard. . . . I have heard them in a living tree—on a sheet of glass— on a stretched iron wire—on a stretched membrane—a tambourine-on the roof of a cab—and on the floor of a theatre. Moreover, actual contact is not always necessary; I have had these sounds proceeding from the floor, walls, etc., when the medium's hands and feet were held—when she was standing on a chair—when she was suspended in a swing from the ceiling—when she was enclosed in a wire cage—and when she had fallen fainting on a sofa. I have heard them on a glass harmonicon—I have felt them on my own shoulder and under my own hands. I have heard them on a sheet of paper, held between the fingers by a piece of thread passed through one corner.

Such was Kate's desire to believe in her own manifestations that, her sister Maggie later wrote, in a confession published in the Sunday edition of the New York World, October 21, 1888: "[S]he told me she received messages from spirits. She knew that we were tricking people, but she tried to make us believe. She told us before we were born, spirits came into her room. . . ." To leave nothing to the imagination, Maggie took the stage at New York's Academy of Music later that night, slipped her foot out of her right shoe, placed it on a wooden stool for all to witness the cause of the sound and began to rap without, apparently, moving her foot. Of the performance, one woman, now persuaded of the sisters' 40-year ruse, wrote in from San Francisco: "I know that the pursuit of this shadowy belief has wrought upon my brain and that I am no longer my old self."

Houdini hangs head first over a crowd in Times Square. With his neck and shoulders curled forward in the straitjacket about his torso, he looks like a hook rising only to be cast again. Houdini relaxes. The crane stops. Houdini thrashes—and after a few seconds, he folds the canvas from his core, dangles it from his right arm. The camera frames only the sky and his form. Rewind the film, and he has fettered himself again—the restraint an extension, the body a stage. Because the jacket dangles, divested of its power, and because the body arches against a cloudless sky, we may assume that those who gaze upon him from beneath the lower frame have sounded their applause and are, perhaps, reaching, though such evidence has not been preserved. Houdini knows the body, knows it's not an instrument for the voice from beyond and could never hold the message for which he waits. Every voice needs a body that beds a pain, troubles a mind, but surely any attempt to embody the ineffable would overwhelm that through which it passes. Here is Houdini lifted like some newborn exposed to gravity and distance, the body alone.

In my favorite picture of her, my mother wears a strapless black lace ball gown. She is at a round table, looking down at her fingertips playing at the edges of a wine glass. She seems to be in the midst of a story as men on either side lean toward her like legs of an isosceles triangle. The glass of white wine stands tall before her hands, which linger, dripping long fingers with large knuckles. These hands angle daintily toward the rim of the glass. I remember how she used to make the glasses whirr. She passed her index finger quickly along the surface of the wine and then circled the lip of the glass again and again until a magnificent sound came on slowly as if always there, then expanded like a gas filling every corner of the room. She would wink and look the other way when the notes had reached their peak and people at other tables hushed to search the room for an origin.

The voice is intimate: We each experience our own voice through air and tissue conduction; that is, we both hear our voices and feel the vibration of the sound we emit. This is what I am thinking about as I sit on a red couch in the waiting room at the University of Iowa's Wendell Johnson Speech and Hearing Center. In the opposite corner of the room, a mummified child sits in a blue plastic chair. The plaque above the figure indicates that it is the result of a project completed by children with hearing complications. The figure's torso and head are extremely reclined, and it has no eyes though it holds a mummified book open in its lap.

I have come here to explore the second largest anechoic chamber in the United States, built in 1967. A blonde-haired woman appears and leads me down two flights of stairs, down to the basement. The stairs end at a thick, heavy door, which she pulls open by wrapping her hands around the handle and throwing her body back. Inside, a plank rests on a wire trapeze, which bisects the cube room. The ground is the same distance below our feet as the ceiling is above us. The walls, floor and ceiling are covered in fiberglass wedges designed to absorb sound.

"Hear that?" she asks.

"No, what is it?"

"The whirring of that light above us is so loud. Let me turn it off. Don't worry. I won't shut you in here. It would be too disorienting."

In an anechoic chamber, the only sound that exists is the sound that derives from a source. In other words, a sound that cannot be accounted for may be an illusion triggered by the brain; this is an environment in which one may discover how the body leads itself astray. The first anechoic chamber in the United States was built in 1940 at Bell Labs, in Murray Hill, NJ, and was once cited by Guinness World Records as the "world's quietest room." I turn away from the door as the woman goes out to extinguish the light. In the dark, my ears strain to grasp something, but the only thing I hear is a sort of static that I imagine could be confused with the workings of the ear itself. I pronounce an "h" as if too exhausted to complete the mundane English salutation. It seems to follow as far as my breath endures on exhale.

We are strangers to our own voices. Psychiatrist D. Ewen Cameron knew this. In 1953, he claimed that one way to get a defensive, or psychologically blocked, patient to confront his own psychological problem was to record his voice and play it back. But not just once. Cameron devised an experiment in which patients remained in an isolated room for days—in some cases, weeks—listening to their own voices repeat for 16 hours a day through a microphone planted in a pillow.

In these experiments, negative expressions made by the subject in an initial interview, which included an exploration of the psychological problem, were played over and over in an attempt to break the subject down. Cameron called this technique "psychic driving" and claimed it would break through the patient's defenses, draw out inaccessible material and set up a dynamic implant, which could later facilitate access to previously inaccessible material. Occasionally, he paired the driving with treatments of electroshock therapy. Occasionally, he paired it with LSD. As his experiments progressed, Cameron wondered: Would it be possible to wipe a person clean and begin again?

In a 1956 scientific article entitled "Psychic Driving," Cameron recounts a success story. The problem: a 50-year-old woman suffering from feelings of "inadequacy and profound ambivalence toward her husband." Cameron claims that as a result of his experiment, the woman realized her mother was at fault:

> *The following statement was driven some 15 or 20 times: "That's what I can't understand—that one could strike at a little child." [The patient] has reference here to the fact that her mother used to take out all her own frustrations and disappointments and antagonisms on the patient during her early childhood—even going so far, when the patient was 7, as to tell her, "I tried to abort you, too, but you just wouldn't abort."*

Listening to her own voice in distress, the patient later said, "I can see that it was really my mother who damaged me. . . . It gives me one of those 'all gone' feelings."

Cameron's experiments in psychic driving were part of the CIA's Project MKULTRA, which began in 1950. The goal was the control of the human mind against such fundamental laws of nature as self-preservation. Project MKULTRA was a 25-year, $25-million exploration in response to the strange confessions being produced by American prisoners of war in Korea. The CIA was convinced that the Soviets had come up with a new, powerful brainwashing technique. Further alarm arose with the arrest of two Soviet agents in Germany. The agents were said to be armed with identical plastic cylinders containing hypodermic needles, the contents of which would cause a victim to become amenable to the will of his captor. In addition to Cameron's psychic driving, Project MKULTRA's experiments studied the effects of sensory deprivation, radiation, LSD, Thorazine, Sernyl, mescaline, hypnosis, magic and a variety of sexual positions test-run in brothels as agents watched.

In 1951, Cameron's McGill University colleague, psychologist D. O. Hebb, conducted experiments on student volunteers to explore the effect of a lack of external stimuli on the human brain. These experiments were devised to limit the subject's ability to perceive his or her environment. The subject would lie on a bed in a partially soundproof room within a room. He or she lay for hours, days, in the darkness beneath the hum of the air conditioner—hands and forearms fitted with cotton gloves and cylindrical cardboard cuffs to limit tactile sensation; eyes covered by translucent goggles, which allowed only a hazy light, to prevent patterned vision; and head placed in a U-shaped foam-rubber pillow. If at any point the subject felt he could not go on, he could press a panic button.

Although Hebb preferred to use the term "perceptual isolation," many people still apply the term "sensory deprivation" to the methods used in his early experiments. Both terms are misleading. While it is possible to deprive the eyes of light, the same cannot be done with hearing. Although a subject may be placed in an entirely soundproof room, there is still the matter of the circulatory system. The subject hears blood coursing through the vessels near the ear, listens to the breath rushing through the chest, notices the rumblings of the stomach. There are heart noises, breathing noises, sounds made by the middle-ear muscles. In some cases, they are mistaken for auditory hallucinations, which the subject recognizes as "dripping water," "typewriter," "howling dog."

Most subjects in Hebb's experiments indicated that, as the test wore on, they came to believe that the experimenter had deserted them, though that was never the case. Some subjects reported that they felt as if another body was lying beside them in the cubicle, but that was never the case. One subject drew a picture to show how he felt at one point and said it was as if there were two of him and he was momentarily unable to decide whether he was A or B.

Before leaving the house where my mother died, I went looking for her. There was a stillness in her room that could have been mistaken for order. I searched through the hangers to which her blouses and jackets clung tenuously by pale buttons, through the yellow legal pads on which she kept her days' lists. I searched as if she, like a paper doll, had been cut from the background of the world and could be found in the space left behind. "I am willing to believe," said Houdini when asked about Spiritualism, "but of all I have seen, I have never found anything that couldn't be explained by human effort. My mind is open. I am a human being, and I have loved ones on the other side. I would like to get in touch with them if it were possible."

After an initial period of sleep in the chamber, Hebb's subjects would lapse into daydreaming. Although some had planned to spend the time thinking over some mathematical problem, they quickly found they could not maintain concentration. Their thoughts wandered to the past. They imagined traveling from one land to the next, envisioning each step.

One subject made up a game of listing, according to the alphabet, chemical reactions and the scientists who had discovered them. At the letter "n," he was unable to think of an example. He tried to skip "n" and go on, but "n" kept coming back. "N" demanded an answer. He tried to dismiss the game altogether but could not. He endured the game for a short time. And finding that he was unable to control it, he pushed the panic button.

The experiments associated with MKULTRA were explored as methods of truth-seeking. In an attempt to explain things people had a hard time explaining, the CIA even decided to hire a magician. They found a professional New York magician and asked him to write a "Magic Manual" for $3,000. They wanted to know how to "perform a variety of acts secretly and indetectably." They wanted to know how to read minds and transmit thoughts, possibly across long distances like oceans. They wanted many other things as well:

They wanted to know if rubber could be produced from mushrooms.

They wanted to know if water witching could locate an enemy submarine.

They wanted to know how to achieve the controlled production of headaches and earaches; twitches, jerks and staggers.

They wanted to know how to induce amnesia.

They wanted to know how to reduce a man to a bewildered, self-doubting mass.

And they wanted to know how to direct him in ways that might lead to the construction of a new person.

Of his colleague at McGill University, Hebb said:

Cameron was irresponsible — criminally stupid — in that there was no reason to expect that he would get any results from the experiments. Anyone with any appreciation of the complexity of the human mind would not expect that you could erase an adult mind and then add things back with this stupid psychic driving. . . . He was the victim of his own kind of brainwashing—he wanted something so much that he was blinded by the evidence in front of his eyes.

"[W]e see man governed by instinctive drives and by long-buried, long-forgotten memories," Cameron said in a 1962 speech given during McGill University's Reunion Weekend Seminar on The Mind of Man. He continued:

Logic and reason are held in admiration, but an extraordinary amount of thinking is non-logical. . . . [W]e recognize that the mind of man sometimes accords meanings destructive of his well-being and even imperiling his ultimate survival.

Hebb later admitted that his own experiments in perceptual isolation were used to explore the effects of brainwashing. In 1961, at Harvard's Symposium on Sensory Deprivation, years after he had completed his experiments, Hebb explained:

The work that we have done at McGill University began, actually, with the problem of brainwashing. We were not permitted to say so in the first publishing. What we did say, however, was true. . . . 'Brainwashing' was a term that came a little later.

There is a form of soft torture used in the early stages of brainwashing. The effects—in extreme cases, a breakdown of the subject's sense of self—are seldom discussed. You are the prisoner of war, and the guard hands you a blank sheet of paper. He says, "Write out your autobiography in as much detail as possible." You write for hours, days. You hand over the record. He thanks you, may commend your attention to detail. He hands you another sheet of paper. "Write out your autobiography." There appears to be no end.

"Anechoic" literally means "without echo." The anechoic chamber at Harvard University was supposedly the source of inspiration for John Cage's 1952 classic, "4'33"." In 1951, he entered the room, expecting to hear silence. Instead, he claimed to have heard two sounds, one high and one low. The engineer in charge informed Cage that the high sound was his nervous system and the low one was his blood. "What we require is silence," Cage had said in his 1950 "Lecture on Nothing," before his visit to the chamber. "What silence requires is that I go on talking."

Houdini escaped from chains; cuffs; cuffs with Bramah locks; Bean Giant cuffs; French letter cuffs; Rohan's cuffs; Krupp's cuffs ("I was in that cuff half of an hour, and it seemed like an eternity"); a Black Maria en route to a prison in Siberia; a galloping horse; a sea monster; a crazy crib; a giant football; a US mailbag; a fragile paper bag; a wet sheet; a lit cannon; a leather belt; a packing case; a rotating wheel; a rolltop desk; the Water Torture Cell; a hot-water boiler; a water mill; a glass box; a "ghost box"; the "Metamorphosis box"; the "Milk Can"; milk churns; the "Mirror" cuffs; an "invincible bracelet"; irons; leg irons; "bridge jumpers"; iron boilers; an iron-ringed wicker basket; manacles; shackles; straitjackets; sailcloth sacks; safes; cells in Brooklyn, Buffalo, Cleveland, Detroit, Missouri and Rochester; cell no. 3 in DC; cell no. 2 on Murderer's Row; trunks; locked trunks; roped trunks; snow tires; Boston tombs; diving suits; and a coffin with screwed-down lid. He remains in the coffin originally fashioned for a performance from which, now, he is forever expected to emerge.

In Iowa, after inching onto the wire trapeze, across to the middle of the chamber, I ask my guide whether the engineer was accurate in his explanation of the two sounds as the nervous system and circulatory system. She looks me squarely in the eyes and replies, "I don't know about silence. I don't work with silence." In the neurology of the 1930s and 40s, certain areas of the human cortex were called "silent." In his 1941 book, "Epilepsy and Cerebral Localization," neurologist Wilder Penfield writes that these areas of the cortex "are called silent only because it is found that their destruction produces no detectable interference with mental or psychical function. This is due to the replaceability of those areas. . . ." In the darkness of the anechoic chamber, I knew it might be wrong to infuse the approximation of silence with meaning or hope, to find comfort in an environment that prides itself on the purity of experience, but I found comfort in thinking that here was a place where each sound was, at least theoretically, ensured of an origin.

I woke at 4 a.m. and tiptoed downstairs to find her bed empty. The covers were thrown back, and I noticed that the indentation of her body in the mattress had grown smaller. I pushed open the swinging door to the small adjoining kitchen until it bumped against something on the other side. I pushed the object forward using the weight of the door and stuck my head through the opening to find her sitting on the floor, surrounded by shards of glass, which caught the moonlight from the window and dazzled her sunken outline. She looked up at me, smiling, and said, "Sorry to wake you.

I was just getting a drink of water, and the glass slipped from my hands."
As she spoke, she held her hands up, and we watched as they twitched in
the air, beholden to no one.

FROM THE AUTHOR

One of the first nonfiction writing courses I took at Iowa was John D'Agata's
"Experimental Essay." We were given a series of reading packets that focused on different aspects of the essay (for example, essay as performance,
essays that highlight a central narrator-researcher, and so on). And we
were asked to write our own essays throughout the semester and invited
to mimic the new styles and approaches to which we were being exposed.
We read Lucretius, Seneca, Eliot Weinberger, Velimir Khlebnikov, Myung
Mi Kim, Michel Butor, C.D. Wright, and many others, including excerpts
from Jerome Rothenberg's *Shaking the Pumpkin*. Joe Brainard's "I remember" showed us how a list-like form could illuminate our relationships with
memory, time, and narrative. The Florentine Codex and essays from Sumer
showed us how everyday objects could illuminate one's relationship with
his environment or culture and thus tell us something about how that person perceives his world. This may have driven the initial attempt at "Anechoic," which resembled a journey essay (i.e., you go some place, come
back, what's changed?).

"Anechoic" began with a trip to a flotation tank company in Chicago.
The tanks are provided as a way for clients to achieve total relaxation by
limiting the individual's sensory perception. The tank itself is a coffin-like
chamber filled with Epsom salt and water, the temperature of which ap-
proximates the body to provide a sense of seamlessness between skin and
air. They call the experience Restricted Environmental Stimulation Technique (REST). It was the same name given to neuroscientist John C. Lilly's
research in the fifties, as an alternative to the term sensory deprivation,
which became complicated by the practice of brainwashing. (In specific,
sensory deprivation was an early stage of brainwashing.) Lilly created the
first isolation tank to explore the brain apart from external stimuli in 1954.
The birth of the isolation tank coincided with the popularization of psy-
chedelic drugs in the United States, the use of which influenced research
into the nature of consciousness. It was thought that by limiting the body's
physical experience of the world, one could come to a greater understanding of the brain as well as our perception of reality.

The trip to Chicago resulted in a straightforward, plodding essay that focused on the novelty of the trip and failed to explore the implications with regard to loss and absence. Soon after, a classmate pointed me in the direction of John Cage, whose classic "4′33″" was inspired by a visit to the world's first anechoic chamber. I spent time in Iowa's Music Library reading Richard Kostelanetz's books on Cage, and scanning through some of Cage's own works like *Musicage* and *Silence: Lectures and Writings*. He used methods like chance operations and the I-Ching to create texts and help break through a dominant language or narrative. (Interestingly, and for anyone more interested in a bodily approach to constraints and writing, Matthew Barney of Cremaster fame used physical constraints to create his Drawing Restraint series.) In a pretty literal way, I wanted to know what the ultimate narrative was, that is, how the body determines the self in the world. So I also started dropping by the Medical Library and listening to heart and lung sounds that evidenced particular abnormalities in the body. All of which eventually led me to running the experiment on myself, by visiting Iowa's own anechoic chamber.

The University of Iowa's Wendell Johnson Speech and Hearing Center houses a chamber similar to that of the anechoic chamber. It was engineered to minimize external sound in order to create an environment that could be used to test and optimize hearing aids. There is an extreme difference between limiting the visual and auditory senses. Lying in the pitch-dark flotation tank seemed only to limit my visual frame of reference. But, standing alone in the middle of the chamber, I became more aware of the body's own noises and automation. This created a sense of claustrophobia as well as fragility. I felt singular and alone. I was struggling with my mother's death and my father's absence. But, as Cage indicates, silence is a concept.

This resulted in a new version of "Anechoic," which juxtaposed the sensory deprivation research with that of the anechoic chamber and better reflected the underlying emotional landscape of the essayist. To weave these histories together and ground the reader in the central inquiry, I included personal memories of my mother. These paragraphs came from a separate file that I keep of writing fragments that have been cut from past essays and from my writing journal. The disjunction of this version confused readers. And after reading this draft, Robin Hemley suggested that I look into Houdini's relationship with the Spiritualists, who believed the dead could be contacted through a medium. The inclusion of this narrative helped ground the reader by locating the research in a central inquiry of loss.

When I'd arrived at Iowa, I thought of the essay as a linear, personal narrative in which the writer recounts a series of related events. This approach felt limiting, but I didn't understand how to move past it at the time. How do you describe the intangible, or complicate absence in order to come to a better understanding of it? John's experimental essay class showed me what an essay could be. In specific, we learned that an essay could be a performance, a reflection of the essayist's psychic landscape, and so on. Because, in part, what we notice reflects what we value. In this way, knowledge and experience influence the way we perceive, or experience, the world.

What holds "Anechoic" together is the emotional landscape of the essayist, which is revealed by the subjects and histories to which she attends. At some point, it seems all you can say about a particular loss is "*this* person is no longer *there*." Yet your experience of that particular absence or space continues, and changes.

Round Trip

JOHN D'AGATA (1998)

(Originally published in *Creative Nonfiction*)

1

Isaac, who is twelve, has come involuntarily.

"We insist he grow up cultured," his mother says, leaning over our head-rests from the seat behind. "My father brought me to Hoover Dam on a bus. There is just no other way to see it."

Hours ago, before the bus, I found the tour among the dozens of bro-chures in my hotel lobby. It had been typed and Xeroxed, folded three times into the form of a leaflet, and crammed into the back of a countertop rack on the bellhop's "What To Do" desk in Vegas.

Nearby my tour in the brochure rack were announcements for Colorado River raft rides that would paddle visitors upstream into the great gleam-ing basin of the dam.

There were ads, too, for helicopter rides—offering to fly "FOUR friends and YOU" over "CROWDS, TRAFFIC, this RIVERS & MAN'S MOST BEAUTI-FUL structure—all YOURS to be PHOTOGRAPHED at 10,000 FEET!"

Hot-air balloon tours.

Rides on mountain bikes.

Jaunts on donkeys through the desert, along the river, and up the dam's canyon wall.

There was even something called the Hoover Dam Shopper's Coach, whose brochure guaranteed the best mall bargains in Nevada, yet failed to mention anywhere on its itinerary Hoover Dam.

Brochure in hand, I stood in line at the tour's ticket booth behind a man haggling with a woman behind the glass. He wanted a one-way ticket to Hoover Dam.

"Impossible," the woman said. "We sell The Eleven-Dollar Tour. One tour, one price."

The one-way man went on about important business he had at the dam, things he had to see to, how the tour's schedule just wasn't time enough.

"Sir," she said, through security glass. "I'm telling you, you'll have to come back. They're not gonna let you stay out there."

He bought a ticket, moved on.

We boarded.

Like the ad said, The Eleven-Dollar Tour comes with a seat on the bus, a free hot-dog coupon, and a six-hour narrative, there and back.

Our bus is silver, round, a short-chubby thing. It is shaped like a bread box. Like a bullet. "Like they used to make them," says Isaac's mom.

I turn to Isaac, my seatmate, say, "Hi, my name is John," and he says he doesn't care, and proceeds to pluck the long blond lashes from his eyelids, one by one, standing them on his wrist, stuck there by their follicles.

It is at this point that Isaac's mom leans over our headrests and tells me that Isaac is a good boy, "talkative, really," that he just happens to be grumpy today because "Mother and Father" have insisted that he accompany them on this "educational tour." Isaac's mother tells me that to keep Isaac entertained in Las Vegas they are staying in a new hotel—the largest in the world, in fact—with 5,000 guest rooms, 4 casinos, 17 restaurants, a mega-musical amphitheater, a boxing ring, a monorail, and a 33-acre amusement park, all inside an emerald building. She presents the brochure.

I say, "Wow."

Then Isaac's dad, looking up from another brochure he holds in his lap, says, "You know, kiddo, this Hoover Dam looks pretty special!" And then come statistics from the paragraph he's reading.

The feet high.

The feet thick.

The cubic yards of concrete.

Of water.

The 3 million kilowatts.

And the plaque.

"Let me see that." Isaac's mom takes the brochure and reads the plaque's inscription to herself. She shakes her head.

"Do you believe that? Isaac, honey, listen."

Isaac's eyes roll far away. His mother's voice climbs up a stage.

She is just loud enough to be overheard. Just hushed enough to silence all of us.

It is her voice, and the quiet, and the words on the plaque that I think might have made the whole trip worth it even then, even before we left the

tour company's parking lot and learned there'd be no air-conditioning on
the six-hour ride, even before we stood in line for two hours at the dam;
before the snack bar ran out of hot dogs and the tour guide of his jokes;
before the plaque was laid in 1955 by Ike; before the dam was dedicated in
1935 by FDR; before the ninety-six men died "to make the desert bloom";
or before the Colorado first flooded, before it leaked down from mountains, carved the Grand Canyon, and emptied into the ocean. Even before
this plaque was cast by a father and his son in their Utah blacksmith shop,
there was the anticipation of this plaque, its gold letter riding on the backs
of all creators. And Isaac's mother's voice, even then, I believe, was ringing
circles somewhere in the air: ". . . the American Society of Civil Engineers
voted this one of the Seven Modern Wonders of the World!"

*These are the seven wonders of the world: a beacon, a statue, gardens, pyramids,
a temple, another statue, and a tomb. I have set eyes on them all—this Lofty fire
of Pharos, and the statue of Zeus by Alpheus, and the Hanging Gardens, and the
Colossus of the Sun, and the Huge Labor of the High Pyramids, and the vast tomb
of Mausolus, and the House of Artemis mounted to the Clouds—and I tell you,
as a scholar and as a wanderer and as a man devoted to the gods, they are and
always will be the Seven Greatest Liberties man will ever take with Nature.*

(ANTIPATER OF SIDON, from his lost guidebook, c. 120 B.C.)

2

Our driver maneuvers lithely through the streets filled with rental cars. I
tilt my head into the aisle. There is his green-sleeved arm, his pale, pudgy
hand that is dancing on the gearstick rising out of the floor. His head, bob-
bing above the rows of seats in front of me, seems to bounce in rhythm
with his horn. He honks to *let* pedestrians cross.

He rearranges his hair.

Leans a little forward.

Fluffs a cushion at his back.

We are idling at a crosswalk. We are there seven minutes, when suddenly, out of the air, our driver's voice comes coiling.

*On the right side of us is Flamingo Hotel where Elvis Presley owned a floor
of that hotel on our right side.*

*On the left side of us is the Mirage Hotel where Michael Jackson owns a
floor of that hotel on our left side.*

His words emit circles, whip bubbles around our heads. His sentences
wrap around the bus and greet themselves in midair. All the way to the

dam the bus rumbles inside this cloud, the date slips steadily away, the tour transforms into a silent scratchy film that is slowly flitting backward through frames of older dreams.

We sit among neo-Gothic images heaping up from the pages of a souvenir borrowed from Isaac's grandfather, a 1935 photographic essay entitled, "The Last Wonder of the World: The Glory of Hoover Dam." On its brittle pages machines still throb, light still beams from the book's center spread.

A full, glossy, long-shot view of the generator room reveals round, sleek, plastic bodies lined up like an army, surrounded by looming concrete walls adorned with pipes of gleaming chrome. Everything stands at attention. Nothing but light is stirring. The whole scene is poised forever to strike against an enemy that never breached the river's shore.

Gambling wasn't legalized in our state until 1935 is when they legalized gambling in Nevada.

The patterns in these pictures are like wax dripping from candles, islands coagulating from spurts of lava, liquid steel pouring out of kettles into rifle molds. Buick frames, the skyscrapers of Chicago. The round machines spin their energy like spools, all of it rolling off their bodies, through the pages, over the slick, curved surface of the next machine, which is identical to the last: which is blinking the same, rounded the same, parodying his sentences revolving around our heads, and shielding our tour from starts and stops, from *In the beginning*, from *Ever after*, from *Now* and from *Then*, and from any time—from all time—in which this vacuous progression cannot fit, because its round body is nowhere near the right shape for the boxy borders of dates.

Just to let you know, folks, our tour company's been on the road since 1945 is how long we've been traveling this road.

I mention to Isaac that the machines resemble something I once saw in *Doctor Who*, and he says, "No they don't"—which is the first thing he has said to me in an hour.

"It's more like *Star Trek*'s Plasma Generation," he says. But when I tell him I don't quite follow him, we decide that something from *Batman* suits our conflicting descriptions best.

What we do not know at this moment, however, is that in 1935, when the dam was opened, Batman was about to make his debut in comic strips. So was Superman, and other superheroes—summoned from Krypton or Gotham City to defend our country against impending evils—their bodies toned flawlessly as turbines. They came with tales of an ideal Tomorrow. They came jostled between two wars, buffering our borders against enemies on every side, encircling the country with an impenetrable force field, and introducing at home a new architecture of resistance: round, sleek, something the old clunky world slipped off.

A lot of these trees and most of this grass is brought in from out of state.

A lot of these trees and most of this grass is brought in from Arizona.

These are the same curves I once found in my grandmother's basement. Toasters so streamlined they're liable to skid off the kitchen counter. A hair dryer filched from Frankenstein's brain-wave lab. A Philharmonic radio taller than my ten-year-old body, and reeking of Swing—leaking tinny voices, platinum songs, and the catch-me-if-you-can whorls from Benny Goodman's silvery tube.

My grandmother's is the world that dropped the bomb—itself a slick object—so elegantly smooth it managed to slip past American consciousness, past enemy lines.

Afterward, in her world, "Atomic" was a prefix attached to the coming world and all the baubles to be found there. But in that present, at the opening of Hoover Dam, the designers of the future could only have guessed what atoms looked like.

And still their imaginations leaped instantly to *round*, to *fast*, to *heralds of the future*.

3

During the sixth century, St. Gregory of Tours compiled a list of the seven wonders of the medieval world which demonstrates an inaccurate knowledge of history. He retained four wonders from the original list, but made three additions of his own: Noah's Ark, Solomon's Temple, and the Original Tree of Life—which, he claimed, had been discovered in the underground archives of a church in his native France. But St. Gregory, of course, was wrong. The remains of the Tree of Life were used to construct the Crucifix on which our Saviour died—now housed, of course, in the Holy Cross Church in Rome.

(from my grandmother's library, G.B. Smith's *Remembering the Saints*)

4

"There's this computer game I like so I guess that counts right? It's not the real world but it lets you do really awesome stuff that's pretty cool so you can call that a wonder I bet. But I gotta go to my friend's house to play it though 'cause my parents won't get it for me cause they think it's too violent. Hey you can't write this down or I'm not talking man. It's called

Civilization. You start with two guys—a guy and a girl—and they're like at
the start of the world or something. But after all the animals are made and
stuff. And then—um—you have to make babies because the whole point
is to you know start the civilization. So the computer keeps asking you
what you want to do. Like if you want to have babies at a certain time or
if you wanna be a hunter and gatherer or start farming and all that. So at
the same time the computer has its own family that it's starting and you
have to be in competition with them. So you start your family and all that
and you become a village and . . . that's all the boring stuff. But you have
to do it to start up the game. So before you know it you're like the leader
and everything and people start gods and that kind of stuff and there's
laws that you get to make up like if you want people to steal or how many
wives you can have. And all of a sudden the computer calls war on you and
you have to fight them 'cause if you don't then the game ends 'cause the
computer can kill all your people. So there's whole long parts when you
gotta learn how to do battle and you decide if you wanna use your metal to
make weapons or not and how many people you'll make fight 'cause after
you play a long time you learn that if you keep some people in the village
during the war you can make them keep making weapons and stuff and
help the fighters who are hurt. And usually if you make it through the war
with some people left then the computer won't kill you off 'cause it'll let
you try to start the village again. So all that happens and—um—every now
and then the computer lets you know that someone in the village makes
an invention. Like if they use the well to try to make a clock or they build
a building with stones that has a roof so you can put more floors on top of
it and—you know—then cities start. Then people start sailing down the
river and they find other places to live and there are like whole new civili-
zations that the computer controls that you get to find. Now it all depends
on how you act with the new people that tells whether or not you start a
war or something or if you join their village and team up your forces. When
that happens the computer gives you a lot more technology. So all that
goes on and like thousands of years go by and pretty soon it starts looking
like the modern world and you're controlling a whole country. Then your
goal is to get control of the whole world which only one of my friends has
done but then there's always this little place you don't know about that
starts a revolution and then the whole world starts fighting and everyone
ends up dead. I've never gotten that far though. I've controlled a couple
countries before and I usually make them all start a colony in space and
what's great is that if you tell them to fly to a planet in the solar system
then the computer isn't programmed that far and it lets you do whatever

you want for a little while until it just ends the game 'cause it doesn't know how to continue 'cause it can't compete with you if you just keep inventing new stuff it hasn't heard of. So sometimes I get like three countries to go up there and they start this whole new civilization and there are new animals and just the right amount of people and all the buildings are beautiful and built with this river that turns hard when you pick up the water and you can shape it how you want. So there's all this glass around and it's awesome but it only lasts like a year because the computer gets freaked out and ends up stopping the game. The game always ends up destroying the world."

5

When the Canal was being completed, the renowned sculptor Daniel Chester French and the best-known landscape architect of the day, Frederick Law Olmstead, were hired to decorate it. After a careful survey, the two artists refused the commission. So impressed were they by the beauty which the engineers had created that they declared, "For we artists to add to it now would be an impertinence."

1. The Panama Canal, 1914

MY LIST

"Hello, Joe Miller here."

"Hi, sir. I'm wondering if maybe you could help me out. I'm trying to find the American Society of Civil Engineers' list of the Seven Modern Wonders of the World. Are you the right person to talk to?"

"Yeah, yeah that's me. I think the list you're talking about is pretty old, though. We just announced a new list you might be interested in."

"A new list?"

"The 1999 Modern Wonders of the World."

"Oh. Well, actually I guess I'm interested in the old Modern list."

"Well that's forty years old! This new one we have is a lot more impressive. I think this is what you're looking for."

"Well, could you maybe tell me about the first list anyway? I can't find it mentioned anywhere in my library. I kind of need it."

"Well, that'll take some time . . . Let me get back to you . . ."

A common witticism on that bleak Depression day when this spectacular skyscraper opened its doors was, "The only way the landlords will ever fill that thing is if they tow it out to sea." But such pessimistic sentiments were wrong, as pes-

simists always have been in America. The population of the building now is that of a small city!

2. The Empire State Building, 1931

MY GRANDFATHER'S LIST

"Just put down the Statue of Liberty.
That's all I want you to put down."

How do you dig a hole deeper than anyone has ever dug, fill it with more concrete and steel than has been used in any other public works campaign, and do it all in the middle of California's busiest harbor, swiftest current, most stormy shore? No, no! it would be sheer folly to try—but they did it anyway!

3. The San Francisco-Oakland Bay Bridge, 1936

MY MOTHER'S LIST

1. The Twin Towers
2. The Apollo Space Program
3. PCs
4. Cannabis
5. Picasso
6. August 9, 1974 (Richard Nixon's resignation)
7. Cape Cod

Then the fun begins. The aqueduct's route crosses two hundred forty-two miles of terrain that looks as if it had been dropped intact from the moon: a landscape of mountainous sands, dry washes, empty basins—one of the hottest, deadliest wastelands in the civilized world. . . . And this conduit, man's longest, spans it all!

4. The Colorado River Aqueduct, 1938

ISAAC'S MOTHER'S LIST

"Oh, I know these. One must be the Brooklyn Bridge. I practically grew up on that thing! The Eiffel Tower has to be on there. Probably the Sears Tower, too. The Washington Monument. Niagara Falls. What about the Pentagon? And the Hoover Dam, of course."

Flying over the city, below the left wing of the plane, you will see Chicago's Southeast Works, one of the largest and most advanced sewage treatment facilities in the world. It is a veritable modern city, as spanking-looking as if sealed in a fresh-washed bottle, and as motionless and silent as a hospital at night.

5. The Chicago Sewage Disposal System, 1939

GUY-IN-A-BAR'S LIST

1. A rapid development in our fine and visual arts
2. With all of our technological advancements,
   a continued sadness among the people
3. Our ignorance of environmental problems
4. Magic
5. The Internet
6. Alaska
7. Hoover Dam

A certain stopper was the fact that the Coulee could only rise to 550 feet. At that height it backed up the Columbia River into a 150-mile-long lake. Any higher and it would have flooded Canada.

6. The Grand Coulee Dam, 1941

JOE MILLER'S LIST

"Yeah, this is a message for John D'Agata. I have that information you requested. This is the 1999 list of Modern Wonders of the World:

> one is The Golden Gate Bridge;
> two, The World Trade Center;
> three, The U.S. Interstate Highway System;
> four, The Kennedy Space Center;
> five, The Panama Canal;
> six, The Trans-Alaskan Pipeline;
> and seven is Hoover Dam."

It lofts up with the majesty of Beauty itself, and you marvel at what manner of men could have conceived the possibility of building such a wonder.

7. The Hoover Dam, 1935 (from *America the Beautiful: An Introduction to Our Seven Wonders*)

6

Perhaps the Book of Genesis is the first and most famous list of wonders. Today, however, such rosters of remarkable things are common in America.

Whenever I visit a city for the first time, I always notice the gold stars on storefronts—"Voted Best Barbershop," ". . . Mexican Food," ". . . Auto Repair." My brother, who prides himself on his ability to spot "quality trends," as he calls them, has sworn for years by *Boston Magazine*'s annual "Best Of" issue.

He says that living by the list is like living in a perfect world. And the list has grown so comprehensive each year that, these days, my brother seldom has to live without perfection. He has found, for example, a "professional scalper" with the best last-minute Bruins ticket deals, a laundry known for having the best-pressed cuffs, and a sportsman's lodge with the best range for skeet shooting—a sport my brother has taken up simply out of awe of it being listed.

Another purveyor of perfection has gone so far as to publish a book-length list, entitled The Best of Everything, which includes the Best Sexy Animal (the female giraffe), the Best Labor-Saving Device (the guillotine), the Best Vending Machine (a mashed-potato dispenser in Nottingham, England), and the Best Souvenir (a shrunken head from Quito, Ecuador).

Not to be outdone, proponents of the worst things in the world have published *The Worst of Everything*. On this list can be found the Worst Nobel Peace Prize Recipient (Henry Kissinger), the Worst Item Ever Auctioned (Napoleon's dried penis), the Worst Poem Ever Written ("The Child" by Friedrich Hebbel), and the Worst Celebrity Endorsement for a Car (Hitler, for the Volkswagen Bug: "This streamlined four-seater is a mechanical marvel. It can be bought on an installation plan for six Reichsmarks a week—including insurance!")

Now Isaac's mother leans over our seats and shows us both another brochure.

"Just think how happy they all must have been," she says, unfolding an artist's rendition of the future across our laps. "I sure wish I lived back then. You know?"

1939. Queens, New York.

She, Isaac, and I have just paid our fifty cents, and before us—miles wide—are promenades, sculptures, buildings, and glittery things, all laid out in perfect grids. "So bright and lovely," she says, "it makes me want to close my eyes." Even the people around us shine, sweaty inside their wool suits and skirts. There are thousands of them, Isaac decides—just like the people who walk around EPCOT.

"You know," he says. "The kind who you can't really tell are real or not."

We buy frankfurters, a guidebook, little silver spoons at every exhibition. We are here because—even as far west as Nevada, even as far into the future as 1999—we have heard that this is the greatest fair ever orchestrated on earth.

We start with Isaac's mom's list: the Gardens on Parade, the Town of Tomorrow, the House of Jewels, the Plaza of Light, Democracity.

Then we visit Isaac's list: the Futurama, the Academy of Sports, the Court of Power, the Lagoon of Nations, the Dome of the Heinz Corp.

And by the time we visit my list we have stumbled smack into the middle of the fair, inches from its epicenter, squinting back up at those dazzling fair trademarks known in our guidebook as *Trylon* and *Perisphere*. The obelisk and the globe stand like silence behind the roaring and spurting of ten giant fountains.

The two of them are like fountains behind the silence of our gaze.

One of them is stretched so high it scrapes the color from the sky. The other is arched playfully on its own curved back.

The obelisk, we read, is 610 feet tall ("That's 50 feet taller than the Washington Monument!" our guidebook claims). The sphere is 180 feet in diameter ("The largest globe in the state of New York!").

Both objects are words that never before existed. And despite all the euphoria surrounding them in '39, all the family photos posed in front of them, the silverware and shaving kits and Bissell Carpet Sweepers that bore their images, *Trylon* and *Perisphere* never made it into our lexicon.

At the foot of them, I can't see why.

One is like a list, the other is like a wonder. But I don't say this aloud.

"An arrow and a bull's eye!" one of us blurts out. And so they are. Perfectly.

Or one is like an ancient scroll unrolled, the other is an orb of undecipherable glyphs. One is how we describe a fantasy; the other is what we've secretly dreamt.

Shoulder to shoulder, we three look them up, then down. Our mouths hang wide—with *awe*—filled with them.

I remember the first list of wonders that I ever knew. One year, an old man on our street told my mother that he had once been a college professor, a master of Latin and Greek. Within days I was studying classics with him. I had just turned eight.

My tutor, Mr. Newcomb, lived alone among statuary and plaster casts of temple friezes. Tapestries padded his walls. I met with him each day in the barest room of his house: a desk, two chairs, a lamp, a rug, and seven hanging woodcuts of the seven ancient wonders.

Some days, instead of reading, Mr. Newcomb beguiled me with trivia about the hanging wonders on his walls. And some days, strewn over the years, he divulged their secrets. Why, for instance, the curse of the Pyramids in fact is real; where, in Turkey, the Colossus' body parts are actually hidden; what, according to Vatican documents, which Mr. Newcomb alone had read in Rome, Napoleon "felt" as he pissed on the charred remains of Diana's great temple.

Later, Mr. Newcomb's woodcuts of the seven ancient wonders became mine once he had died. At that point, however, I had only managed to grasp the first conjugation in Latin, so for years after, until I could return to Latin in school, the ancient wonders lived beside me in a parallel present tense.

I have them still. They hang around—dark, worn—reminding me of the last wonderful secret my tutor left: that he had never studied Latin, never read the classics. That he had never traveled to Rome, nor much farther beyond our town.

He had never actually liked school.

Yet what he had was curiosity. Crustiness. An air of scholastic formality. He had a dustiness that was reliable. A home adorned, tastefully, lessons always prepared for me, cookies, milk, stories that kept me rapt. He had a knack, which was his lure, for both the mundane and fantastic.

The black-breasted roadrunner, my favorite bird, is that black-breasted roadrunner there.

The bird hurries past our bus, darting up the mountain pass as we slowly descend its peak. I am awakened by our driver's voice and my ears popping as we slide into the valley. Everyone else, everyone except for Isaac and the one-way man, is asleep. They chat across the center aisle.

"I'm gonna live there," says the one-way man, when Isaac asks what he'll do when we arrive at the dam.

"You can live there?" Isaac asks.

"Well, I'm gonna," says the man.

Isaac's mom, I know, would want me to intervene here, tell Isaac the man's just joking with him. Tell Isaac the one-way man is crazy.

But when Isaac starts talking about his computer game, and the one-way man explains how the concave wall of the Hoover Dam would be awesome for skateboarding, it is they who stop, mutually—nowhere conclusive and without any care.

They sit back in their seats, stare forward awhile, and fall asleep.

7

continents, days per week, Deadly Sins, Epochs of Man according to Shakespeare, hills of Rome, liberal arts, perfect shapes, planets in the Ptolemaic system, Pleiades in Greek myth, Sacraments, seas, Sleepers of Ephesus, wives of Bluebeard, wonders of Yemen, Years War

FROM THE AUTHOR

If I had a process while trying to write this essay I am unaware of it.

I know that what I first tried to write was "At the Dam," an essay that had been written a few decades earlier by Joan Didion.

I love that essay.

Sometimes, when I was younger, I wanted to be that essay—not just to have written it but to be able to inhabit it, like drag, to feel its sentences so intimately inside me that the power of Didion's prose might somehow cause an infection.

I brought a copy of the essay with me when I first visited Las Vegas. I was with my grandparents, and we were only there on a pit-stop overnight. But I begged them to make the hour-long car ride down the Strip from our hotel, through the fuming desert, up the Black Mountains, down the orange canyon walls, and along the single-laned highway across Hoover Dam.

What I'd wanted to do was take my photocopy of the essay out of my pocket at the dam and begin to read it aloud to the other tourists who were there, waiting for a chance to get inside of the dam in order to tour its turbines. We would all listen rapt as Didion described a place that was eerily empty of us, and then we'd all look out over the rim of the dam and see it for what it was—not a marvel of engineering, nor a monument to the West, but a testament to the spirit of imagination itself, that thing that I had an inkling I wanted to be a part of but which I hadn't yet figured out how to access on my own, nor even if I had any right to do so.

All I had, in other words, was that essay. And so I wanted to be it.

Years later, after that visit with my grandparents, and just after I finished college and was about to enter Iowa, I spent a summer working as a barback, selling condoms, landscaping, and delivering ice cream cakes and balloons while dressed as a rainbow-costumed clown, trying to raise enough money to make the trip back to Vegas. I took a bus tour to the dam, because I couldn't afford a rental car, and when we finally arrived at Hoover I forgot my copy of "At the Dam" on my seat on the bus. I'd been distracted by my seat mate who wouldn't stop talking about a video game that sounded sort of like something I had played before myself and sort of like something fake.

But anyway the dam was nice. They had made a lot of changes. I remember that I found it as inspiring as I had years earlier as a teen, but a little different this time without Didion's essay ringing in my ears.

When we reboarded, my seat mate continued talking as if an hour-long tour of Hoover Dam hadn't interrupted our conversation, and I used the back two pages of "At the Dam" to make a couple notes.

But beyond that, whatever process that was involved in writing my own version of Hoover Dam has since been lost to me. The only process that matters, really, is the one that helped me figure out that I was not Joan Didion but was in fact myself.

Bruce Springsteen and the Story of Us

HOPE EDELMAN (1992)

(Originally published in *The Iowa Review*, reprinted in *The Pushcart Prize XXI*)

The first time I heard a Bruce Springsteen song performed live was in 1979, when I was in the tenth grade and Larry Weinberger and A.J. DeStefano stood in our high school parking lot shouting all the words to "Thunder Road" from start to finish, zipping right through that tune at fast-forward speed. Eyes squeezed shut into brief black hyphens, shoulders pumping to an imaginary drum beat, they sang to an audience of ten or twelve sophomores sprawled against the hoods of their parents' old cars, their red and green and blue looseleaf binders strewn right side up and upside down like blackjack hands along the pavement at their feet.

This was October, the second month of the school year, and the time between 3:40 p.m. and dinner was still a flat landscape of vast and open hours. A single cigarette slowly made its way around the circle, passed between the tight Vs of fingers and held just long enough for each of us to blow a smoke ring for effect. Across the parking lot, students called to each other by last name ("Yo, Speee-VAK!"), car doors slammed, engines revved like short-lived lawn mowers. Larry and A.J. finished their song and started on "Jungleland," pausing after, "The Magic Rat drove his sleek machine over the Jersey state line" just long enough to allow:

"Into Rockland County!"

"The Ramapough Inn!"

"Yo mama's backyard!"

"Hey! Your sister's bedroom, ass*hole*."

We all knew the words to Springsteen's songs, and we knew, firsthand, most of the places they described. Some of them practically *were* in our parents' backyards. We were living in New York, just over the New Jersey border in the tiny towns that dot the bottom of the state map like scattered flecks of black pepper, a county filled with minor suburbs most frequently described by their relative position to somewhere else: thirty-three miles northwest of Manhattan, less than a one-hour drive from two international airports, and a half-tank of gas north of the Jersey shore.

Springsteen Country, our bumper stickers read, though most of us took thick black magic markers and crossed out the second R. Springsteen County was far more accurate for a place where high school principals considered "Jungleland" appropriate music to play over the homeroom P.A. system; where parents routinely dropped off their children in front of Ticketron offices fortified with sleeping bags and pastrami sandwiches, returning the next morning to carpool them to school; and where sixteen-year-olds held parties in empty parking lots on heavy, humid, late-summer nights, where they sat on the hoods of cars and swirled beer around in the can, listening to Springsteen sing about a barefoot girl on the hood of a Dodge drinking warm beer in the soft summer rain. It was enough to make you wonder where the night ended and the song began, or if there really were a difference, at all.

Those were our years of music, back when we still could find simple, one-step answers to life's most complex problems in the lyrics of the songs we sang, back when a deejay's mellifluous voice could still smooth out all the rough edges of a day. In those years, the late '70s and early '80s, we plucked our role models from the FM dial—Bruce Springsteen, John Cougar, Joan Jett, a cast list of sensitive survivors, underdogs with good intentions, minor idols who neatly met our critical adolescent need to constantly feel wronged without ever actually doing anything wrong, and we aligned our frustrations with the lyrical mini-dramas scripted for us in advance. Our mythology was created and recycled, and recycled and recycled, every day.

Though we liked to imagine ourselves as the kind of characters that peopled Springsteen's songs—he was, after all, *writing about us*—the fit was never quite right. We had pretty much the same anxieties, but the socioeconomics were all wrong. He sang of working-class kids stuck in dead-end towns who grabbed their girlfriends by the wrists, leapt into their rebuilt '69 Chevys and peeled out of town in search of their futures. Our hometown was an upper-middle-class suburb where a college education was more an expectation than an exercise in free will. Most of us would grow up to become just what our parents had planned, and to do just as they had done. *Doctor, lawyer, C.P.A.* But in the time we had before our decisions became too intractable to erase, we were free to try on and shrug off whatever clothing best fit our erratic moods. Even the most intelligent, even the most affluent among us had visions of a utopia free of parents, P.E. teachers, and pop quizzes. Springsteen offered us his version of that place, his promises surrounding us like audio wallpaper—hogging the airwaves on our car radios, piped into our homerooms, pumped into every store in our local indoor shopping mall, encircling us with songs of hot desire and escape.

This was 1978, 1979, and in the magazine interviews we passed from desk to desk in social studies class Springsteen told us he would never change, would never, essentially, grow up. His was a world of perpetual adolescence, an eternal seventeen. "I couldn't bring up kids," he told *Rolling Stone*. "I couldn't handle it. I mean, it's too heavy, it's too much. . . . I just don't see why people get married. It's so strange. I guess it's a nice track, but not for me."

Back then, like us, Springsteen was still living among his history, shuffling along the Asbury Park boardwalk with his hands jammed down deep in the front pockets of his jeans but his eyes fixed on the gulls that dipped and cawed on the horizon. He held tight to the Jersey towns where he began, always swore he'd never forget the people or the place, but he also knew where he wanted to go, and this duality pervaded his songs like a restless, wanton motif. His lyrics told us precisely what we wanted to hear: that when the pressures of adulthood started squeezing us too tight we could just peel out, leaving skid marks as our contemptuous farewell, and his music could, in the course of only three minutes, transform a solitary harmonica wail into a full-band battle cry, the cymbals crashing *one, two, three* like a bedroom door slamming shut over and over again.

But I'm talking early Springsteen here, vintage Springsteen, those pre-1980 songs that put you in a fast car and took you on a one-way ride through images that came quick and fast as lightning, no time to bother with a chorus you could return to and repeat when you lost your place in the stream of consciousness lyrics that rambled on and on like Kerouac sentences in search of a period. The songs that gave you hope there was a simpler, gentler world out there somewhere, and that the happiness missing from your own backyard could be found in the next town. This was back before he cut his hair short and sprouted biceps, back when the guitar chords still came down angry and loud and an unshaven, scrawny Springsteen rooted himself behind the mike with a guitar pressed tight against his groin, his shoulders and neck twitching spastically in time with the beat. Back when you could still tell a lot about a man by the lyrics that he sang, and when you thought Bruce Springsteen knew a lot about you, as you lay alone on your twin bed with the door slammed shut and the hi-fi turned up to 9, listening to him play the piano introduction to "Jungle-land" the way he did it every time, with his left hand firmly anchored in the bass chords as his right hand skittered manically up and down the soprano notes, flailing like a frantic fish, fluttering like wings.

When I met Jimmy T. I was seventeen and still a virgin, and three weeks later I was neither anymore. We did it for the first time on a Saturday afternoon in his lumpy double bed underneath guitars that hung suspended from a ceiling rack like electric pots and pans. He had a chair jammed under the doorknob and WPLJ turned up loud enough to mask our noise, and sometimes when the radio hit a bass note, a guitar string buzzed above my head. Two hours of songs must have played that afternoon, but the only one I remember is Springsteen's "Hungry Heart," because as soon as he heard the opening chords Jimmy T. started to hum and thrust in rhythm to the song. *Got a wife and kids in Baltimore Jack, I went out for a ride and I never went back.* Jimmy T. assured me that losing his virginity at age thirteen made him eminently qualified to relieve me of mine without unnecessary pain or pomp. He was right, on both counts, but I was disappointed nonetheless. I'd been prepared for several unsuccessful attempts, searing pain, and the kind of hysterical bleeding Sylvia Plath had described in *The Bell Jar*. The ease of it made me wonder, at first, if we'd done it right.

I was the last among his friends to lose it but the first among mine, and when I left his parents' house I drove straight to my friend Jody's, walked down the hall to her room, sat down carefully on her white-ruffled canopy bed, and started to cry.

"Holy shit . . . ," she whispered, and when I nodded she threw her arms around my chest, and hugged me, hard.

"Holy shit!" she shouted, bouncing her butt up and down on the bed. "Holy SHIT! TELL ME WHAT IT'S LIKE!"

What was it like? What was any of it like? Like one long manic car ride on an open stretch of road with a driver whose license had wisely been revoked. And I'm not talking just about the sex part. It was like that all the time with Jimmy T. He could get a whole room of people singing with no more than five words of encouragement and a chord on his guitar, and when we went to the movies he'd have met everyone in our row and even collected a phone number or two by the time I came back with the popcorn and Junior Mints. The intersection of a precocious intellect with a cool-guy delivery had him performing monologues about hypothetical conversations between Hitler, Santayana, and Christ ("So, the Nazi dude would have said to the formerly Jewish dude, man . . .") to his small group of smoking-section disciples during lunchtime, after he'd cut three classes that morning and had to beg his English teacher to give him a passing grade. His mother once told me his I.Q. was 145, a fact I found suspicious considering he'd never learned how to spell.

Jimmy T. Just look at his name. James Anthony Spinelli was the full version, but he wouldn't answer to James or Jim and he always included the T. For Tony. When I reminded him that his middle name was Anthony, and shouldn't he then be Jimmy A.? he gave me a crooked half-smile and raised his open palms in a shrug. I told him Jimmy T. sounded like a name he got from a fourth-grade teacher with too many Jimmys in one class, and he laughed and created a list of last names he might have had, had this been true: Tortoni, Turino, Testarossa. Jimmy Traviata at your service, he'd say, opening the car door for me with a flourish of the wrist and a bow. Jimmy Tortellini here to escort you to Spanish class. My mother would have called him a man with presence, like Frank Sinatra or Tom Jones. The kind of man, she said, who can take your heart away.

Jimmy T., I'm certain, would have considered this a compliment. In fact, if it'd been on paper, he probably would have tried to autograph it. At seventeen he already envisioned himself as a celebrity of sorts, with an existence worth chronicling as it unfolded. Write the story of us, he used to say, assigning the task to me, because I was the one who would conform to the rules of grammar and could spell. But he was the storyteller among us, the one with the elaborate narratives of drag races and secret meetings with record executives, and of playing his guitar in smoky SRO bars where audiences lifted their brown beer bottles and shouted for more. Stories I would have immediately thought unbelievable had they not been told with such authority, such grace. Write the story of us, he would say, the "us" squeezing implied chapters between its two characters, but when I tried I could never get past our first, unremarkable conversation at a party in a cheap motel room at the New Jersey shore. The people who appeared on my pages were insipid and one-dimensional, nothing at all like the characters we aspired to be, and my efforts turned into crumpled wads of paper I tossed against his bedroom walls.

I spent most of my after-school hours between those walls, preferring to close a bedroom door against the silence of Jimmy T.'s house than against the disorder of my own. This was 1982. The summer before, my mother had died of cancer, quickly and unexpectedly, leaving my father to care for three children, ages seventeen, fourteen, and nine. When we returned from the hospital he looked at us and blinked quizzically, as if to ask, Have we met? and I realized for the first time how fragile a balance life must be, if it can be tipped so swiftly, so dramatically and irrevocably, by the force of a single event. Only after my mother was gone did I understand she'd been the only adhesive that had held us all together, and as the empty Scotch bottles multiplied on the kitchen counter my father began to spout increasingly weird and existential rhetoric about how the individual is more important than the unit, and how we all must learn to fend for ourselves. I'm doing just *fine*, thank you, he hollered when he found me one evening pouring honey-colored streams of alcohol down the avocado kitchen sink. And I don't need *you* or anyone *else* to tell me how to live my life. Then don't you tell me how to live mine, I screamed back in a defensive panic, and he yelled *Fine!* and I yelled *Fine!* and everything, perhaps, would have been just fine, except that very soon I began to feel like a tiny, solitary satellite orbiting way out there, connected to nothing and no one, even after my father apologized and sent me on vacation to Florida to show how much he really meant it. I just smiled and kept saying everything was fine.

That was the fall I became obsessed with J.D. Salinger, read each of his books four times and began to quote esoteric Zen koans at wholly inappropriate cafeteria moments, and for an entire week that winter I ate nothing but ice cream and wore nothing but black. When teachers kept me after class to ask how I was doing, I said, with great conviction, I am doing just fine. But when you're out there spinning solo, it's only a matter of time before you get close enough to someone else's gravitational pull. That spring, Jimmy T. came trucking across the dirt-brown motel room carpet, black curls flapping and motorcycle boots clomping with each step, to sit next to me on the orange bedspread. He was a senior with a fast car, a reputation, and a Fender Stratocaster electric guitar. I didn't dare say anything as plebian as hello.

Our first, unremarkable conversation: He said So, and I said So, and he said, Hope? and I said Jimmy T., and he said Yeah and I said Yeah, and he said, Cigarette? and pulled a pack from his back pocket, and I said Match? and pulled a book from mine, and he said Thanks, and I said Thanks, and he said Shit! I know you can use words with more than one syllable because I see you walking out of that AP English class every day.

It didn't take me much to fall in love at seventeen—the graceful arc of a smooth-shaven jaw, the smell of freshly washed hair, the sound of a telephone ringing at precisely the moment of the promised call. After Jimmy T. and I returned from the beach that Sunday, we intertwined our fingers and we held on tight. Two weeks later, we were officially in love.

We spent every afternoon together, in his bedroom at the top of the stairs. Jimmy T. played songs he said he'd written for me, on the beat-up acoustic guitar he'd bought with birthday money when he was twelve. He and his friend George had written a song on it they'd sold to a record label the previous year, a tune Jimmy T. played for me over and over again as I sat crosslegged on his bed. We kept the curtains drawn. His room was dark and womblike, like a tight hug, and far removed from the bright yellow-and-green pep of my own. The verve of my bedroom had become a hypocrisy in my father's house, where dust had settled on the living-room tables and a television droned constantly in the background to give the illusion of discourse. The downstairs bedroom that once had been my sanctuary from mother-daughter strife had transformed into something foreign and surreal. I'd grown much older than seventeen that year, but every time I walked into my room the geometric mobiles and kitten posters along its perimeter told me I'd once been that age, and not so very long ago.

Jimmy T.'s room, on the other hand, was testimony to postmodern teen-age chaos: stereo components and recording equipment stacked schizo-phrenically against the walls; cassette and eight-track tapes scattered like loose change across the floor; Muppet dolls hanging in nooses from the ceiling; six-year-old Bruce Springsteen posters taped to the sliding closet doors; and pages and pages of handwritten sheet music layered like onion skin on top of his dresser, desk, and bed. Jimmy T. was working on a proj-ect, he said, a big one that the record company was anxiously waiting to see. It would take him another two years, he said, maybe three. He couldn't reveal its content yet, but he said it had the potential to change the world. Three years, maybe four. He didn't think the world could wait much longer than that.

He'd chosen music as his medium, he said, because it was the most in-fluential, *the most powerful* forum for widespread philosophical reform, our last-gasp hope to save our youth from an impending spiritual decline, and he was certain he'd be the one who'd one day use his guitar to make the difference that mattered. But he'd have to get moving soon, he said, seeing as how he was already certain he wouldn't live past forty.

"I mean, shit," he said. "Look at Springsteen. He's already pushing thirty five. All right, the man's a genius, he's changed my life, but how many years does he really have left? Okay, I'm seventeen now, right? So say I take off at twenty, maybe twenty one. Can you *imagine* how much I'd get done if I got started then?"

He told me this the night we met, as we walked along the beach be-fore dawn. It was no surprise that our conversation quickly skidded into music, one of the few common denominators that fused the three distinct groups—Italians, Blacks, and Jews—that comprised our high school student body. In English class that year we all read Shakespeare and Keats, but our real poets were the ones whose song lyrics we carefully copied onto our spiral notebook covers. When our teacher asked three students to bring in their favorite poems for the class to interpret the next day, Elisa Colavito showed up with the lyrics to "Born to Run." It was worth every five-paragraph essay we had to write that year to see Mrs. Bluestein squinting at the blackboard, trying to scan and analyze *Just wrap your legs 'round these velvet rims, and strap your hands 'cross my engines.*

My yearbook is filled with handscribbled verses like these, all the Jackson Browne and James Taylor and Bruce Springsteen aphorisms we reached for in moments of passion or distress. *I don't know how to tell you all just how crazy this life feels. Close your eyes and think of me, and soon I will be there. Baby, we were born to run.* They were the greatest hits of pre-packaged sentiment, providing me with words that sounded like what I thought I was supposed to feel. I had no blueprint for emotion, no adult I trusted to tell me what I should do with my mother's winter coats, or how to feel when I heard my siblings crying alone in their rooms, or what to say to a father who drank himself to sleep each night. In the absence of any real guidance or experience, Jackson Browne's advice to hold on and hold out was as good as any I could divine on my own.

Discussing music our first night together gave Jimmy T. a convenient chance to introduce his favorite topic—Bruce Springsteen—and engage in open idolatry, which he did at every available moment. By our senior year, Jimmy T. had recreated himself almost entirely in the musician's late '70s image, adopting the appearance (long, dark hair, faded jeans, half smile), the voice (a gravelly just-got-outa-bed-and-smoked-a-packa-Marlboro grumble), the transportation ('69 Chevy with a 396, and a motorcycle, no license), and the look (chin down, eyes up, head tilted slightly to one side) we saw on album covers and in music-magazine photo spreads. Jimmy T. wasn't content to merely listen to the man; he actually wanted to be him. Which meant that I, in turn, got to be his Wendy-Annie-Rosie-Mary-Janey, his co-pilot in passion and impulse. It gave me a clear persona, straight-forward and well-defined. The first time we walked hand-in-hand between the rows of metal lockers, I metamorphosed from the girl whose mother had died of cancer last year into the girl who was dating Jimmy T.—the girl who rode tandem and helmetless on his motorcycle, the girl who didn't care about safety or the law. I'd been waiting all year for someone to hand me a costume that fit so well.

It wasn't a bad deal. After all, the scenery changed every day and I never had to drive.

There are two kinds of men, my mother told me when I was sixteen: the ones who need you, and the ones who need you to need them. I eyed my father closely the year after she died, looking for some kind of clue about him, but his actions were too inconsistent, his silence too enigmatic, to help me decide either way. From across the kitchen I watched him, a big, awkward man with a woman's apron tied around his waist, carefully measuring ingredients into a microwaveable casserole dish as his glass of Scotch and soda sweated droplets onto the counter at his side. He insisted on cooking every night, but after dinner he retreated to his room where he fell asleep, snoring loudly, by nine. "He *has* to go to bed this early, so he can wake up for work at five," my sister insisted, in that horrible "Don't FUCK with me . . . please?" tone we all mastered that year. But I knew that sometimes in the middle of the night she went to stand outside our father's room, listening for his breathing, and when she didn't hear it she opened the door a crack just to make sure she saw his chest rise and fall. I knew, because sometimes when I came in late at night I went to check for it, too.

Jimmy T. and I worked out a system: lying on my bed downstairs, I waited until the last floorboard creaked above my head before I dialed his number. I let it ring only once, hanging up before either of his parents could get to the phone. When I heard his engine idling in the street I climbed out my sub-basement window, crawled across three feet of slippery bark chips and rough shrubs and then sprinted across the lawn to the Chevy's passenger door. I held my breath until the moment when the cool metal door handle connected with my palm, that concrete smack of arrival, exhaling with relief as I landed with a soft thud in his vinyl passenger seat.

We navigated the back roads after midnight, with a Springsteen tape in the cassette deck and a Mexican blanket folded on the back seat. Night was when we made our mark. "Welcome to my beaudoir," Jimmy T. liked to say, gesturing toward the open blanket as I unzipped my jeans. "Would Madame like a mint on her pillow, or perhaps the services of a personal valet?"

We fucked behind a grade school, right beside the jungle gym. We fucked in the backyards of kids we were certain hated us at school. We fucked in a park, in a parking lot, and on a dock along the Hudson River while three geese fought it out over half a bagel. It's a miracle we never got caught. We learned how to be quick about it. Maybe that's why.

Jimmy T. always sang along with the tape as he drove me back to my father's house. He had a pretty good voice, on-key with a slight Jell-O quiver when he held onto the low notes and a scratch against the back wall of his throat when he reached for the high ones. It was a tight match to Springsteen's, and when he sang with the tape I had to listen hard to distinguish between the two. Jimmy T. drove with his left hand on top of the steering wheel and his right hand resting against the back of my neck. The damp summer breeze carried the scents of lawn clippings and moist tree bark through the open windows and into our hair. I tried to come up with ways to extend time so I wouldn't have to go home so soon. If I surfed the FM dial I could usually find a driving song that would buy me three or four minutes more. Sometimes I had to fight the urge to slide my left sneaker on top of Jimmy T.'s right one and press the accelerator to the floor. This was my fantasy: the two of us speeding deeper and deeper into the woods, with his right arm across my shoulders and my left palm resting against his thigh, like a couple in a tiny, private theater with a windshield as our screen.

I knew other girls like me in high school who saw their boyfriends as their saviors, turning to them for the nurturing and attention they couldn't get from home. We were everywhere, holding on to our textbooks with one hand and our boyfriends' belt loops with the other as we maneuvered through the halls; scratching their names into our arm skin with safety pins during study hall, making little love tattoos; sitting knee-to-knee in Planned Parenthood conference rooms while a counselor named Joe waved flat-spring diaphragms and Pill packets in the air as he talked about "shared responsibility." Outside in the waiting room, another group sat clutching their bouquets of ten-dollar bills, waiting to file in. There were so many of us, so many rooms of women, all waiting to be saved.

When Jimmy T. and I were juniors, the year before we met, his best friend Billy D'Angelo died. The local newspaper reported it as an accident, no other victims involved. It happened in late May, just a few weeks before Billy would have graduated. I'd known Billy from fifth-period lunch, when we sometimes stood in the same circle in the smoking section outside with our shoulders hunched together to protect our matches from the wind. It was no secret that his grades hadn't been good enough to get him into any college, or that his parents were beginning to turn up the volume about enlisting in the military. "The fucking *army*, man," he said, flicking his cigarette butt into the grass. "Like I'm really going to cut my hair and do push-ups. Right."

Wild Billy, his friends called him, after Springsteen's song "Spirit in the

Night." It's sort of a lonely song, about old friends and drugs and a single night's attempt to get away from it all, but Billy didn't seem to mind the name.

I didn't know Billy all that well, but up until the time he died I still believed the universe was a largely benevolent place run by a judicious management. In this cosmos of my imagination, people didn't die young. My mother was still alive, and though she'd been diagnosed with breast cancer the previous spring, it hadn't yet occurred to me that she might actually do something as radical as die. Her own optimism blanketed the family with a false security, allowing us to believe we could all go on living just as we always had, treating cancer and chemotherapy as temporary boarders on a month-to-month lease.

Before Billy died, death was more than just an abstraction to me. It was damn near incomprehensible. When it caught up with him, it caught up with me, too, and I was left struggling to understand the insidious speed and finality of it. One day Billy was cupping his hand around a lit match, trying to light a cigarette in the wind, and the next he was gone, a quenched flame. For the first few days after he died, I kept half-expecting him to sidle up next to me outdoors with an unlit Marlboro dangling from his mouth. I just couldn't wrap my mind around the idea that someone who'd always been there could suddenly be so . . . well, *nowhere*, as far as I could see.

The accident—which is what we were calling it then—had happened on a Saturday night, in a state park about fifteen miles north of town. Jimmy T. and Billy and their crowd of high school friends used to go up there after dark and race cars on the narrow roads that hugged the mountain curves. Billy had convinced Jimmy T., don't ask me how, to lend him his '65 Mustang for the ride. Kimmy Rinaldi, Billy's unofficial fiancée, pulled him over to the gravel shoulder and pleaded with him not to race. Afterward, she said she'd just had a bad feeling about that night. Not bad like you were on an airplane and suddenly thought it might be on its way down, she told me, but bad enough to say something, you know? Billy told her not to worry, popped a quick, dry kiss against her mouth, and caught the key ring Jimmy T. tossed his way with a quick twist of his wrist.

What happened next happened quickly. Moments after the two cars squealed off, everyone jogged up the road to see beyond the first bend. Jimmy T. was the first to arrive, just in time to see the Mustang take a sharp right turn off the edge of the road and to hear the sickening crash and thump of metal against granite and bark as the steep forest rejected the car all the way down the mountain's side.

Jimmy T. took off running to where the other driver stood, already out of his car, pounding its roof with a meaty fist and crying without tears. *Crying without tears*, they said. "I don't get it, man. He was on the *inside*. I don't *get* it man. I don't get it." A couple more people ran over, and there was a bunch of noise and some crying, and a lot of spinning around without any real direction before someone decided it would probably be a good idea to call the cops. When Kimmy finally realized what had happened, she started screaming Billy's name, over and over again. It took three people to hold her back, to keep her from going over the edge after him.

The funeral was six days later, in a church around the corner from our school. A wave of students outfitted in tan poly-blend suits and white peasant skirts left after third period that day, all absences excused. After the service, Jimmy T. and some other friends paid their respects to Mrs. D'Angelo and told her how they hoped she'd have 'Wild Billy' engraved somewhere on the headstone. They said they knew Billy would have wanted it that way. She was very kind and courteous and said Bill had been so lucky to have had friends as nice as them, but when the stone went up a few weeks later, it read *William Christopher D'Angelo, Beloved Son and Brother, 1963–1981*, and nothing more.

The story of Billy's death quickly become a dark legend told and retold up and down the hallways of our school, increasing in macabre and explicit detail until even those who'd been there couldn't separate the imaginary from the real. The car did a complete flip as it went over the cliff, or was it two, or three? Billy had called out "Kimmy!" as he went down, or was it "Jimmy!" or "Why me?!" Overnight, Billy became our romantic hero, the boy who'd died at the same fast speed at which he'd lived. Never mind that he'd really spent most of his days red-eyed and only marginally coherent in the smoking area outside. Never mind that his car left no skid marks. In myth you have no mortal limits. You can achieve anything. You can become a god.

I didn't really know Jimmy T. before the crash. His friends later told me that witnessing it had changed him, but they couldn't explain quite how. It made him more . . . reckless, they said, gazing toward the ceiling as if adjectives grow between fluorescent lights. More . . . unpredictable. More . . . well, just *weirder*, you know?

Yes, I wanted to say. Yes. It's easy to pinpoint the effects of a positive change, harder—unless they're clearly pathological—to recognize those that stem from a loss. Those are our tiny secrets, the runaway pieces of psyche we bury under thick layers of silence and defense. We say we're managing. We say we're doing fine. We say we don't need help and people believe us, because they want to believe us, even when our actions clearly indicate the opposite is true.

It took me almost a month after our first weekend at the beach to tell Jimmy T. about my mother, though of course he'd known the story all along. Everyone did, by then. I tried to pass it off matter-of-factly in the car one night—"My mother died last year, you know?"—but before I could even finish the sentence I'd begun to cry. It was still that close to the surface. He pulled into the nearest driveway and held me tight, my hands trapped between his chest and my face. He pulled them away and kissed my eyes, licking my tears like a cat. "Shh," he said. "Don't cry. Jimmy T. is here."

That night was the only night he ever talked with me about Billy dying. He told me his version of the crash story from beginning to end: about the good-luck butt slap he gave Billy before he got into the Mustang; the way Billy drove off with his left fist thrust out the open window and northwest into the air; and how for one crazy moment, when he first saw the car leave the ledge, he thought it might sprout wings and fly.

If only he hadn't given Billy the keys, Jimmy T. whispered. If only Kimmy had complained a little more. If only he'd been driving the car, Jimmy T. said, and that's when he started to cry, a loud, dry, keening sound like an animal left alone too long. I pulled his head to my shoulder and rocked him, my cheek against his hair. There are times when loss will bind you tighter than happiness or humor or music ever can.

College, Jimmy T. said, was just a place where all the problems of the world masqueraded as department names, but I might as well go anyway. "Someone's got to help me undo all the damage that's been done, and they'll take us more seriously if you have a college degree," he explained. Before I'd even met Jimmy T. I'd been accepted at a school in Illinois, and throughout the summer my departure date hung over us like a heavy Great Plains sky. As August melted into September, Jimmy T. still wasn't sure what he'd do in the fall. Maybe take some courses at the community college in town: philosophy or religion, or poetry or film. He once casually mentioned coming to Chicago with me. My evasive "Yeah . . ." surprised us both, and told him not to offer again. We both knew he was only grasping for a plan as he watched his previously reliable audience begin to disperse, moving on to college, the military, and jobs in other states.

This hadn't been the promise. The promise had been that we'd stay young together, live out our dreams, and one day land on the cover of

Newsweek or *Rolling Stone*. It hadn't accounted for the powerful force that smoothly propels white, middle-class kids out of high school and into whatever it is they're expected to do next.

We'd counted on Springsteen, at least, to keep his original vow, but even he couldn't sustain it forever. With the release of *Nebraska* in the fall of 1982, he made the sudden transition from the prophet of one generation's rhapsody to the chronicler of another's demise. The album was a veritable avalanche of fractured dreams, filled with stories of plant shutdowns, home foreclosures, and debtors driven to desperate means.

Springsteen was just describing the times, I suppose, but they weren't my times anymore. The first time I listened to *Nebraska* and heard *Everything dies, baby that's a fact, but maybe everything that dies someday comes back*, was the first time I'd ever listened to a Bruce Springsteen song and thought, You are wrong. You are so completely wrong.

The night before I left for college, I tacked a calendar on Jimmy T.'s bedroom wall and counted off the days until I'd be home for Thanksgiving break. "Seventy four," I told him, with manufactured optimism as he sat sullenly on the edge of the bed, wrists dangling between his knees. "When you wake up in the morning, it'll be only seventy three."

"I know how to subtract."

Overnight, I had become the traitor, he the betrayed. "Don't leave me," I pleaded, as I held onto him at the door.

"What?" he said. "You're the one who's getting on the plane without me."

Which I did, in the middle of September, on a direct flight to Chicago from New York. The first friend I made in my dorm became my closest one that year, a prep school graduate from Massachusetts with Mayflower ancestors and an album collection filled with Joni Mitchell, Johnathan Edwards, and Neil Young. "Bruce Springsteen?" she asked, scrunching up her nose in thought. And then, after a pause, "Isn't he that short guy from New Jersey?" By the second week of school, I'd buried all my cassette tapes in the bottom of a desk drawer. It's frighteningly easy to abandon the familiar when you discover it might be cliché.

Jimmy T. mailed me a letter in late September saying he couldn't contact me again until Halloween, because he was going on the road with his new band. So you can imagine my surprise when, in mid-October, I returned from an anthropology class on a Thursday afternoon and found him sitting alone in the first-floor lounge of my dormitory, his black leather jacket with the chrome zippers at odd angles hopelessly out of place in the

sea of Izod sweaters and wool peacoats from Peck & Peck. He looked like a
page from one short story ripped out and used as the bookmark in another,
and when I first saw him I pulled my books into my chest and took a step
back. He understood that step, he told me later. Hey! he said. Jimmy T. is
no fool.

I didn't know exactly what pushed—or pulled—me back into the protec-
tive pocket of the glassed-in entryway. All I knew was in that moment after
I instinctively withdrew, I suddenly understood something about relationships, something important. I understood there was a third kind of man
my mother never told me about, the kind who you need, regardless of how
he feels about you. The kind who offers you shelter when no one else even
knows how to open a damn umbrella. The kind you can love but can never
stay with for long, because the reason you ran to him in the first place was
to gather the strength you needed to leave.

Jimmy T. stayed with me in Chicago for three days. We argued the whole
time. We apologized in harmony, and then we argued some more. He
wanted me to come back with him. I wanted him to leave alone. He wrote
prose poems and taped them to my mirror when I was in class. *The Chicago
wind blows back your hair, you're living your art, your part. Long camel hair
and scarf.* We couldn't get past metaphor. "My axe has broken strings," he
told me late one night, and I asked him to please for God's sake just drop
the poetry and get to the point.

Our conversation, at the end: He said, I came here to ask you to do something with me, and I said What? and he said, But now I see you won't, and I
said *What?* and he said, I can't tell you, exactly, but it has to do with a quest
I can't fulfill alone, and I said Please. *Please* would you just tell me what
you mean. And he said all right, but you can't tell anyone, you swear? So I
swore, and he nodded, and then he told me, very simply, that he was the
Second Coming of Christ.

After he'd gotten back on the plane alone, after I'd called his mother from
the pay phone at O'Hare and told her what he'd said, after the iceberg in
my stomach finally began to thaw, I spent long nights wondering about the
role I'd played in all this. Could I have prevented it somehow? Could I have
been the cause? As the letters addressed to Jimmy T. came back marked
"Return to Sender, Deceitful Sender" in an angry scrawl, I lay on my bed
and stared at the ceiling, looking for the words that would help me understand.

I was lying like this in my dorm room one night with the clock radio tuned in to Chicago's WXRT when I heard the first few bars of Jimmy T.'s song, the one he and his friend George had sold to the record company, come through on the air. I lay very still, barely breathing, trying to identify whose voice was singing the familiar words. I didn't dare move, too afraid I'd miss the end of the song and the name of the band.

I had to wait through two more songs before the deejay returned. ". . . and before that we heard the Greg Kihn Band," he said, as the music faded away. "Doing a remake of an old Bruce Springsteen tune."

Somewhere in the distance, I imagine, an engine revved and purred. Somewhere far beyond my reach, another boy shifted into high gear and pressed the pedal to the floor, believing he could sail on and on into the night.

FROM THE AUTHOR

The first iteration of "Bruce Springsteen and The Story of Us" was written in a class called "The Art of the Essay" in the spring of 1991. It was taught by Mary Swander, who went on to become a distinguished professor at Iowa State University and the poet laureate of Iowa. We met twice a week at 8:30 a.m., dreadfully early in a frigid Iowa winter.

Mary's objective was to have us craft artistic, well-rounded portraits. We were invited to choose a subject with whom we wanted to spend the whole semester, anyone, living or dead, personally known or not. For five months, we'd write character sketches, recreate conversations (real or imaginary), show our characters in action, and craft razor-sharp physical descriptions. Our texts included James Baldwin's *Notes of a Native Son*, "Shakespeare's Sister" by Virginia Woolf, and excerpts from Mary McCarthy's *Memoirs of a Catholic Girlhood*. Mary had been educated in Catholic schools herself and during breaks she entertained us with stories about nuns she'd known.

Why did I choose Bruce Springsteen? Maybe because I was twenty-six and already feeling sentimental about the breathless excitement of adolescence. Maybe because I was an inveterate New Yorker whose rough edges often felt incompatible with the soft contours of the Iowa prairie. Or maybe I was trying to hold on to a time and place before it became reshaped and mythologized by the passage of time. Probably all of the above.

Mary used a modular approach to portraiture, assigning us a series of short, weekly exercises that might or might not add up to a complete profile in the end. I'd spent four years in journalism school and three years as a magazine editor, and I thought, "You want us to spend a whole semester doing work that could amount to nothing in the end?" I didn't understand the value of process over product, although by the end of the semester I would.

The first three exercises I wrote were about Bruce Springsteen, but for the fourth I found myself drifting off topic and writing about my high school boyfriend, who'd fashioned himself into a lesser facsimile of the man. Which then led to writing about the year after my mother died, the first time I'd attempted to write about that time. Jo Ann Beard was in the class and also writing about the death of her mother, some of which would appear in her 1998 collection *The Boys of My Youth*. In a workshop of one of my short pieces, Jo Ann said, "I don't think this is an essay about Bruce Springsteen at all. I think it's an essay about grief." She was absolutely right. I considered dropping the class to write that story instead, but to Mary's credit, she told me to forget about the class assignment.

"It's good writing," she said. "Just keep going."

I finished a first draft by the semester's end and returned to it several times over the next few years. I couldn't get the point of view right. At first I'd created a present-tense, seventeen-year-old narrator to tell the story with all the naivete and wonder she'd possessed at the time, but she wasn't wise or jaded enough to sense the subtle, darker nuances. Then I tried writing from my current point of view, looking back with more than a decade of hindsight, but that narrator kept inserting too much adult analysis. I needed a narrator who was both as tough and as vulnerable as the teen I'd been and yet enough of an adult to have a sense of what had really happened and the impact it had on a child.

Through trial and error, I eventually landed on a narrator just slightly older than the girl in the story, yet not quite as experienced or cynical as the adult I'd become. As soon as I started writing from her point of view I knew I'd found my storyteller, and the final draft came very quickly after that.

I sent the final version to the *Iowa Review*. The editing process was fairly smooth. As I recall, our only point of disagreement was whether to include the word "fuck". The managing editor felt it was too harsh a word for the narrator to use, but I made a case for keeping it. I'd created a persona with a crass, angry edge, which accurately reflected who I was at the time. I'm glad we left the word in. To me, it captures the kind of gratuitously defiant, cocksure passion both Jimmy T. and I possessed that summer, the perfect blend of fear and freedom that comes from feeling you have nothing left to lose.

Jimmy T. thought of himself as a suburban New York version of Bruce Springsteen, but he was more of a 1980s James Dean to me. I've always thought that if you'd put James Dean in a flannel shirt and handed him an electric guitar, he would have come up with something that sounded like a Springsteen song.

The Rain Makes the Roof Sing

TOM MONTGOMERY FATE (1986)

(Originally published in *Manoa*)

Typhoon Kadiang arrives abruptly, taking down tree limbs and power lines, blowing rain through the screens, cooling the house. When we lose electricity I light a small candle and anchor it on a metal lid with a few drops of hot wax. I sit at my desk in the teetering light and try to read my English Composition students' response to their first in-class writing assignment. I asked them to write a one paragraph response to the question: *What is love?* Not wanting to waste paper, groups of four students shared one 8 1/2 by 11 sheet, carefully tearing it into quarters. Most wrote only a sentence or two.

Due to the wind I can't keep all of the wrinkled scraps of love weighted down, the candle lit, or the rain out, so I move to another room, choosing hot and windless over inconvenient but cool. But without the breeze to distract me, the incessant pounding of rain on metal is barely tolerable. I can't hear myself think. I can't hear anything. I am consumed by the barrage of sound which refuses to diminish, and then, after nearly an hour, amazingly, grows louder.

None of the students who live with us seem to notice the torrent of rain, or at least not to mind. Mhae, though she surely can't hear herself, is playing her guitar and singing with Lita. I watch them for a moment, but can't tell what song they are mouthing. Narissa is studying intensely with a trio of thick candles set up around her. She has positioned them so the flames dance wildly in the wind, but somehow are never extinguished. The shifting light and sinister shadows don't seem to affect her concentration. Eden is outside on the porch talking to her boyfriend under the overhang. Carol, my wife, is reading Jane Smiley's *A Thousand Acres* with a dim flashlight. I dream of Iowa, the place I will always come from. My corn and cows and

October frosts have been replaced by rice and water buffalo and typhoons. I feel like one of Smiley's characters. I too am going nuts.

Love is like the mango—ripe, sweet, everywhere. Everyone eat the mango. Everyone love.

Love is patient and gentle—like slow bubbling rice.

Love is feeling I have with family that we both know.

I love Yang, our carabao. We depend for each other.

My mother nursing her bebe—up all night. Love is what that is.

The students' responses pull me out of my frustration. I am intrigued by the variety. When I give the same assignment at home in the U.S., my students, who are more adept at English, write less concrete responses. Most are close to this: "Love is a strong emotional feeling or bond which a person has for another person or thing." The whole idea of this introductory exercise is to distinguish between writing that tells or explains and writing that shows or reveals, to move from vague, abstract concepts to concrete imagery. It is interesting how the Filipino students seem to more readily give examples, to show love rather than attempt to explain it. I wonder if there are any cultural implications.

Caring is love. How do we care. When they dynamite fish in my place they are not caring about the coral. Now there are no fish. No coral or shell. Now there is no love.

My brothers and I work together. We love to work together. We love each other. We trust each other.

Love is not always so easy. Sometime I am hard up for love. Two boys courting me. They play the guitar for me, but I don't think it is love.

Love is banal.

Love is "banal"? This response, one of the shortest and least concrete, confuses me—in part because I haven't heard the word since we arrived in the Philippines. Love is dull, common, ordinary, and mundane? I wonder if I'm missing something. Could she mean that love doesn't need to be extravagant or complicated, that it's necessary and routine? I don't think so, at least from the little I know about love in Philippine culture. "Banal" would seem to describe what love is not.

I ask Lita for help.

"'Banal' means 'sacred' or 'holy,'" she explains.

"It does? I've never heard that definition."

"That's because you don't speak Tagalog," she smiles.

I tell her that there is also a word in English spelled "b-a-n-a-l." She has never heard of it.

Just then Lita hurries off toward the door. "You're not going out are you?" I ask. "No, no, someone is tapping at the gate." How in the heck did she hear that? How did she distinguish that faint metallic tapping from the roar of the storm?

It is a neighbor. I've forgotten her name again. She wants to borrow a candle. Lita has some extras and goes to get them. The woman, who is sopping wet despite her best efforts with her umbrella, sits down near me in the flickering light and smiles. "Adu!" ("A lot!"), she says, referring to the rain, trying to be cordial. "Demasiado," ("Too much,") I reply. She laughs. It doesn't seem to bother her that we are yelling. "No, no," she shouts, "Mayat!" ("It's good!"). "What?" I ask, reverting to English. She looks confused. "What? What is good?" I ask again. "The rain. The rain is good," she says, now in English. She points to the metal roof. "Listen," she says. The rain is actually beginning to let up—a machine gun instead of a jackhammer overhead. "The roof sings," she says smiling again. "Huh? It what?" I ask. "Listen," she says. "The rain makes the roof sing." She looks at me like we shared a secret. I desperately wish we did. I understood what the sentence means, but not her deep, knowing gaze. I wonder if she knows that my affirmative nod is in ignorance.

Lita returns with the candles. The woman says, "Agiamanak," ("Thanks"), and heads back out into the downpour.

I keep listening, waiting for the watery rhythms and melodies to reveal themselves. But nothing comes. That's all I needed. I had found a specific inanimate target for my general frustration: the rain on the roof. But the neighbor lady comes along and exonerates it. She claims the rain makes the roof sing! I wonder why she is so happy. I wonder what kind of song or what kind of voice she hears. I wonder why I can't hear it. I wonder if I'll ever hear the intricacy of Philippine culture above the constant hum of my own.

The next afternoon the rain almost stops, dwindles to a soft drum. But two days of downpour have deadened my hearing. The depth of the quiet is overwhelming. I find myself yelling, still competing with the imagined sound of rain on metal. When I speak too loudly, Narissa laughs, joking about my needing a hearing aid.

I pull out another folder of student writing. Just to vary things I asked this class (more than half were religion majors) to respond to the question "What is God?"

God is not here. I not believe now because of suffering much.
God is hope.
God walks in muddy fields. He plants seedlings—new life.
God is what always there is.

God is rice. God is rain.

God is rain? Is somebody trying to tell me something? That night after supper the rain completely stops. It's replaced by the frogs in the flooded banana grove near our house. They are not as loud as the rain, but close. I lie awake sweating and listening to the great burping swamp of noise, the slippery green, cold-blooded chorus—swelling and then waning, swelling and then waning, seemingly without reason.

I pay closer attention. After an hour of listening I begin to notice that this is not one huge croaking wave of sound, but a sea of specific croaks with different rhythms, tones, tunes perpetually interrupting each other. Yet despite the seeming entropy, it is clear they are all singing one song. There is a kind of unity in the cacophony, an odd, unexpected harmony, a collection of sounds which are at once chaotic and healing. Harmony: notes that sound good together precisely because they're different. That night something changes. I am beginning to hear things.

The next morning the typhoon is still roaring. Classes are canceled. I slide the capiz shell windows closed and pull out some more student writing.

God is always, but not one thing.

God the source of all things is. God the creator and redeemer.

God? Seguro adda. Diak ammo. But I think yes.

God is espiritu—everywhere. I never wonder no God is here.

The last two responses confuse me. In Ilokano *adda* means "is present," and *diak ammo* means "I don't know." Since there are many Spanish words in Ilokano, I assume that *seguro* means the same thing in this language as it does in Spanish: "certain." But that doesn't make sense: "God is certainly here. I don't know." Then I remember that the spelling of some Spanish words integrated into Ilokano stayed the same but their meanings changed while the islands were being colonized. *Seguro* in Ilokano means "maybe," not "certain" as it does in Spanish. I wonder about the historical implications of that.

Did the early Filipinos respond with *seguro* (certainly)—the unquestioning affirmative—to their Spanish masters, but actually mean or think "maybe" in their unwillingness to yield or acquiesce, in their longing for other options? Now the phrase made sense. "Maybe God is here. I don't know, but I think yes."

There is more multi-lingual confusion in the last response: "I never wonder no God is here." I marvel at how my students balance the regional language (Ilokano), the national language (Filipino), the language of instruction (English), and often a tribal language or two. With my limited Ilokano and non-existent Filipino, I am often confused by the language hopping in their writing. Here, one word caused the problem: *no. No* means "if" in Ilokano. Again I wonder about the colonization process, about Spanish or American conquistadors saying "no" and Ilokanos hearing an "if," hearing possibility in denial or condemnation, seeing a crack of light seeping beneath a locked door. "I never wonder if God is here." I find myself longing for this student's certainty. But I am thinking more about belief in myself than in God. I want to believe that I can fit into an isolated rice farming community in the Philippines. And I want to believe that I should be teaching English—"the language of the colonizer," or "the language of money," as one of my students once characterized it while explaining why English should be considered a foreign language.

I put the papers down and listen to the rain, wanting to hear an "if" beyond all of the "no's" I have accumulated in five months of trying to live in a radically different culture, of awkward groping toward integration and acceptance. I start thinking about the English and Filipino definitions of *banal.* Somehow the irony seems related to the "if" I was looking for. How does one learn to see and hear the *banal* (Filipino) in the *banal* (English)? How does one learn to find meaning and value in what at first appears to be meaningless? These questions hang in my head like laundry in the rainy season: forever dripping, perpetually damp, unfinished.

My students and friends were trying to help me understand. In their immense patience, they were trying to teach me to live in the present tense, to pay compassionate attention to the world, to listen and see carefully enough to discern the possibility of the extraordinary in the seemingly ordinary, to hear the sacred music in the off-centered wooden rubble of two wagon wheels, and a slow, cloppity oxen, pulling a rice farmer and his son back to their land, back to that raw green rectangle of life. They were teaching me that "love is like a mango," that "God is rain," that frogs can croak in harmony, that a "maybe" can be better than a "yes," and that an "if" is not always so far from a "no." They were teaching me about the writing process, but also about the difficult process of crossing cultures.

A few hours later the typhoon finally wanes. The torrents of wind fade and the driving sheets of rain ease to a steady downpour. People take the opportunity to get out of their homes. They emerge from behind bamboo gates to see how the typhoon has left their world. Dozens of mangoes, still too green to bruise, have prematurely blown with soft thuds to the leafy soil. Children collect them in plastic buckets. Then they begin to pick up the wet green tangle of bougainvillea vines and broken acacia limbs. Finally, they sweep up the tattered banana leaves with short stiff brooms made from the ribs of a palm frond. The dust pan is a large cracker tin cut away on one end and wired to a pole.

A vendor walks by with a long pole balanced on the back of his neck and shoulders; at each end of the pole is a silver pail. "Mami . . . mami," he calls, peddling noodles. As the streets begin to drain, horse drawn carriages gradually reappear, taxiing people to the market or on some other errand long delayed. A neighbor rolls up her pant legs and stretches an empty rice sack over her head for protection as she wades across the still-flooded banana grove. Three green coconuts, a hubcap, and a freshly drowned rat float by her on the way. She steps over the open sewer and up onto the street on her way to the corner *Sari Sari* store for some eggs.

I keep listening. The rain becomes light and easy. It softly taps gentle corrugated rhythms. The tapping evolves into a pinging, and I began to detect tinny, dented melodies. They unroll themselves like banana leaves in the sun, their immense hidden beauty revealing itself without warning or effort. A little later my wife finishes her book and asks me if I want to go to the market with her to get some milkfish for supper. I tell her I need to finish my papers. But instead I keep listening to the roof, searching for the quiet, elusive voice of the rain.

FROM THE AUTHOR

Though I had taken a nonfiction workshop with Richard Lloyd-Jones that focused on "the art of the essay," I struggled mightily with this one—with how to write a cross-cultural travel essay. Was this piece about me, or about the new culture, or the conflicts and convergences between the two? I soon learned the answer to that question: "Yes." But how was I supposed to weave together a handful of significant, yet seemingly unrelated experiences, that had happened to occur in the same place?

In Jones's class we discussed an organizing strategy that seemed like it might be useful: the "thematic framing" of an image or moment. We explored how essayists often frame an arresting and emotionally acute image in order to limit and invite the reader's imaginative focus and in so doing also introduce a central theme. One example that came up was the image of a weasel skull forever attached to the throat of a live eagle in Annie Dillard's essay "Living Like Weasels." The weasel had reared, struck, and bit the eagle's throat, but the bite didn't kill the eagle, and the weasel's jaw involuntarily locked shut—an evolutionary trait which insured that its prey wouldn't escape. This allowed the eagle enough time to gut and eat the living weasel, whose carcass would then remain lock-jawed to the feathery neck until it decayed and fell away.

What struck me and others in the class about this provocative image was how expertly Dillard used it as thematic glue. The metaphor somehow pulled together all the other odd meanderings and asides in the piece into a single life philosophy without being didactic or simplistic. And while I had encountered other writers who had used a similar strategy—framed moments/metaphors as thematic anchors—I hadn't yet considered it as a means of knitting together my own disparate stories and anecdotes from the Philippines.

So I started combing my journals for visual images that might suggest the central focus of my writing: the problem/promise of living in a vastly different culture. I soon discovered that much of the writing was from the rainy season (when we spent more time indoors) and that much of the imagery was auditory. I had written several descriptions of the widely varied sounds of the perpetual rain on different kinds of rooftops (and other surfaces). But the broader metaphor didn't hit home until I found the notes I'd scribbled one night about our neighbor borrowing a candle during a typhoon. That night in the rain she heard a lovely music, where I heard a deafening monotony. And somehow, that single framed moment captured the meaningful confusion that was my daily life in the Philippines. Would I ever learn to hear the intricacies of Filipino culture above the great droning blur of my own?

I then began to reconsider the rest of my notes for the essay through the lens of this image/metaphor. And that was when things finally started to fit together. A number of related cross-cultural ironies that were tied to my struggles to teach English to multilingual students now seemed to align. And some of the bilingual paradoxes I discovered were so thematically convenient I was stunned. The opposing meanings of "banal" in Filipino ("sacred") and in English ("ordinary") even allowed me to share a tenet of my writing philosophy: attend to the world with enough patience and compassion to somehow discern the sacred in the ordinary.

It took me nearly two years to finish this essay and several more to get it published. When it first appeared in *Manoa*, the final sentence was: "But instead I kept listening to the roof, to the quiet, miraculous voice of the rain." A few years later, when it appeared in *Beyond the White Noise*, a book of essays, I revised that final sentence, because in retrospect it felt romanticized. The suggestion that I could, by essay's end, finally understand the complexities of the new culture felt misleading. The revision: "But instead I kept listening to the roof, SEARCHING FOR to the quiet, ~~miraculous~~ ELUSIVE voice of the rain." This seemed more honest and accurate. Keep listening and searching for the new culture, even if you don't know what you're looking for, or recognize what you hear.

How I Know Orion

WILL JENNINGS (1997)

(Originally published in *Fugue*)

Tagging the top of the tower meant climbing way past close enough, when close enough was all it took for a flash to streak for ground and shock him off the ladder's rung. So when Bobby fell it was the wires just below his feet that caught him prone across his body. Face to the side and arms stretched out to ward off blows, his hands palm down and flexed above his head. His leg spasms coiled him more tightly in the loose cabling along the tower's span and so he was held there, fixed in the current for the forty minutes it took the Power Company to shut down that section of the Suburban Grid. Thirty feet up, he was still conscious and crying out. He was being slowly burned alive. He was twelve.

Below and in the back of an ambulance, Bobby's mother was lying sedated on a gurney, her lower arms bent straight up at the elbow and her fingers flexing as if trying to shape themselves to hold something much too large for her size. And in the back seat of a police squad two officers had flanked his father and they kept him facing away and they kept the windows rolled up and their motor was running and they were talking to him while he smoked, talking to him as he turned red and pounded the back of the seat in front of him with his fists, talking to him until his head collapsed down in his folded palms and they rubbed his back while he convulsed.

Scattered in small clots were mostly adults who looked gape mouthed and afloat in a stupor so complete it could only form a sound entirely low and like a swell on dark water. All day the air had been humid and almost as warm as July, but the mass of cold Lake Michigan was still shaping out from winter and this mixed without a breeze to form what I had learned to call Halo Fog. Against this haze was the reflected flash of police and fire lights, and there were these stray, piercing yelps and sparks and from some place I couldn't tell where there were oh gods sweet heaven my baby boy Bobby please Bobby please Bobby *please* don't let go we're coming baby coming *soon* Christ Jesus when they gonna get him *down*.

This is what I saw that Friday night, the 11th of May.

Some nights after dinner I'd ride with my Dad, closing out the final calls of his day. Sometimes he'd carry a box of hard looking tools, sometimes just an estimate tucked crisp in its envelope. He mostly carried poise and the pockets of his trade: thin screw driver, circuit tester, pen light, a mechanical pencil for sketches and notes. We would ride out to some house in a nearby suburb and ring the door to be met by a businessman just home from the commuter station and knocking gin while the wife rustled supper. Down into closets, basements or crawlspaces we'd go, checking the cleanness of the burn, gauging the flow of air in exchange. My father would eyeball the rooms, squaring up the volume of a space until he could slide rule what was there against the measured cost of ambition.

This night, my father and I had been out driving to look at the furnace and duct work at a house where the owner wanted to install central air before putting the place up for sale. All the tract homes came with stuff done on the cheap, but it all looked the same under the mug shots of the Realty Pages. My dad had worn his best hitched smile and I could hear the neutral flatter in his voice while his eyebrows twitched past all the sloppy work and cobble he'd uncovered. The owner took pains to point out his own weekend handiwork, "It'll bring in twice what it cost me for sure. . . ." When my father 'suggested' his rough estimate, the guy took it like a soft kick to a sharp target, the kind where your lips curl a smile but your tongue tightens to a dart behind your teeth. I came to think that growing up meant learning how to talk in this sort of polite exchange, like being paid back in Canadian money, where things meant less than you'd guess but looked and felt almost just the same.

That particular night we walked out into the particulate gauze of dusk, and I counted the street lamps forming halos as they came on a bit too soon even for this time of the spring.

A Friday in May and we were headed home down the old Glenview market road, the crumbly two lane black top still high crowned from when before there were sewers this far west. And nearing the Milwaukee Road feeder tracks, bouncing up off the fog were lights and then a few cars pulled over and then it was surely something very wrong because there were cops and

a fire truck with its ladder up but reaching nowhere, and the Rescue Pul-
monator guys with their tanks and hoses and nothing to do but lean. And
what looked like a hearse but was really a private ambulance.

Our first guess was somebody'd been clipped by a train, but there wasn't
anything twisted or shorn in sight: no rumpled wrecks, no scraped and
idling diesel. And stiffening in our skin as we got closer, we started to piece
the goings on: there was something or maybe somebody up on the wires of
the highline tower and no one was doing anything. There were blue flash
sparks. And as I leaned out the window I heard what sounded like the soft
pinch of a yell.

My father's inclination has always been to keep driving and so that is
what we did. But traffic had bottlenecked and there was no way out but to
go through and to go through at a crawl. The last person I saw as we went
by and cleared on the other side of the tracks was Peter Harvey, a guy from
my grade at school, standing slouched in who I'd guess to be his mother's
arms and he was crying and pleading something he didn't do didn't mean
to do didn't anyone believe him he was so sorry.

Of course nothing made the evening news. And it wasn't until Saturday
afternoon that I could reconstruct what I had seen on Friday from the
others in the Scout Troop. We were off in an open field learning how to tell
both compass and stars by plotting out the shape of assigned constellations. We were stepping them off by metered paces and placing sticks into
the ground to represent each major star. But mostly we were hearing and
telling all we knew about the night that Bobby Sellars climbed the high
pole by the tracks and fell into a blue gray flash that held him like a mag-
net.

Now he was slowly dying in the Burn Unit at Evanston Hospital.

The first leg is One-hundred-sixty-five degrees for 37 paces.

Blood was the problem, somebody said.

And mark. Now take a reading of 37 degrees and step-off 90 feet.

They couldn't keep it in him. 20 units. 30 units. 55 units.

*Mark. Triangulate your start to present position. What are the angles
formed by these lines?*

And none of us knew what a unit was exactly but only that they seemed
not to stay for long enough to fix.

Peter Harvey had been out walking the family Chow, Tuffy, when Bobby
came scissor kicking over the hedge which ran like a fence in his yard.
Both freed from their supper tables on a Friday in May, foggy or not, they
decided to walk out along the tracks. At some point because there wasn't

enough on the ground to hold their attention, Bobby goaded Peter into goading him to do something anything stupendous. Bobby was good at these ploys. He'd constantly drift from the older grade playground to the younger during recess and get some little kid to dare him to stand atop the very top of the jungle gym and then he'd fake his fall and act as if he'd been killed.

The highpole was singing its frazzle in the mist above them.

Saturday evening and Orion is roaming the southwestern sky. Walking the alleys home from confession at St. Joseph's, I am stalking him, tracing as his stick figure comes apart behind the crowns of trees just beginning to leaf, losing him entirely behind the dormers of angular houses beginning to light in their windows. As I walk along he emerges and assumes his flesh and fable, his boxy upper body and a trophy belt of stars like silver conch.

I am walking the alleys to be safe from cars, to not be so easily seen. For reasons not entirely clear, I've begun to think that visibility is dangerous. Or at the very least, its own undoing. In every movie we watch in school, it's always the obvious kid who gets hurled from the playground equipment: he wouldn't use BOTH hands. Everyone knows this long before the camera spins into the sound of a melon dropped to the floor.

At Scouts we talk about cars, sex, what's the best and worst way to get killed, TV shows, and sometimes sports. Some kids know the underhood details of every Stock Car, Drag Rail, and New Model *Super Sport*. Some swear they know the underneath workings of girls and why this adds up to sex. A few have spent hours applying New Math to what they glean from the backs of their baseball cards. I watch a lot of television and try to make up stories to prove I know something about everything, which no one of any consequence ever believes.

When we talk about the best ways to die, we make it happen in a war or in some way that ensures a lengthy buildup which results in a quick, painless end. When we think about the worst ways, someone'll say "drowning," then "burned in a fire," and then finally we think about being picked out at random, taken someplace and tortured. Deep in some woods, we think about never being found.

Bobby is alive tonight and I have put two quarters in a slot and selfishly lit a dozen votive candles, spacing them out in the rack, connecting those already burning, to draw a shape which appears familiar and, hopefully, brave. Some parents in the PTA have gone to the hospital to give blood, to sit with Bobby's family. My mom and dad have said they can't imagine what that wait would be like and then they tell me to be careful.

Walking the last shortcut home through Pinkowski's Nursery, the tall trees and houses give way to an open field just turned for a summer crop of sweet corn and pumpkins. Along the dirt track which ends at the corner of my street, a set of telephone and electrical lines loop from pole to pole. And looking up I can see him clearly, becoming brighter as I am walking home and into this night, stretched out with his arms above him and legs bent to his side across the wires.

Boys who fall from the sky. I have been thinking about this for weeks. It bothers me, even though I don't quite picture them clearly enough. Most times they are wearing these leather jackets with sheep's wool lining, and these pull-down hats of the same stuff, too. Sometimes it's Bobby and I pretend to see him because his face is one I know for real. The rest of the time they all look like Sergeant Saunders from *Combat* or *The Man From U.N.C.L.E.*, Robert Vaughn. Only younger. Lots younger. These aren't dreams, really. I mean, what happens is I sometimes think of things like this, and maybe try to solve them before I can actually *go* to sleep.

It's 1966. The hit song on the radio is all about men in green berets who jump and die. I am small, blond, shy, and always in the middle of whatever line there is to form. So I also tend to picture myself looking kind of military, with sunglasses, and posed. In those pictures I have a reddish tan, silvery sunglasses, spine like a ram-rod and neatly rolled sleeves which reveal lean, muscular arms.

Sleep is often a hard place to be so deliberate, to calculate entry by clock or the end of a television hour. So lying in bed, I try to make sleep the type of place where I can come to it sideways. I ball up to one side and often it's just a phrase which appears first. A phrase I can repeat in a thoughtless sort of dawdle. *Boys who fall from the sky.* And letter by letter, as these words take place, they begin to form a certain shape against the dome of what I know to be sleep. Somehow, and I'm not exactly sure just when this happens, I only know that it does, these letters and words repeat and repeat until their pictures begin to stand in place. And once they are fixed there, I begin to move beneath them and into the soft hold of the night.

Even this late into spring we have to run The Humidifier to keep my sinuses from leaking so that my eyes don't get caked shut by morning and my mom doesn't have to slowly dissolve the gunk with a warm wash cloth until I can see again. The Humidifier is brown enameled tin and big as a kitchen wastebasket. It sits right next to my bed. The water inside jiggles a bit while its motor hums and the effect is this drone where if I cover my ears just a bit with my pillow, it sounds like the cruising engines of a bomber plane near contrail altitude. Or at least the way those things sound on our TV.

I sometimes think about being in one of those planes, nestled in a hunch of sheepskin and fatigue, prone against the curve of its fuselage as we'd fly on and on through the night. I like to picture how the sky and the stars would look from up there and I imagine everything changed, the constellations further apart and harder to gather, the sheer bristle of too many stars turning a bit hypnotic, like the reflections of snowflakes coming straight at you through your headlights on the highway after dark.

There are a few things you learn in the way you're intended. The rest, my Dad says, you do things you mostly don't want but you do them anyway because your whole life just isn't about the stuff you want or like to do. Sometimes when he smokes one last Lucky before turning out the kitchen light, my father looks like he's reading from a book, which he does quite often, but these sometimes he's just looking at his own hands.

Boy Scouts started out to be a promise made to us by other kids' dads. We were going to cook hobo bread from dough on a green stick, dig a trenchline and call it a *perimeter*. Instead, Boy Scouts turned into a kind of playacting I do well but that I don't much enjoy. The pictures lied, I think, like when we bought my sleeping bag and the box had this scene where the long flap into which the thing rolls up can also be strung up like a little awning above your head. You're supposed to whittle sticks to do this right. But the flap is never long enough once you unroll the thing for the first time.

First Aid is actually this elaborate drill we do in a high school gym in front of judges and kids who bleed iodine and don't move. We mush a Klondike Derby with dog sleds in winter, but no dogs and no snow, and so we have to pull the sleds over cinder horse paths ourselves. When we build towers from lashing staves and binder's twine, we do it indoors, in the gym, again, and we never get to climb to the top and do semaphore. I had practiced semaphore until I could make the flags snap. When we do semaphore we stand a hundred feet apart and I am thinking the whole time why it is we just don't yell.

There are times when disappointment unfolds and I think it deliberate and pointed, maybe even pointed at me, but at the very least the result of some adult who should either step in or step out to make things happen right. What I can't quite figure is how what's deliberate and gets done by adults turns out feeling entirely random.

It's the same with stars. Who's to say how a constellation should be made up of those six over there, but not the seventh? Or eighth? So far in school we've been learning how the Chinese invented gunpowder and rockets first and mapped out stars for navigation, same as the Phoenicians. Greeks and Vikings, too. And I've wondered if they all picked the same stars to make the same shapes, or if maybe one had a bear and the other drew a camel and wouldn't one or the other require more, or fewer dots to connect?

Sandy Estrin is this kid who is pretty smart but wants to always play shortstop, you *know* the type. He says his dad told him how some stars aren't even really there anymore at all. And "all we ever get to see is their reflection, *anyway*," he says. So if light takes *that* long to travel, the star itself might've been destroyed by meteors or somesuch even *before* the Chinese. What happens when the dipper springs a leak, I'm thinking. For days I sat in class while Mrs. Sand traced the dotted tracks of various explorers and I thought about Amerigo Vespucci and Ponce de León, halfway out into nowhere from the coast of Spain when suddenly the lights start to go out one by one in the middle of the sky. Only there's so many stars, they can't be sure. As their wakes disappear behind them they try to adjust, circling without reference, waving their sextants which are handy as hammers.

Another dad is supposed to be teaching us about both reading maps *and* the stars. The thing is you can't read maps at night and you can't pick out constellations during the day. Time and dads being what they are, it's not entirely clear that we can fix this.

Mr. Sail's thought out this course that's drawn to carry us across the sky, but in a way where we can walk it, tracking the point of a needle which bobs and floats its way to North from stick to stick, from star to star, and step by step. For the past several months I have been going out after school and into this vacant lot to practice the lines of Orion, who is the hunter's constellation. He is supposed to be Greek, I think, and has his own story. But what I've found by this time of spring is that he lays out plain at night and high in the sky. Once I'd learned how you can tell him first by the belt, I began to notice stepping out each night to carry kitchen scraps to trash, or looking up from the patio stoop after clicking my dog to her chain: I'd see him and see him first of any, even the dippers big *and* small. Belt first, then the legs and arms and while everybody, including the books they give us at Boy Scouts, wants to imagine a club in his hand and a pelt which dangles from his waist, mostly I see him stick-like and stretched out as if he's fallen in his tracks. Or maybe I think he's stalking this group of deer in another hemisphere and is hiding prone just where he is and not actually walking anywhere, which is how he is supposed to look from down here. Maybe I picture him flat because that is how he is in the field when I step him off in practice, in silence, off by myself and by degrees.

Mr. Sail is Marty's dad, and he's short and thick and looks out from behind and over these roundish lenses, bottle bottomed and floating on thin gold wire. His beard is all the colors of our hedges in winter, and tight like the wooden handled brush my mom keeps under the sink. He speaks with short puffs off of Chesterfields, his round, black eyes looking first to you and then quickly out to wherever it is he wants you to know. He explains to me the difference between near- and far-sighted probably six times before I start to remember—and each time it's the horizon where he finally fixes.

"A surveyor turns what he sees into lines. And numbers. Long, wide, high and low. We set a baseline and all of our measurements read from there. . . ." When we first get to where we are going, this is how the morning begins. And I am fumbling with the case to my Silva Ranger, a newer and fancier compass than I am used to. It has this "sighting mirror" which unfolds at a right angle to the base, but for the life of me I have no idea just how this is supposed to help. I decide if I ever get lost I could use this mirror part to sun-blink search planes, and just as they would be about to bank away from where I am, then my glint would catch them and they would double back on some dare or intuition and then they'd see the large and elaborate Universal Distress Code figures I'd have paced out with rocks and smudge pots below: "AM OK. NEED FOOD AND MAP." *". . . and from there we translate the land into a language any surveyor can understand. Even if they don't speak a word of English. The stars and constellations are like this, too, see . . . the universe is full of patterns. . . ."* But that would be a lie, and what I'd really want that plane to know was that I needed more than a map, I needed instructions. Maybe even an entire rescue.

We ride on Saturday mornings to this field far out between some western suburbs, the four of us who are trying to earn merit badges in both stars and surveying, and we are riding in Mr. Sail's work truck. It's a Tradesman Van with custom nooks and slots to hold all of his necessary chains and sighting posts. There is also this special, padded case which rides on a gyro-like pivot, and in there is the center of his work, which is optical and polished, and he calls it a Transit. At first I thought it might be like a telescope, but Marty told me its lenses *"drop out too fast to infinity . . . too fast to pick up stars."* I have no real idea what he means, except something like being near-sighted. Still it looks to me a lot like a smaller version of the machine they use at the planetarium to plaster stars across the black dome of their indoor sky.

Sometimes we pretend it's really a Norden Bomb Sight, the kind, Mr. Sail says, *"that, and along with a few thousand boys who fell from the sky is what won the war in Europe."* As we pass through village intersections we each take up positions in the van: navigator, ball turret and tail gunners, and Marty is the bombardier. We chatter back and forth the way they do on Twelve O'clock High, starring Robert Stack, which is this Friday night show about the air force over Germany. Bandits and bogies appear in the shape of Chevy Monzas and Mercury Comets and these we grease or splash with lots of chukka-chukkas and ammo to spare. AK-AK and Flak are what we make of pot holes and the rumble over railroad tracks. At some point Mr. Sail tells Marty:

"Bombardier, she's your plane. Take us in to Primary."

And brushing back his surfer bangs, Marty leans over this boxed up gizmo and waits and waits and waits.

Then he says:

"Away."

Some of these mornings out in tall grass, my feet get wet in a hurry and then for the rest of the morning I am cold and make mistakes. By the third week I learn to bring two extra pairs of sweat socks, balled up and stuck down into my lunch sack. Warm and dry, my attention to detail improves. Constellation Map & Compass is the official name for the game we are doing. At least that's what Mr. Sail calls it and expects us to, too. He has this idea where he might write this booklet and try to sell it to the Boy Scouts. But months of stamping out star shapes in wet grass, poking sticks at every turn, and we are not convinced this is such a good idea.

When we started to come here, there was still snow on the ground, and then for a few more weeks our feet left obvious tracks in the mud. For a while, the paths we stamped spelled out a larger shape and when my steps or bearing began to warble, Orion's rough outline would emerge from the tangle underfoot. Enough to hold me, enough to find a fix and decide my compass should be wrong. But now we are nearly into June and we've just the dew to mark our tracks.

The Saturday after Bobby died we stayed long into the afternoon, drilling over and again until what had been close enough became exact, and exactness became as rote as any driven rule. We didn't go to the funeral because it was small, because it was only for family, because it would be just too hard to have that many kids to remind his parents what they'd lost. We'd repeat the details we knew over lunch, at recess, and out here in the taller grass, shaping and reshaping the myth until the truthful story hardly mattered at all. He was our size, he was our age, and he was fearless.

As the morning lengthens, our paths evaporate, and we are left with only what we can hold in our heads and in our hands. It occurs to us out walking along these lines, or standing off alone and where we plant these sticks in turn, that no one but birds, or people in planes, and maybe even the stars themselves could ever tell what it is that we end up drawing.

FROM THE AUTHOR

"How I Know Orion" began as a meander and found its bearings in a dawdle. I'd been trying to write an essay about an eleven-year-old boy's capacity to engage abstract existentialism. That and paper routes, walking the same path from one necessary point to the next and how that meditative labyrinth of suburban streets, rutted dirt alleys, and backyard short cuts could free a kid's mind to wander and ponder the very nature of, well, life. And death. Especially death. And especially the death, it would turn out, of a friend from school who was my same age, same general shape, but a far different demeanor.

I have always loved Lynda Barry and her ability to be who she is now and still speak in the rhythms, digressions, and spaces between that often mark the language of children coming more fully into the world. It's a problem many writers have to acknowledge: you can't speak like an eleven-year-old decades and decades after the fact—at least not without copping to it or tipping your hand, or facing the audience and breaking the fourth wall. In Carl Klaus's "Forms of the Essay" class we read Margaret Mead's "A Day in Samoa" where the narrative voice wants to be both a part and apart at once, to be the ubiquitous fly on the wall, though a fly who can rest at once in situ and then alight upon the authority of science. The day emerges just before sunrise and *not* when the lab's clock ticks one second beyond midnight. Mead's observations lap along the shore of the village lagoon, casually rousing the reader from an imagined lull. Then in the fourth sentence, it happens: "Cocks crow, negligently. . . ." And there you are. In a village. In Samoa. At dawn. And now you're sitting next to someone else's construct of *negligence*, left out to bake in the sun and eventually go bad. No one, not even the rooster wants to claim it. To write through the lens of being eleven, at eleven, when you are long past eleven, means you will have to claim this voice in another way. It might be craft, it could be structure, but it cannot be gimmick.

When I started to write the first draft, it was for a workshop with Patricia Foster, who had just joined the NWP faculty. I had the occasion to go back to where the story took place and decided to engage in some basic immersion technique. I walked my old paper route three days in a row at the same time of day I had walked it when I was eleven. It was early spring, the same as when the essay begins. And this made me think of the other destinations to which I'd regularly walked: to school and back, to church for Saturday confession, and that prompted the memory of when and how I learned to use a map and compass in Boy Scouts, from a friend's father who was a surveyor. He assigned each of us a constellation, which we plotted on paper and then transferred to a large, open grassy field. The physicality of retracing literal steps and routes provided the expected prompts one usually associates with nostalgia: that rusted No Outlet sign, the contractor stamps on sections of sidewalk, the house that used to be canary yellow and has since been muted into more acceptable pastel. But the repetition also recreated time spent in motion, traversing the again and again. And this allowed my mind to wander and so notice the more obvious (as they seem to me now) points in a constellation of metaphor.

The original draft began with an account of just such a walk to set up the premise of an eleven-year-old's capacity for pondering the continuum of time and place, of what was ephemeral, and wondering if anything really lasted very long or even long enough. And, who, if anyone, was in charge? Patricia selected the piece as one of three to be workshopped when Joy Harjo visited for a few days. Harjo cut to the chase. "Begin with the boy on the wire," she said, "It's the only place to begin." So the narrative problem then became how to lead with the vivid and visceral. It nearly scuttled me . . . not a simple cut, delete, cut and paste, and then spackle and caulk transitional gaps.

So I went back to the geographical center of those places and visited them. Again. And I walked those routes again. And again. It happened, again, to be at almost the exact time of year as the original and central event of the essay: a boy climbs a high power line tower on a misty night, slips, and falls into a tangle of lines and straps. It takes days before he dies. And that was it: it took days. Meaning, it didn't happen all at once and we certainly didn't know all the details at once. Instead, the communal ownership of that story took weeks and months to finally transfer and assemble. Each of us put it together in roughly the same way, using the same tools, but perhaps stamping its final narrative into our own assignation of shapes.

On that last visit, I was cutting through the yards of houses where the dirt road for a nursery had once been a neighborhood shortcut. I was uneasy about my deliberate choice to trespass, a nervousness the very telling of this story was beginning to engage. A car door slammed in the drive of the closest house. Hidden by the civil dusk of early evening, my eyes focused sharply in alert. I froze in my steps and waited as the moment passed. I had not been seen. My focus relaxed and drew back to a wider field, taking in the shapes of trees, rooflines, the darkening dome of night. In stark contrast to the sky were the looping wires of aboveground power and telephone lines. Behind them and just emerging were the lights that shaped Orion. From where others might notice, he was likely still the hunter. But from where I stood, he seemed prone, falling into the wires, forever mortal. I was late for a dinner already, but at that moment dinner was out of the question. I'd seen the shape of my essay. My only choice was to go write.

Grammar Lessons

The Subjunctive Mood

MICHELE MORANO (2001)

(Originally published in *Crab Orchard Review*, reprinted in *Best American Essays 2006*)

Think of it this way: Learning to use the subjunctive mood is like learning to drive a stick shift. It's like falling in love with a car that isn't new or sporty but has a tilt steering wheel and a price you can afford. It's like being so in love with the possibilities, with the places you might go and the experiences you might have, that you pick up your new used car without quite knowing how to drive it, sputtering and stalling and rolling backward at every light. Then you drive the car each day for months, until the stalling stops and you figure out how to downshift, until you can hear the engine's registers and move through them with grace. And later, after you've gained control over the driving and lost control over so much else, you sell the car and most of your possessions and move yourself to Spain, to a place where language and circumstance will help you understand the subjunctive.

Remember that the subjunctive is a mood, not a tense. Verb tenses tell *when* something happens; moods tell *how true*. It's easy to skim over moods in a new language, to translate the words and think you've understood, which is why your first months in Spain will lack nuance. But eventually, after enough conversations have passed, enough hours of talking with your students at the University of Oviedo and your housemate, Lola, and the friends you make when you wander the streets looking like a foreigner, you'll discover that you need the subjunctive in order to finish a question, or an answer, or a thought you couldn't have had without it.

In language, as in life, moods are complicated, but at least in language there are only two. The indicative mood is for knowledge, facts, absolutes, for describing what's real or definite. You'd use the indicative to say, for example:

I was in love.

Or, *The man I loved tried to kill himself.*

Or, *I moved to Spain because the man I loved, the man who tried to kill himself, was driving me insane.*

The indicative helps you tell what happened or is happening or will happen in the future (when you believe you know for sure what the future will bring).

The subjunctive mood, on the other hand, is uncertain. It helps you tell what could have been or might be or what you want but may not get. You'd use the subjunctive to say:

I thought he'd improve without me.

Or, *I left so that he'd begin to take care of himself.*

Or later, after your perspective has been altered, by time and distance and a couple of cervezas in a brightly lit bar, you might say:

I deserted him (indicative).

I left him alone with his crazy self for a year (indicative).

Because I hoped (after which begins the subjunctive) *that being apart might allow us to come together again.*

English is losing the subjunctive mood. It lingers in some constructions ("If he *were* dead," for example), but it's no longer pervasive. That's the beauty and also the danger of English—that the definite and the might-be often look so much alike. And it's the reason why, during a period in your life when everything feels hypothetical, Spain will be a very seductive place to live.

In Spanish, verbs change to accommodate the subjunctive in every tense, and the rules, which are many and varied, have exceptions. In the beginning you may feel defeated by this, even hopeless and angry sometimes. But eventually, in spite of your frustration with trying to explain, you'll know in the part of your mind that holds your stories, the part where grammar is felt before it's understood, that the uses of the subjunctive matter.

1. with "Ojalá"

Ojalá means *I hope* or, more literally, *that Allah is willing.* It's one of the many words left over from the Moorish occupation of Spain, one that's followed by the subjunctive mood because, of course, you never know for sure what Allah has in mind.

During the first months in Spain, you'll use the word by itself, a kind of dangling wish. "It's supposed to rain," Lola will say, and you'll respond, "Ojalá." You'll know you're confusing her, leaving her to figure out whether you want the rain or not, but sometimes the mistakes are too hard to bear.

"That Allah is willing it wouldn't have raining," you might accidentally say. And besides, so early into this year of living freely, you're not quite sure what to hope for.

Each time you say *Ojalá*, it will feel like a prayer, the "ja" and "la" like breaths, like faith woven right into the language. It will remind you of La Mezquita, the enormous, graceful mosque in Córdoba. Of being eighteen years old and visiting Spain for the first time, how you stood in the courtyard filled with orange trees, trying to admire the building before you. You had a fever then, a summer virus you hadn't yet recognized because it was so hot outside. Too hot to lift a hand to fan your face. Too hot to wonder why your head throbbed and the world spun slowly around you.

Inside, the darkness felt like cool water covering your eyes, such contrast, such relief. And then the pillars began to emerge, rows and rows of pillars supporting red and white brick arches, a massive stone ceiling balanced above them like a thought. You swam behind the guide, not even trying to understand his words but soothed by the vastness, by the shadows. Each time you felt dizzy you looked up toward the arches, the floating stone. Toward something that felt, you realized uncomfortably, like God. Or Allah. Or whatever force inspired people to defy gravity this way.

Later, after ten years have passed, after you've moved to Oviedo and become fascinated with the contours of language, the man you left behind in New York will come to visit. You'll travel south with him, returning to La Mezquita on a January afternoon when the air is mild and the orange trees wave tiny green fruit. He'll carry the guidebook, checking it periodically to get the history straight, while you try to reconcile the place before you with the place in your memory, comparing the shadows of this low sun with the light of another season.

You'll be here because you want this man to see La Mezquita. You want him to feel the mystery of a darkness that amazes and consoles, that makes you feel the presence in empty spaces of something you can't explain. Approaching the shadow of the door, you'll each untie the sweaters from around your waists, slipping your arms into them and then into each other's. He will squint and you will hold your breath. *Ojalá*, you'll think, glimpsing in the shadows the subjunctive mood at work.

2. *after words of suasion and negation*

In Oviedo, you'll become a swimmer. Can you imagine? Two or three times a week you'll pack a bag and walk for thirty-five minutes to the university pool, where you'll place clothes and contact lenses in a locker, then sink into a crowded lane. The pool is a mass of blurry heads and arms, some of which know what they're doing and most of which, like you, are flailing. You keep bumping into people as you make your way from one end of the pool to the other, but no one gets upset, and you reason that any form of motion equals exercise.

Then one day a miracle happens. You notice the guy in the next lane swimming like a pro, his long arms cutting ahead as he glides, rhythmically, stroke-stroke-breath. You see and hear and feel the rhythm, and before long you're following him, stroking when he strokes, breathing when he breathes. He keeps getting away, swimming three laps to your one, so you wait at the edge of the pool for him to come back, then follow again, practicing. At the end of an hour, you realize that this man you don't know, a man you wouldn't recognize clothed, has taught you to swim. To breathe. To use the water instead of fighting against it. For this alone, you'll later say, it was worth moving to Spain.

Stroke-stroke-breath becomes the rhythm of your days, the rhythm of your life in Oviedo. All through the fall months, missing him the way you'd miss a limb, your muscles strain to create distance. Shallow end to deep end and back, you're swimming away. From memories of abrupt mood shifts. From the way a question, a comment, a person walking past a restaurant window could transform him into a hunched-over man wearing anger like a shawl. From the echo of your own voice trying to be patient and calm, saying, *Listen to me. I want you to call the doctor.* In English you said *listen* and *call*, and they were the same words you'd use to relate a fact instead of make a plea. But in Spanish, in the language that fills your mind as you swim continually away, the moment you try to persuade someone, or dissuade, you enter the realm of the subjunctive. The verb ends differently so there can be no mistake: requesting is not at all the same as getting.

3. with "si" or "como si"

Si means *if. Como si* means *as if.* A clause that begins with *si* or *como si* is followed by the subjunctive when the meaning is hypothetical or contrary to fact. For example:

If I'd known he would harm himself, I wouldn't have left him alone.

But here we have to think about whether the if-clause really is contrary to fact. Two days before, you'd asked him what he felt like doing that night and he'd responded, "I feel like jumping off the Mid-Hudson Bridge." He'd looked serious when he said it, and even so you'd replied, "Really? Would you like me to drive you there?" *As if* it were a joke.

If you knew he were serious, that he were thinking of taking his life, would you have replied with such sarcasm? In retrospect it seems impossible not to have known—the classic signs were there. For weeks he'd been sad, self-pitying. He'd been sleeping too much, getting up to teach his Freshman Composition class in the morning, then going home some days and staying in bed until evening. His sense of humor had waned. He'd begun asking the people around him to cheer him up, make him feel better, please.

And yet he'd been funny. Ironic, self-deprecating, hyperbolic. So no one's saying you should have known, just that maybe you felt a hint of threat in his statement about the river. And maybe that angered you because it meant you were failing to be enough for him. Maybe you were tired, too, in need of cheering up yourself because suddenly your perfect guy had turned inside out. Or maybe that realization came later, after you'd had the time and space to develop theories.

The truth is, only you know what you know. And what you know takes the indicative, remember?

For example: You knew he was hurting himself. The moment you saw the note on his office door, in the campus building where you were supposed to meet him on a Sunday afternoon, you knew. The note said, "I'm not feeling well. I'm going home. I guess I'll see you tomorrow." He didn't use your name.

You tried calling him several times but there was no answer, so you drove to the apartment he shared with another graduate student. The front door was unlocked, but his bedroom door wouldn't budge. You knocked steadily but not too loud, because his housemate's bedroom door was also closed, and you assumed he was inside taking a nap. *If* you'd known that his housemate was not actually home, you would have broken down the door. That scenario is hypothetical, so it takes the subjunctive—even though you're quite sure.

The human mind can reason its way around anything. On the drive to your own apartment, you told yourself, he's angry with me. That's why the door was locked, why he wouldn't answer the phone. You thought: If he weren't so close to his family, I'd really be worried. If today weren't Mother's Day. If he didn't talk so affectionately about his parents. About his brother and sisters. About our future. If, if, if.

When the phone rang and there was silence on the other end, you began to shout, "What have you done?"

In Spain, late at night over *chupitos* of bourbon or brandy, you and Lola will trade stories. Early on you won't understand a lot of what she says, and she'll understand what you say but not what you mean. You won't know how to say what you mean in Spanish; sometimes you won't even know how to say it in English. But as time goes on, the stories you tell will become more complicated. More subtle. More grammatically daring. You'll begin to feel more at ease in the unreal.

For example: *If* you hadn't gone straight home from his apartment. *If* you hadn't answered the phone. *If* you hadn't jumped back into your car to drive nine miles in record time, hoping the whole way to be stopped by the police. *If* you hadn't met him on the porch where he had staggered in blood-soaked clothes. *If* you hadn't rushed upstairs for a towel and discovered a flooded bedroom floor, the blood separating into water and rust-colored clumps. *If* you hadn't been available for this emergency.

As the months pass in Spain, you'll begin to risk the *then*. His housemate would have come home and found him the way you found him: deep gashes in his arm, but the wounds clotting enough to keep him alive, enough to narrowly avoid a transfusion. His housemate would have called the paramedics, ridden to the hospital in the ambulance, notified his parents from the emergency room, greeted them after their three-hour drive. His housemate would have done all the things you did, and he would have cleaned the mess by himself instead of with your help, the two of you borrowing a neighbor's wet-vac and working diligently until you—or he—or both of you—burst into hysterical laughter. Later this housemate would have moved to a new apartment, just as he has done, and would probably be no worse off than he is right now.

You, on the other hand, would have felt ashamed, guilty, remiss for not being available in a time of crisis. But you wouldn't have found yourself leaning over a stretcher in the emergency room, a promise slipping from your mouth before you could think it through: "I won't leave you. Don't worry, I won't leave you." *As if* it were true.

4. after impersonal expressions

Such as *it is possible, it is a shame, it is absurd.*

"*It's possible* that I'm making things worse in some ways," you told the counselor you saw on Thursday afternoons. He'd been out of the hospital for a few months by then and had a habit of missing his therapy appointments, to which you could only respond by signing up for your own.

She asked how you were making things worse, and you explained that when you told him you needed to be alone for a night and he showed up anyway at 11:00 p.m., pleading to stay over, you couldn't turn him away. She said, "*It's a shame* he won't honor your request," and you pressed your fingernails into the flesh of your palm to keep your eyes from filling. She asked why you didn't want him to stay over, and you said that sometimes you just wanted to sleep, without waking up when he went to the bathroom and listening to make sure he came back to bed instead of taking all the Tylenol in the medicine cabinet. Or sticking his head in the gas oven. Or diving from the balcony onto the hillside three stories below. There is nothing, you told her, nothing I haven't thought of.

She said, "Do you think he's manipulating you?" and you answered in the mood of certainty, "Yes. Absolutely." Then you asked, "*Isn't it absurd* that I let him manipulate me?" and what you wanted, of course, was some reassurance that it wasn't absurd. That you were a normal person, reacting in a normal way, to a crazy situation.

Instead she said, "Let's talk about why you let him. Let's talk about what's in this for you."

5. *after verbs of doubt or emotion*

You didn't think he was much of a prospect at first. Because he seemed arrogant. Because in the initial meetings for new instructors, he talked as if he were doing it the right way and the rest of you were pushovers. Because he looked at you with one eye squinted, as if he couldn't quite decide.

You liked that he was funny, a little theatrical and a great fan of supermarkets. At 10:00, after evening classes ended, he'd say, "Are you going home?" Sometimes you'd offer to drop him off at his place. Sometimes you'd agree to go out for a beer. And sometimes you'd say, "Yeah, but I have to go to the store first," and his eyes would light up. In the supermarket he'd push the cart and you'd pick items off the shelf. Maybe you'd turn around and there would be a whole rack of frozen ribs in your cart, or after you put them back, three boxes of Lucky Charms. Maybe he'd be holding a package of pfeffernusse and telling a story about his German grandmother. Maybe it would take two hours to run your errand because he was courting you in ShopRite.

You doubted that you'd sleep with him a second time. After the first time, you both lay very still for a while, flat on your backs, not touching. He seemed to be asleep. You watched the digital clock hit 2:30 a.m. and thought about finding your turtleneck and sweater and wool socks, lacing up your boots, and heading out into the snow. And then out of the blue he rolled toward you, pulled the blanket up around your shoulders, and said, "Is there anything I can get you? A cup of tea? A sandwich?"

You were thrilled at the breaks in his depression, breaks that felt like new beginnings, every time. Days, sometimes even weeks, when he seemed more like himself than ever before. Friends would ask how he was doing, and he'd offer a genuine smile. "Much better," he'd say, putting his arm around you, "She's pulling me through the death-wish phase." Everyone would laugh with relief, and at those moments you'd feel luckier than ever before, because of the contrast.

Do you see the pattern?

6. *to express good wishes*

Que tengas muy buen viaje, Lola will say, kissing each of your cheeks before leaving you off at the bus station. *May you have a good trip.* A hope, a wish, a prayer of sorts, even without the ojalá.

The bus ride from Oviedo to Madrid is nearly six hours, so you have a lot of time for imagining. It's two days after Christmas, and you know he spent the holiday at his parents' house, that he's there right now, maybe eating breakfast, maybe packing. Tonight his father will drive him to Kennedy Airport, and tomorrow morning, very early, you'll meet him at Barajas in Madrid. You try to envision what he'll look like, the expression on his face when he sees you, but you're having trouble recalling what it's like to be in his presence.

You try not to hope too much, although now, four months into your life in Spain, you want to move toward, instead of away. Toward long drives on winding, mountain roads, toward the cathedral of Toledo, the mosque at Córdoba, the Alhambra in Granada. Toward romantic dinners along the Mediterranean. Toward a new place from which to view the increasingly distant past. You want this trip to create a separation, in your mind and in his, between your first relationship and your real relationship, the one that will be so wonderful, so stable, you'll never leave him again.

Once you've reached Madrid and found the pensión where you've reserved a room, you'll get the innkeeper to help you make an international call. His father will say, "My God, he can't sit still today," and then there will be his voice, asking how your bus ride was, where you are, how far from the airport. You'll say, "I'll see you in the morning." He'll reply, "In seventeen hours."

The next morning, the taxi driver is chatty. He wants to know why you're going to the airport without luggage, and your voice is happy and excited when you explain. He asks whether this boyfriend writes you letters, and you smile and nod at the reflection in the rearview mirror. "Many letters?" he continues, "Do you enjoy receiving the letters?" In Spain you're always having odd conversations with strangers, so you hesitate only a moment, wondering why he cares, and then you say, "Yes. Very much." He nods emphatically. "Muy bien." At the terminal he drops you off with a broad smile.

"Que lo pases bien con tu novio," he says. *Have a good time with your boyfriend.* In his words you hear the requisite subjunctive mood.

7. in adverbial clauses denoting purpose, provision, exception

How different to walk down the street in Madrid, Toledo, Córdoba, to notice an elaborate fountain or a tiny car parked half on the sidewalk, and comment aloud. You've loved being alone in Spain and now, even more, you love being paired.

On the fifth day you reach Granada, find lodging in someone's home. Down the hallway you can hear the family watching TV, cooking, preparing to celebrate New Year's Eve. In the afternoon you climb the long, slow hill leading to the Alhambra and spend hours touring the complex. You marvel at the elaborate irrigation system, the indoor baths with running water, the stunning mosaic tiles and views of the Sierra Nevada. Here is the room where Boabdil signed the city's surrender to Ferdinand and Isabella; here is where Washington Irving lived while writing *Tales of the Alhambra*. Occasionally you separate, as he inspects a mural and you follow a hallway into a lush courtyard, each of your imaginations working to restore this place to its original splendor. When you come together again, every time, there's a thrill.

He looks rested, relaxed, strolling through the gardens with his hands tucked into the front pockets of his pants. When you enter the Patio of the Lions—the famous courtyard where a circle of marble lions project water into a reflecting pool—he turns to you, wide-eyed, his face as open as a boy's.

"Isn't it pretty?" you keep asking, feeling shy because what you mean is: "Are you glad to be here?"

"*So* pretty," he responds, taking hold of your arm, touching his lips to your hair.

The day is perfect, you think. The trip is perfect. You allow yourself a moment of triumph: I left him *so that* he would get better without me, and he did. I worked hard and saved money and invited him on this trip *in case* there's still hope for us. And there is.

Unless. In language, as in experience, we have purpose, provision, exception. None of which necessarily matches reality, and all of which take the subjunctive.

On the long walk back down the hill toward your room, he turns quiet. You find yourself talking more than usual, trying to fill the empty space with cheerful commentary, but it doesn't help. The shape of his face begins

134 : GRAMMAR LESSONS

to change until there it is again, that landscape of furrows and crags. The jaw thrusts slightly, lips pucker, eyebrows arch as if to say, "I don't care. About anything."

Back in the room, you ask him what's wrong, plead with him to tell you. You can talk about anything, you assure him, anything at all. And yet you're stunned when his brooding turns accusatory. He says it isn't fair. You don't understand how difficult it is to be him. Your life is easy, so easy that even moving to a new country, taking up a new language, is effortless. While every day is a struggle for him. Don't you see that? Every day is a struggle.

He lowers the window shade and gets into bed, his back turned toward you.

What to do? You want to go back outside into the mild air and sunshine, walk until you remember what it feels like to be completely alone. But you're afraid to leave him. For the duration of his ninety-minute nap, you sit paralyzed. Everything feels unreal, the darkened room, the squeals of children in another part of the house, the burning sensation in your stomach. You tremble, first with sadness and fear, then with anger. Part of you wants to wake him, tell him to collect his things, then drive him back to the airport in Madrid. You want to send him home again, away from your new country, the place where you live unencumbered—but with a good deal of effort, thank you. The other part of you wants to wail, to beat your fists against the wall and howl, *Give him back to me*.

Remember: purpose, provision, exception. The subjunctive runs parallel to reality.

8. after certain indications of time, if the action has not occurred

While is a subjunctive state of mind. So are *until, as soon as, before,* and *after.* By now you understand why, right? Because until something *has happened*, you can't be sure.

In Tarifa, the wind blows and blows. You learn this even before arriving, as you drive down route 15 past Gibraltar. You're heading toward the southernmost point in Spain, toward warm sea breezes and a small town off the beaten path. You drive confidently, shifting quickly through the gears to keep pace with the traffic around you. He reclines in the passenger's seat, one foot propped against the dashboard, reading from the *Real Guide* open against his thigh. "Spreading out beyond its Moorish walls, Tarifa is known in Spain for its abnormally high suicide rate—a result of the unremitting winds that blow across the town and its environs."

You say, "Tell me you're joking." He says, "How's that for luck?"

Three days before, you'd stood in Granada's crowded city square at midnight, each eating a grape for every stroke of the New Year. If you eat all twelve grapes in time, tradition says, you'll have plenty of luck in the coming year. It sounds wonderful—such an easy way to secure good fortune—until you start eating and time gets ahead, so far ahead that no matter how fast you chew and swallow, midnight sounds with three grapes left.

In Tarifa, you come down with the flu. It hits hard and fast—one minute you're strolling through a white-washed coastal town, and the next you're huddled in bed in a stupor. He goes to the pharmacy and, with a handful of Spanish words and many gestures, procures the right medicine. You sleep all day, through the midday meal, through the time of siesta, past sundown, and into the evening. When you wake the room is fuzzy and you're alone, with a vague memory of him rubbing your back, saying something about a movie.

Carefully you rise and make your way to the bathroom—holding onto the bed, the doorway, the sink—then stand on your toes and look out the window into the blackness. By day there's a thin line of blue mountains across the strait, and you imagine catching the ferry at dawn and watching that sliver of Morocco rise up from the shadows to become a whole continent. You imagine standing on the other side and looking back toward the tip of Spain, this tiny town where the winds blow and blow. That's how easy it is to keep traveling once you start, putting distance between the various parts of your life, imagining yourself over and over again into entirely new places.

Chilly and sweating, you make your way back to bed, your stomach fluttering nervously. You think back to Granada, how he'd woken from a nap on that dark afternoon and apologized. "I don't know what got into me today," he'd said. "This hasn't been happening." You believe it's true, it hasn't been happening. But you don't know *how true*.

You think: He's fine now. There's no need to worry. He's been fine for days, happy and calm. I'm overreacting. But overreaction is a slippery slope. With the wind howling continuously outside, the room feels small and isolated. You don't know that he's happy and calm right now, do you? You don't know how he is today at all, because you've slept and slept and barely talked to him.

You think: If the movie started on time—but movies never start on time in Spain, so you add, subtract, try to play it safe, and determine that by 10:45 p.m. your fretting will be justified. At 11:00 p.m. you'll get dressed and go looking, and if you can't find him, what will you do? Wait until midnight for extra measure? And then call the police? And tell them what, that he isn't back yet, and you're afraid because you're sick and he's alone and the wind here blows and blows, enough to make people crazy, the book says, make them suicidal?

This is the *when*, the *while*, the *until*. The *before* and *after*. The real and the unreal in precarious balance. This is what you moved to Spain to escape from, and here it is again, following you.

The next time you wake, the room seems brighter, more familiar. You sit up and squint against the light. His cheeks are flushed, hair mussed from the wind. His eyes are clear as a morning sky. "Hi, sweetie," he says, putting a hand on your forehead. "You still have a fever. How do you feel?" He smells a little musty, like the inside of a community theater where not many people go on a Sunday night in early January. He says, "The movie was hilarious." You ask whether he understood it and he shrugs. Then he acts out a scene using random Spanish words as a voice over, and you laugh and cough until he flops down on his stomach beside you.

Here it comes again, the contrast between what was, just a little while ago, and what is now. After all this time and all these miles, you're both here, in a Spanish town with a view of Africa. You feel amazed, dizzy, as if swimming outside yourself. You're talking with him, but you're also watching yourself talk with him. And then you're sleeping and watching yourself sleep, dreaming and thinking about the dreams. Throughout the night you move back and forth, here and there, between what is and what might be, tossed by language and possibility and the constantly shifting wind.

9. *in certain independent clauses*

There's something extraordinary—isn't there?—about learning to speak Spanish as an adult, about coming to see grammar as a set of guidelines not just for saying what you mean but for understanding the way you live. There's something extraordinary about thinking in a language that insists on marking the limited power of desire.

For example: At Barajas Airport in Madrid, you walk him to the boarding gate. He turns to face you, hands on your arms, eyes green as the sea. He says, "Only a few more months and we'll be together for good, right sweetie?" He watches your face, waiting for a response, but you know this isn't a decision, something you can say yes to. So you smile, eyes burning, and give a slight nod. What you mean is, *I hope so*. What you think is, *Ojalá*. And what you know is this: The subjunctive is the mood of mystery. Of luck. Of faith interwoven with doubt. It's a held breath, a hand reaching out, carefully touching wood. It's humility, deference, the opposite of hubris. And it's going to take a long time to master.

But at least the final rule of usage is simple, self-contained, one you can commit to memory: Certain independent clauses exist only in the subjunctive mood, lacing optimism with resignation, hope with heartache. *Be that as it may*, for example. Or the phrase one says at parting, eyes closed as if in prayer, *May all go well with you.*

FROM THE AUTHOR

The idea for "Grammar Lessons: The Subjunctive Mood" presented itself one evening at The Mill restaurant in Iowa City where, over beer and pizza, I was listening to a grad school friend describe the difficulty of learning French. She was doing fine, she said, with the vocabulary and most of the grammar, but the subjunctive mood was killing her. I'd experienced something similar while trying to learn Spanish, and as she talked, my thoughts drifted to other bars and other restaurants, to the cathedral in Oviedo, the mosque at Córdoba, the Alhambra in Granada. I thought about the year I'd spent living in Spain, time that had seemed conditional, outside reality, laced with hope and fear. A subjunctive time, I realized suddenly, in the dim light of The Mill's front room.

I had just read John D'Agata's essay, "Martha Graham, Audio Descripton Of," published in the *Georgia Review*, and been taken with its disjunctive structure, and so I decided to write an essay in the form of a grammar lesson, subtitled with rules for usage that would each be followed by a narrative example. The narratives would reveal a larger story about how I'd moved to Spain in order to separate temporarily from a boyfriend who struggled with mood disorder. I knew right away it was a good idea, and I also knew that the concept of grammar was larger than this one piece. The metaphor was so rich that it seemed worthy of a thesis, if not an entire book.

The next morning I dug out my old Spanish grammar book and translated the rules for using the subjunctive mood into my computer. Then I started writing the examples, and in a couple of weeks the essay was complete. Although writing it was emotionally intense, it was also strangely easy.

Before sending the essay out to literary journals, I submitted it to a Master's Workshop run by visiting writer Phillip Lopate, who chose to discuss it publically. Lopate liked the essay very much, liked the story and the narrator, was sure I could publish it somewhere right then. But, he added with a frown, it didn't hold up to re-reading. There was nothing new to discover the second time around, he said, and so the essay felt like a one-trick pony.

He wanted to see deeper ideas, stronger resonances, a more profound message. He just thought it could be more, he said. Right? Couldn't it be more?

Yes, I thought, it certainly could.

I put the essay away for a few weeks, then revised it thoroughly, beginning a cycle that would play out over and over again. My professors Carol de St. Victor, Carl Klaus, and Susan Lohafer commented on drafts, as did friends and classmates, and I kept revising to incorporate their feedback. When grad school ended and I moved to the east coast, I unpacked the essay and tried again. It was a good essay, I thought, but it still didn't stand up to rereading. And then, eventually, it wasn't even good anymore. It was broken. The spark of life that had sizzled in the early draft was gone.

Over the next two years, I tried several times to revive my dead narrative. I found a hard copy of the first draft and used it to remind myself of the emotion, the sweat-inducing danger I'd felt when I first started telling truths that might not make my narrator sympathetic. I brought elements of that draft into the newest one, massaging it until the essay seemed to cohere once again. But something was still off.

Then I moved back to the Midwest and settled into a teaching position, where I joined a writing group comprised not of creative writers but of scholars from various disciplines. That turned out to be an important choice, because as I revised the essay yet again to give to them, I viewed it as if through the eyes of strangers, people less interested in funky structures and literary techniques than in a captivating story.

The most pivotal scene of the essay took place in a restaurant in Córdoba, Spain, with dialogue I remembered perfectly. But the scene wasn't yet powerful enough, and as I tried to figure out why, I remembered that the real conversation hadn't happened in Córdoba at all. It had happened in a pensión in Granada, just down the hill from the Alhambra. Somehow, early in the drafting process, I had convinced myself it would be easier for readers to stay in Córdoba rather than move on to Granada. That's a lazy way of thinking if ever there was one, since readers will go anywhere you take them, but I hadn't wanted to do the work of getting them there.

In my experience, the danger of fictionalizing creative nonfiction isn't that you might be found out. It's that letting your imagination run off with real life can mess up your story. Writing about actual events means "reading" your experience in an interpretive way, honoring the complexity and coaxing meaning from it, but the act of slipping fiction into nonfiction often involves simplifying reality. Or tidying it. Or in some way taking the wind out of its sails.

So the last step of revision for this essay involved overhauling that section by paying close attention to what had really happened and, in the process, facing down one of the essay's hard truths: that it's possible to love someone with all your heart, so much you'll do almost anything for him, and at the very same time, want him out of your life.

Rewriting that section brought me back to why I'd started the piece to begin with, and it allowed me, finally, to craft an ending that seemed utterly true. Most importantly, with that final revision I began to see how the essay might stand up to re-reading. I gave it to the writing group and then sent it to the *Crab Orchard Review* essay contest, which it won, and the following year it appeared in *Best American Essays 2006*.

All told, it took six years to finish what began as an easy essay.

JUDY! JUDY! JUDY!

ELENA PASSARELLO (2008)

(Originally printed in *Let Me Clear My Throat*)

[Music] cannot even be judged by the human ear alone, since it is directed toward those immeasurably complex and unpredictable psychological and physical reactions of the entire human organism, and toward its qualities of imagination and remembered experience.

RALPH KIRKPATRICK, "On Concert Halls"

I. OVERTURE: "The Trolley Song," "Over the Rainbow,"
"The Man That Got Away."

They wait for her in a high-domed ellipsis of unsteeled brick and masonry. She is thirty minutes late and the Hall has filled with their anxious fabric, perfume, and breathing. As they scan the back corners of the red stage wall, they wonder if her singing sounds the same. If it is still coltish and limber, like it was at the Palace in '51, or on *Lux Radio Theatre* a dozen years before that. If she can still belt, still swing. If she's as fat as they say she is.

Their eyes wander to the gap in the ceiling, the only change to the Hall's anatomy in 70 years. Even the seat frames are the same as that day in 1891 when Carnegie christened it "Music Hall," hoping to keep his name out of things. He hired an amateur cellist to design the shoebox-shaped room, simpler than the ladies of the Oratorio Society might have preferred: no gilded proscenium or frescoes. Its smooth-walled arch leaps over each velvet seat and shades it like an awning, like that famous phonograph cone into which the puppy sticks his nose. This is the Victorian equivalent of wiring space for sound.

The conductor starts his overture, the trumpets smashing through the one about the trolley, about the rainbow, about the man that got away.

There is no bill of song; the programs in the audience's hands only say "Act One: Judy" and "Act Two: More Judy," plus a personnel list and an ad for Steinway. The full orchestral sound shoots from center stage, out past the vacant mic, and into the Hall, where it splinters. Each wave of the overture races to discover the hard surface it will hit first.

Those long and close walls make the music slap the sides of the Hall before it shoots up to the roof. Because the walls reflect sound first, the wavelength that touches the audience's right ears is infinitesimally different from the signal that goes left, deepening the work of the brass, reeds, drums, and strings. This small difference between left and right makes the sound bleed into other senses: the ticketholders can stroke it like fur, taste the flavor of it, wrinkle their noses at the musk it sprays. After bussing the walls, the music rocks up and then back to the carpeted floor, then fades into the curtained flanks, adding rhythm and even more shape.

We call that map of sonic travel the "presence" or "warmth" of this Hall, a hall that some call the first Stradivarius of American architecture. And though we may not know it, that presence is the reason we sit in the Hall, in any room, really, and wait to hear a voice sing to us. We're waiting for the moment in which sound fills a room and then changes from wavelength to wave: a thing we can surf on or drown in. A moment with undertow that hits us in the places where we move. Though, in these situations, we all choose to sit still while it strikes us.

The conductor looks offstage right, and there she stands. Tiny in flats, despite five inches of coif and a spangly jacquard wrap. Her brown eyes glisten with something wet, but he cannot tell if it is a Ritalin glaze or tears. She is twisting the fire curtain in her fists, tipping forward a bit into the folds of asbestos so that the front rows cannot see her. In her hiding spot, she shouts her trademark warm-up into the fabric. It inflates her, pump by pump, with each syllable. The conductor can spy on her from his podium. Though, at point blank range of the overture, he cannot hear her voice. He can only watch her tiny jaw mouthing the words of the warm-up: FUCKEM FUCKEM FUCKEM FUCKEM FUCKEM FUCKEM FUCKEM FUCKEM.

II. ACT ONE: "When You're Smiling,"
"Almost Like Being in Love / This Can't Be Love,"
"Do It Again," "You Go to My Head,"
"Alone Together," "Who Cares," "Puttin' On the Ritz,"
"How Long Has This Been Going On?" "Just You, Just Me,"
"The Man That Got Away," "San Francisco."

Her first concert was in a hall much like that of yours or mine: a little red-walled room that rarely seats more than one. Its acoustics are unparalleled. She lay, awash in sound, as voices and white noise traveled the scaffolding of her mother's tissues, skeleton, and plasma. Sound vibrated the length of her mother's spine, down through her pelvic arch, and into that snug listening room of liquid and muscle. There, it provided the most all-encompassing sonic experience a body will ever know, so powerful that we register it before we are even wired to open our eyes or make fists. Imagine the added power of that omnipresent first hall if it were shoved under the keyboard of a movie house's piano every night, four shows a night. This was the bill of sound in her hall, from the day in the second trimester when she grew ears to the warm night in June when her father closed the theater to carry his wife to the Itasca Hospital.

She showed up having bathed for nine months in reprise after reprise of "Ain't We Got Fun," "Toot, Toot, Tootsie," and "(Tamale) I'm Hot for You." She was as expert in these melodies as she was in her mother's voice, the closest voice, the voice that boomed around her to prove the difference of a body at rest and a body in peril. Sound and emotion vibrated the fluid in any extra space around her. Lyrics lapped against her body; so did patter. She kicked to the sound of stop-time, vamps, and waltzes. She wiggled in the ripples of a dotted eighth note, and ballads slowed the beat of her heart.

Legend has it that, less than two years later, in the very same movie house, she first sang for an audience, yelling the only verse she knew of "Jingle Bells" until her throat gave and her father dragged her off. For a decade after, her tiny voice stretched its legs, first through every Minnesota social hall with a curtain and baby grand, then through the Twinkle-toe Kiddie Revue, the Kinky Kid Parade, *Big Brother Ken's Kiddies Hour*, the Beverly Hills Pickfair, the *Los Angeles Examiner*'s all-star Christmas Benefit, the Second Annual Alfalfa Festival, the Vitaphone Kiddies movie shorts, and two weeks at the Chez Paree with Georgie Jessel.

Jessel changed her name from Gumm to Garland the year her voice broke. Weight and sinew had tipped it backward, dissolving the helium pitch of childhood, and then coaches built wind power and muscle strength around the hormones that waxed the cracks in her vibrato. By the time she sang "Zing! Went the Strings of My Heart" in the MGM offices, the test pianist had to run out of the room. He must have told Louis Mayer that from her tiny mouth came more sound than there was space in the office, and that it was still in there: a sweet warble banging the leaded windowpanes to get out. "The Little Girl with the Big Voice," they decided to call her, and they did, nearly as often as they called her the name that she'd christened herself: "Judy."

Tonight, this 70-year old Hall shakes when she leaves the wings and pump-walks to the center stage microphone. New York women in organza slippers and kidskin gloves actually stand on the seats of their carpeted chairs to see her. But she begins the first song without a diva curtsy or the Jolson *pietà* arms, instead just skating out on the ease of the melody. The first phrase of "When You're Smiling" floats away, minus the showy *rallentando* wind-up of Durante or Louis Armstrong: *whenyahhsmiiileeeeeeeeeeeeeng.* Her voice swells and recedes with the long notes of the last two vowels, and that loose vibrato feels even more silvery in the treble of a mid-century mic. But the voiced lyric does not live alone in the Hall; it meets the voices of the ticket holders. So there, one electrified voice leaps into an SRO crowd, and begets that crowd's choral push-back of deafening, unmiked sound.

Three thousand sets of cords touch 400 times a second, entreating the help of the whole body. Backs contract, ankles shake, feet tighten in wing-tips. Each body is its own Hall as their physical architecture boosts the air in their throats, playing to their personal rafters, their crown molding, their buttresses. And as their bodies buzz with reflected sound, the Hall outside of them shakes further.

Variety will call tonight "the greatest evening in the history of show busi-ness," but maybe what happens has less to do with "show" than with the high-five between the crowd's roar and her infamous voice. They yell "Judy! Judy! Judy!" for her big sound, which can turn a Hall into that tiny red room to which we all had tickets years ago.

Dozens will report—in the *World Telegram*, in the *Herald Tribune*, and fifty years later in *Vanity Fair* and on NPR—that they wept a little with her first "When You're Smiling," shot from the stage like an arrow from a five-foot-tall crossbow. Perhaps they were frightened that, without the soft comforts of fluid and skin around them, this makeshift womb on 57th Street wouldn't weather such a full-bodied vocal event.

As she sings to them, they sneak wary glances at the ceiling three balco-nies above their heads, where the sound finally pools. The bridge in "When You're Smiling" turns into a medley, and she sings a rag-rhythm *forget your troubles, c'mon get happy! WHEN! YOU'RE! SMILIN!* and they clamor.

Feel my heart, they say to the man on their right, and he does. Their chests hum with resonance from without and from within. *See?* they say. *I swear to Christ this whole damn place is gonna cave.*

III. ACT TWO: "That's Entertainment,"
"I Can't Give You Anything But Love," "Come Rain or Come Shine," "You're Nearer," "A Foggy Day," "If Love Were All," "Zing! Went the Strings of My Heart," "Stormy Weather," "You Made Me Love You / For Me and My Gal / The Trolley Song," "Rock-a-Bye Your Baby With a Dixie Melody."

When the set moves through a string of up-tempo numbers, she pounces on them, the drums racing to keep up like the back legs of a spurred horse. She meets the staccato wordplay of Cole Porter and Fred Fisher with a pleasingly baffled, Great Lakes response, like Steve Allen earnestly over-pronouncing every syllable of "Bee-bop-a-lula." The fastest songs run their course in less than ninety seconds, the applause from the previous number barely waning by the end of the tune that follows, and their lyrics are often interrupted by the bop of her chin or shoulder pad on the microphone. Like the blaring horns behind her, she is somehow allowed to land on either side of her brassiest pitches in "Come Rain or Come Shine" and "Puttin' On the Ritz" without doing any damage to the integrity of the melody. This turns each up-tempo song into a survival struggle, a bout from which she rises off the mat again and again, with style.

The ballads offer something else: a disturbing emotional vertigo, as if the floor is stripped down to a narrow eyebeam that holds the sound, the space, and the evening together. She walks it solo, one note in front of the other, and they all hear her beckoning them to meet her, first at the bench she shares with her pianist, and then closer even, into the cabin of her open mouth. She whispers in and out of tune: *and I believe / that since my life began the most I've had is just a talent to amuse.* And then a flattening six final notes in mezzo-forte belt: *HI, HO! If LOVE Were ALL!*

And then there are the swells in her end-notes. She builds little dwell-ings—caves, tents, awnings—in the bulges of the song, and the audience ducks with her into each new brassy schematic. In "For Me and My Gal," she tightens her grip on the swell, mimicking the musculature of a grin. She pushes her palate down for the swells in "The Man That Got Away," loosening the vowel, then rolling it from her teeth to her tonsils like a dram of Armagnac. She caps the "ah" swells in "How Long Has This Been Going On?" with strange punches of extra breath. After many swells, she puts a catch into the next note, like a hole in the floor she must step over to pre-vent from falling into the basement. The catches halt the meter each time, and she seems surprised by it, as if she has never sung "Come Rain or Come Shine" or "The Trolley Song" before. Her audience, in turn, is surprised by the sheer number of places she goes after catching herself. Dips, runs, trills, rolls—they never knew there were so many ways to be this loud.

Lenny Bruce isn't here, and he certainly isn't one of the hundred men who run down from the cheap seats after the finale. But he will play the LP pressing of this concert a hundred times, like nearly everyone with a hi-fi did in 1961. Later that year, he will tell another crowd in another kind of hall—one curtained and padded to make the acoustic dead-zone necessary for speech—that the Judy encore kills him. Not because of the way she builds three floors to "Rock-a-bye Your Baby": first a lilting schmaltz, then a stripper-rhythm belt, and then a top-level blare so raucous she growls the last syllables. Not in how her voice, already twenty-three songs in, still flips and shimmies and blasts past the fire exits. Not even in those men at the stage reaching for her, shrieking right into her little face.

IV. ENCORE: "Over the Rainbow," "Swanee," "After You've Gone," "Chicago."

It's only *after* "Rock-a-Bye" that Lenny Bruce starts to pay attention, he says. This is after she has calmed the crowd underfoot, who beg her for "Swanee!" and "Chicago!" and for her to "just stand there!"

She looks out at the Hall and says, "I know, I know. I'll sing 'em all and we'll *stay all night!*" At the prospect of being locked in the Hall with her until dawn, they all roar, and right then, she mutters to them at a half-octave drop, "I don't ever wanna go home; I never . . . ," trailing off. This is the moment that does Bruce in.

Because, he says, her voice falls out of sync at the word "home." This "home" she intones is not a showbiz exclamation, like the set list's songs of homes in San Francisco, Chicago, or Dixie. Here, the word "home" sounds nothing like the Kansas "home" Judy-as-Dorothy Gale sighed in Oz, or the Saint Louis "home" Judy-as-Esther Smith summoned after "Have Yourself a Merry Little Christmas." Tonight, "home," Lenny Bruce says, is no comfort, not in Real-Live-Judy's thirty-eight-year-old mouth. This home, to him, sounds "scary."

Bruce compares her low, stammered "home" to a child in bed, begging his mother for a fifth glass of water, not because he is thirsty, but because his room is built too flat, with far too many echoes and shadows to bear. He'll drink water all night long, though he is full and exhausted, rather than have her leave. Because a hand holding a glass to your lips is better than a dark, quiet room in which you float alone. Even if such a room is what we are all supposed to want, a place where thoughts can roam without accompaniment, without the need for performance.

Judy's muttered "home" reminds Bruce how foreign it feels—if you are a human like him or like Judy—to try to be close to someone inside the home, a house without rhythm or red velvet, without the amplified sounds of someone's hands or voice or heartbeat.

"Lotta *tsuris*," Bruce says of Judy, his voice shaking along with his head. "Lotta dues."

He might hear in her paid-up voice the "home" on Beverly Drive, where she escaped in 1950, two days after MGM fired her from a musical she didn't want to do in the first place. She locked herself in the home's master bath, smashed a drinking glass and sawed at her neck with the shards, as if to say, *here! If this is what you want, take it out of me. Clone it. Fucking bronze it; I don't care.*

Or perhaps he hears in her "home" the cold tile of his own quiet room, where his housemate will find him, blue and naked with a cord around his arm, just five years after this show.

Or he might hear the cramped London home where Judy will live by the end of the decade. One June evening, she will lock herself into *its* tiny bathroom. Instead of breaking a drinking glass, this time she will fill one with water and slide far too many Seconal past her throat. Six hours later, when her fifth husband climbs through the bathroom window and lifts her body, it will moan at him a little, though it will feel hard and cold to his touch.

Or maybe Lenny Bruce hears the sterilized walls of the Westminster Hospital, where the on-duty pathologist will scalpel a Y shape into Judy's torso days after her death. He'll follow either the Rokitansky or the "En Masse" method of autopsy, both of which take the larynx fairly early. Both require him to use his thumbs to separate the muscles that connect larynx to trachea, like popping beans from a pod, until he holds her voice box in his hands. He will then tie a string around it, lifting it out of her neck and placing it next to her on the table, so that it hovers outside her body like a droopy balloon.

In the pile of offal to be burned, he will leave the two white porous tabs, tinier than baby teeth, which hung on the walls of her throat for 572 months. They are a few millimeters larger than they were during her days on the MGM lot, slackened from cigarettes and Blue Nun wine, from encores and rage blackouts and bad patter and orgasms. They will not make it across the pond to the Frank E. Campbell Funeral Chapel, a room of spartan plaster on Madison Avenue with pews for two hundred. Regardless, over ten thousand people will wait, not to sit in that chapel hall, but to walk past her last white metal box, which she will, of course, leave uncovered to let in the light.

There will be velvet walls—blue, this time—and glitter. And at eleven p.m., the Funeral Director will ask police if they can keep allowing people to pass through the threshold. He will leave the doors to the chapel's hall open long into the warm night so that people can stay inside and, in silence, answer Judy's hand-sewn mouth.

FROM THE AUTHOR

I decided to write about Judy Garland one Saturday at the Iowa City Public Library, when I was smack in the middle of another essay on screaming and death. I'd been researching the infamous movie sound clip called the Wilhelm Scream, and since Garland's *A Star is Born* features a famous Wilhelm, I found a DVD copy and reserved a library viewing carrel so I could hear the scream in context. This was before everything was on You-Tube, when you actually used viewing carrels as a part of your research.

Back then, my sense of Judy was limited to *The Wizard of Oz* and that trembling, pants-less Judy impersonation that Mike Myers did on *SNL*. I'd never been very impressed. But that day, when I watched her sing "The Man that Got Away" to James Mason, I got so overwhelmed I sweated up the back of my chair (belated apologies to the library patron who used the carrel next). I forgot to listen for the Wilhelm Scream. I just got sucked up into the Judy tornado, as have many before me.

Even through those subpar headphones, I heard why I *had* to write about this visceral, tricky singing. Hers is one of the most evocative voices I've ever heard, and I'm a girl who spent five years of her life doing little more than listening to evocative voices. But Judy's is not the best voice, the most perfect voice, or even the most universally understood voice. It might, however, be the voice that produces the most alarming *tension* in the listener. Her vocal power is frightening, but something frighteningly vulnerable lives inside her as well. She sounds both born to sing and as if singing is bound to kill her. Some might say that it did. My goal from day one was to summon some of those taxations and tensions through writing.

Since I was making a whole thesis of essays on the human voice, I first thought she could be the book's Virgil. Judy could help me convey a lot of basic vocal information—a sort of laryngeal tour guide—that in turn would deliberately describe the particulars of her legendary voice. I saw these interstitial essays—little Judy cameos—standing between my longer pieces on Wilhelm Screams, war cries, Howard Dean, etc. After inhaling all the Judy content I could hunt down, I wrote a few shorts in first person, spoken in this mock-Judy, midcentury lexicon. "Hello, young lovers. Won't you follow me down my throat?" "Explore the thin mucosa of my vocal folds when I sing the vibrato in 'Get Happy'." "Do nothing—absolutely *nothing!*—until you hear from me, belting an alto-top D in the mask."

Okay, the sentences weren't that terrible, but they were close.

When the little essays flopped in workshop (of course), one member of my cohort pinpointed why in a very kind way. It isn't easy to make Judy Garland talk to a reader, he said, because her voice is often so loud in the reader's brain already. You can't easily script words for the mouth that has been singing "Over the Rainbow" to a reader since his parents had a Beta-max. I would take it further and say you can't easily put a direct *description* of that voice into a reader's ear, either. Directly discussing Judy's voice was like staring straight at the sun.

If I wanted to write an essay on Judy, I would need to find another entry point—a narrative focus on some related, but indirect subject that allowed access to the voice and persona of Judy, but did not attempt to embody them. I needed to address Judy in an indirect, peripheral way. So I saved my research and a few dozen of my least nauseating sentences in a file, hoping to come back to them when I was smarter.

Three years deeper into my voice project, a couple things happened. First, the fiftieth anniversary of Judy's Carnegie Hall comeback concert caught a bunch of media buzz. Then my friend got pregnant. When I heard her news, I trumpeted some of my recent findings on how the fetus, which didn't even have ears yet, would feel her voice as ripples in the gelatinous liquid of her womb, caused by vibrations that pulsed down her bones and converted her widening pelvis into a band shell. While my friend was merely grossed out by my totally awesome research report, something ignited in my own brain. This was the entry point I had been looking for back in Iowa City: Carnegie Hall was a figurative womb, one which Judy knew how to rock thanks to what she learned while in a literal womb back in 1922.

I decided I could articulate the tension in Judy's voice by discussing both of these types of architecture—hall and womb—and the tensions they produce in their audiences. I spent a month digging up info on the engineering of Carnegie Hall to match what I'd already learned about the sonic engineering of the womb. I forced myself through lectures on dome height, absorption coefficients, and audio-architectural compromise. And I must have listened to *Judy at Carnegie Hall* five hundred times; its playlist ended up becoming the structure of the essay.

I think my peripheral approach is why this draft is more successful than the abominable speaking for Judy that I did in the earlier versions. While my core intentions for both drafts were identical, working with those two removed-but-related topics allowed me to write in a way that sort of triangulated the Judy sound, rather than aiming right at it. In short, this was the essay that taught me sometimes it's better to approach an iconic piece of culture from the side rather than head-on.

The Bamenda Syndrome

DAVID TORREY PETERS (2009)

(Originally published in *The Best Travel Writing 2009*;
Winner, Solas Grand Prize for Travel Writing)

In mid-June of 2003, Raymond Mbe awoke on the floor of his dirt hut. A white moth had landed on his upper lip. In a half-sleep, he crushed it and the wings left traces of powder across his lips and under his nose. The powder smelled of burnt rubber and when he licked his lips, he tasted copper. Outside the hut, his eyes constricted in the sunlight. A steady dull thud, like a faraway drum, filtered through the trees. "I hate that noise," Raymond told me later. "The sound of pounding herbs with a big pestle. Every time I hear it, I know that a short time later they will stuff those herbs up my nose."

Two hours later, Raymond's nose burned as the green dust coated the inside of his nostrils. A muscular man in a white t-shirt cut off at the sleeves held Raymond's arms twisted behind his back. Across a table from Raymond, a loose-jowled old man in a worn-out fedora had measured out three piles of crushed herbs.

"Inhale the rest of it," said the old man.

"Please," Raymond pleaded, "I have cooperated today. You don't have to force me."

Deftly, the man in the sleeveless tee twisted Raymond's elbows upward, leveraging Raymond's face level with the table-top. Raymond considered blowing away the herbs. He found satisfaction in defying them, but already his arms burned with pain. He snorted up the remaining piles of green dust. From his nostrils ran herbs coated in loose snot. The piles gone, Raymond's arms were given a final yank and released.

"Oaf," Raymond muttered and wiped his face with his shirt. No one paid attention; already the old man had motioned to an androgynous creature in rags to approach him. Four other patients stood in line waiting for their turn.

In the bush that ringed the compound Raymond pretended to relieve himself. Glancing around him to make sure no one watched, he fell into a crouch and crept into the foliage. The scabs on his ankles split anew at the sudden effort. Pus seeped down onto his bare feet and he briefly remembered that he had once had a pair of basketball shoes. They had been white, with blue laces.

One hundred yards or so into the bush, he emerged onto a small path that ran in a tunnel through the foliage. Raymond stood up and began walking, brushing aside the large over-hanging leaves as he went. In places, the sun shone through the leaves, shaping a delicate lacework on the path. The tunnel dilated out onto the bright road. It had been three months since Raymond had seen the road. Under the mid-morning sun, heat shimmered off the pavement and mirages pooled in the distance. The road appeared empty.

"So, I did it. I placed a foot on the road. Very close to where I had last seen my mother. Then I walked across."

"Oh it was terrible," said the tailor who works alongside the road, "We heard him screaming and laughing down on the road. He was like an animal or something possessed. I was scared."

In June, I traveled to a village named Bawum, outside the city of Bamenda in the Anglophone Northwest Province of Cameroon, to interview a priest named Father Berndind. Bawum consisted of a single road, high in the cool grasslands, lined for a mile or so with cinderblock dwellings and the occasional open-front store. Behind the houses ran a network of dirt footpaths connecting poorer thatch-work houses built of sun-dried brick or *poto-poto*.

Berndind had launched a campaign to eradicate the practice of witchcraft from his parish. Plenty of priests wanted to do away with witchcraft; Berndind was unique because he waged his campaign from a seminary that bordered the compound of a witchdoctor. His neighbor was Pa Ayamah, a healer renowned for his ability to cure cases of insanity caused by witchcraft.

I went to Bawum with a post-graduate student named Emmanuel, a thoughtful, good-natured guy who grew up in one of the sun-dried brick houses across the road from both Ayamah and the seminary. We agreed that he would introduce me to both Berndind and Ayamah as a friend rather than a foreign research student if I paid for food and transportation.

He had written a Master's thesis on F. Scott Fitzgerald's *The Great Gatsby*. "It's funny," he said, "You come from America to study Cameroonians, and all I want to do is study Americans."

We arrived on a Saturday night. Emmanuel took me to Mass the following morning to meet Berndind. The church was bright and airy, but struck me as weirdly out of place among the green underbrush and dirt paths. It was built in a pre-fab style; the type of church that I remember having seen in lower-middle class areas of Iowa and Nebraska. On closer inspection, I saw that parts of the church had been hand-built to look pre-fabricated. Inside, I felt underdressed. I was the only man not wearing a sportcoat. In Yaoundé, fashion tended towards the sort of suits worn by comic-book super-villains; lots of bright color, wide pinstripes, and shimmery ties. From the somber colors assembled in that church, I gathered that the trend did not extend out into the provinces.

I felt better when a young man who wore a ratty blue t-shirt and taped-together flip-flops wandered in. He was short and strangely proportioned, a squat upper body rested on thin legs, like a widow's walk on Greek-revival columns. He plunked himself down in the pew in front of me. Seated, his feet barely brushed the ground. Halfway through the Mass, he craned his head around and stared at me. He pointed at my chest and whispered loudly, "Hey! I like your tie! Very shiny!"

A wave of heads spun around to appraise my clothing choice. "Um. Thank you." A few older men glowered at me and I blushed.

After the Mass, while I waited outside the church to meet with Berndind, I saw the boy walk by and slip into a thin trail that led into the bush. "What's the story with that guy?" I asked.

"Oh, that's Raymond." Emmanuel said, "Nobody pays any attention to him. He's a patient at Pa Ayamah's."

"I wasn't there," said Emmanuel's sister, "But I heard about it. They had to take him back bound at the wrists and ankles."

"Your teeth have worms in them," George Fanka told Emmanuel. We had stopped to visit Emmanuel's Aunt Eliza, before going to Bawum. "That's why they hurt. They are filled to bursting with worms."

"Worms?" Emmanuel asked.

"I am good with worms," George Fanka assured him. "I can pull worms out of pile also."

George Fanka did not fit my idea of a native doctor. He was my age and sported a Nike track suit. He styled his hair like a mid-Nineties American rapper and a cell phone hung from a cord around his neck. A few years prior, Emmanuel's Aunt Eliza had come down with a mysterious illness. She spent a good chunk of her life savings on doctors unable to give her a diagnosis before she hired George Fanka to come live with her and treat her. She was a bulky, ashen-faced woman whose frequent smiles were followed by equally frequent winces. Once too ill to stand, under Fanka's care, she had recovered enough to walk into the town center.

The night I met George and Aunt Eliza, we sat in her cinderblock living room drinking orange soda. For more than two hours George talked about his abilities as a healer. "Well, Sir," he said when conversation turned to successful treatments, "I come from a long line of doctors. It's in my blood. My uncle is a famous doctor."

"That's why he came here," Emmanuel said, nodding at his aunt. "She needed someone who could live here and George's uncle recommended him."

"Everyone in my family has the ability. There are contests you know. Yes, contests. Contests." George repeated certain words, as though his audience were intermittently hard of hearing. "All the doctors get together and we compete to see who is the best. I won a contest, you know." He talked quickly and eagerly.

He took a swig of orange soda, smacked his lips, and hurried on. "I won a contest and that's how I lost my toes. Well, only on one foot but that's how I lost them. I'm a diviner; that's what I do best."

"Wait, you lost your toes?"

"On my right foot." Abruptly, he dropped his soda bottle on the table. Emmanuel lunged forward to keep it from spilling. George didn't notice; he was already bent over in his chair, tugging off his Nikes. He gripped his sock by the toe and pulled it off with a flourish, like a waiter revealing a prized entrée.

He was right. His right foot had no toes. There was a line of angry, puckered scars where his toes had been. They looked disturbingly like anuses. Aunt Eliza said something in a flustered Pidgin to George, who was proudly inching his foot towards my face. Emmanuel moved as though he were going to intercept George's foot, but when he saw me lean in for a better look, he leaned back and asked, "Are you scared?"

"No," I said, "Just caught me by surprise."

"Yes, sir!" said George, ignoring the interruption, "My toes were burned off by lightning. After I won the contest, I was too proud—I had been playing with my abilities too much. So someone threw lightning to hit me, but it just got my foot."

George was still holding his foot high in the air, speaking from between his legs. I peered closely at his foot. "Take a good look!" George said gleefully.

A number of people in Cameroon claimed the ability to throw lightning. I had asked about the phenomenon repeatedly, but while everyone said it was possible—and some had even promised to introduce me to people who could do it—tracking down lightning-throwers seemed to be a wild goose chase. An English anthropologist named Nigel Barley had spent a year with the Dowayo tribe in Northern Cameroon asking about lightning rituals, only to find that their method of directing lightning was to place marbles imported from Taiwan in little bowls set on the mountainside. My own investigations into the phenomenon were inconclusive. My best lead, a professor at the University of Yaoundé, had suggested that lightning could be thrown by coaxing a chameleon to walk up a stick.

Nonetheless, there have been some very strange lightning strikes across Africa, many of them having to do with soccer. On October 25, 1998, 11 professional soccer players were struck by lightning in a crucial game in South Africa. Two days later, 11 Congolese soccer players were killed by a second lightning strike, this time a ground steamer. The worst lightning strike ever recorded occurred at a third soccer game in Malawi, when lightning struck a metal fence, killing five people and injuring a hundred more. The official response of African soccer officials to the lightning strikes speaks to the common interpretation of these events: they banned witchdoctors from the African Nations Cup.

I had no idea what toes burnt off by lightning might look like, but if I had to imagine, they would have looked something like the scarred puckers lined up on George's foot. I wondered if he had maybe cut his toes off himself, or lost them in an accident, but the wounds looked cauterized, like they had drawn up into themselves.

"Yes, sir," George continued from between his legs. "It might have been another jealous healer, or maybe the spirits thought I was too bold."

I asked George if he could throw lightning. He dropped his leg and cried, "Certainly not! I am a healer and a Christian." He fixed me with an offended expression and wagged his finger back and forth. "That sort of thing is not what I do. What I do is, see, hold on . . ." He grabbed an empty glass from in front of him. "I make soapy water and I tell it what a person's illness is. Then I look into the water and I can see which kind of herbs I need to find. The next day I go out into the forest and get them."

"I get headaches," I said. "Do you have something for that?"

"And my teeth hurt," Emmanuel said. George looked up my nose and at Emmanuel's teeth. I needed to sneeze more, he told me. Emmanuel, he diagnosed, had teeth full of worms. We made an appointment to return the next day for treatment.

Pa Ayamah's compound looked similar to all the other compounds that dotted the green hills of Bawum: a few huts of sun-dried brick in a clearing surrounded by dense bush. In places, the sun sparkled through the tall trees and sent shadows flitting across soil padded smooth by human feet. Even in rural Cameroon, I had expected an insane asylum to look somewhat clinical—whether or not it was run by a witchdoctor. I saw none of the usual tip-offs: no nurses, no white buildings, no corridors or wards. Only the weathered, hand-painted sign, "Pa Ayamah—Native Doctor," marked that I had found the right place.

In front of a smattering of brown huts, dusty men in chains shuffled about an open yard. Others not chained had their feet encased into makeshift stocks of rough wood. Everyone smiled at me, as if I were a regular stopping in for an evening beer at the neighborhood bar. A man with his hands tied to his belt tried to wave in greeting and nearly pulled himself over. He grinned ingratiatingly, obviously wanting me to share the joke. I managed a disoriented smile and realized that I had never before seen anybody tied up. A very old man with sunken eyes approached me and held out his hand. Without thinking, I reached to shake it, but recoiled when I saw that it was purple with infection.

"Antibiotics?" the man said hopefully.

Behind me, Raymond burst out from one of the huts, barefoot, pulling on a t-shirt as he ran. "Hey! I saw you at church!" he cried.

I turned with relief away from the old man. "Oh yeah," I said, my voice more eager than I intended, "I remember!"

"You do?" Raymond came to a stop in front of me.

"Yes. I do."

"And I remember you!"

We beamed at each other.

"What's your name?" Raymond asked.

"Dave."

"Antibiotics?" the old man said again, thrusting his purple hand towards me.

"No, no!" Raymond said loudly, leaning in towards the old man. "He's a missionary."

"What? No, I'm not."

"But you're white. And I saw you at church."

"I'm a student. I came to talk to Pa Ayamah"

"Never seen a student here," Raymond commented. "But, oh, come, I'll show you where Ayamah stays." He grabbed me by the arm and pulled me away from the old man, whose parched voice faded as I walked off. "Antibiotics?"

Raymond led me on an impromptu tour of the compound, tugging me along by my sleeve. A good portion of Ayamah's land was devoted to raising corn, planted in rows of raised dirt. Beyond the cornfields were small houses, where women related to the patients lived and prepared food. Raymond confessed that he had no relations among the women, but many of the patient's families couldn't afford both the treatment and food, so a female relative was sent to care for the patient. The few women I saw did not give me the same welcoming smiles as their relatives. I tried to say hello to a pretty girl beating laundry in a soapy bucket. She returned my greeting with a sneer, as if she had caught me attempting to watch her bathe.

Beyond the women's huts were the patients' quarters. The huts were small and dirty, each with a fire pit in front. An aging man with a barrel chest and wooly hair chased chickens with a broom. He was laughing and shrieking. When he cornered a chicken, he spit on it and clapped his hands delightedly. "That's where Pa Ayamah is," Raymond said. I followed his finger to a long building with a tin roof. "You can just go in."

"Thanks for showing me around," I said extending my hand. "It was nice of you."

Raymond shrugged and clapped me on the shoulder. He was significantly shorter than me and had to reach up to do so. "Oh, I know how it is. I used to be a student myself."

Clouds hung low in a leaden sky the morning Emmaunel and I presented ourselves at George Fanka's door for treatment. Fanka had exchanged his Nike track-suit for a red Adidas shirt and assumed a businesslike air, though his cell-phone medallion still hung from his neck. He led Emmanuel and me to a small wooden shack, consisting of two rooms, padlocked shut. The first had a bed, a small stereo, and was decorated with magazine cutouts of American popstars. A large stuffed baboon guarded the second room. "I'll sell you the monkey," George said to me.

"I couldn't get it through customs."

George shrugged and led us inside the second room. Most of the room was taken up by a large table, filled with old water bottles that contained many colored liquids. Red, brown, and green tree barks lay ground up in newspaper. I sat with Emmanuel on a bench and sniffed at the air, which smelled stale, like corridors of a natural history museum. George perused a few bottles and handed me a little bit of brown powder twisted up in cigarette cellophane. "For your headaches. It is a type of tree bark, okay? You snort a bit of that and then you will sneeze for a while and your head will clear."

I nodded. George pulled out a dirty flat head screwdriver. "Let's get rid of those worms," he said to Emmanuel. "They are in your gums." George poured a white suspension over a cotton ball and directed me to hold a piece of paper below Emmanuel's chin; from my position I had a clear view into his open mouth. I hesitated when I saw the screwdriver poised above Emmanuel's teeth, suddenly worried about tetanus. But, I reasoned, when performing oral surgery with a screwdriver, is the status of one's tetanus shot really the primary concern?

"Hold the paper steady," George chided.

Emmanuel's gums looked inflamed, the inside of his mouth very pink. George rubbed the cotton ball across Emmanuel's gums. Little white spots appeared against the pink, then what looked like whiteheads began to form in the gums between the teeth. George reached in Emmanuel's mouth. He pinched one of the whiteheads between the screwdriver and his thumbnail and began to pull. The whitehead stretched and began to pop out in segments. George grunted and forced another finger into Emmanuel's mouth. The last segment of the white-head thing popped out with a little spurt of blood. George held it up for my inspection. It was a small, white, segmented worm, squirming, and covered in blood. It was about a four or five millimeters long, and fat like a maggot.

"They die fast in the open air," he said, and dropped it onto the piece of paper I held. The worm curled up slowly and was still.

"Fuck," I said. I had watched carefully for any sleight of hand, and saw none. The worm had just appeared, a fat zit growing in stop-motion capture. I wanted to be skeptical, but the disconnect between my eyes and brain created a dead spot in my thoughts. I felt seasick. "Fuck," I said again.

"You say that a lot," said George, dropping another worm on the paper. "Uh-oh, I only got half of that one. If they die in there, they rot." Emmanuel winced. His gums bled profusely by the time George got the other half out and still the whiteheads seemed to swell of their own accord. By the time he was done, George had pulled four more worms out of Emmanuel's mouth.

A few days later, I asked Emmanuel if his teeth felt better. "I think so," he said, "but I also went to a dentist who told me the pain was from an infection. He gave me medicine for it. So I don't know if I feel better because of George or the medicine. I'm glad I covered all the options."

A prominent American biologist who visited the University of Yaoundé was skeptical of my story. He had not heard of such a worm. When I returned to the United States, I went to my university library and looked up parasitic worms. To the best collective knowledge of Western biologists, there are no segmented parasitic worms that live in human mouths anywhere in West Africa. Apparently, the worms I'd seen did not exist.

Pa Ayamah was a tall man with folds of skin hanging off his face. His eyes looked coated with oil and slipped around, as if the sockets were too big for them. He spoke no English; Emmanuel translated for us. The three of us sat in a line of rickety chairs, pushed against the far wall of a dark dirt-floored room. Ayamah sat very still, but his stillness seemed to come more from a force of energy held back, like a coiled spring waiting to be released, rather than any sense of relaxation or ease.

Ayamah began by announcing that he was of the sixth generation of healers to specialize in the mentally ill. He was the sole heir to two hundred years of practice. Ayamah spoke to Emmanuel, not me, and Emmanuel waited until Ayamah finished before he translated the words.

"He says that the knowledge will die with him," Emmanuel said. "His sons have left him to try to become businessmen in the cities."

Ayamah spoke again, sharply, and stared at the empty space in front of him when Emmanuel translated. "They will end up as market boys. He says that they have forsaken their heritage to be market boys. He finds it shameful." Ayamah wore an old fedora with a snakeskin band. He took it off after he began to speak in earnest. According to him, there were three causes of mental illness. The first was God, by which Emmanuel explained he meant fate and I understood to mean natural causes. The second reason people went crazy was because they neglected their ancestors. Finally, Ayamah said, people might go crazy because one of their enemies placed a curse upon them.

"What happens after people go crazy?" I asked. Ayamah puckered his lips and blew in exasperation. He gave a response that lasted over a minute. Emmanuel cleared his throat and gave a one word translation, "Encopresis."

"Uh, that means shit-smearing, right?"

"Yes, and they fight with it. Many things having to do with shit."

"What does he do about it?" I gave up any pretense of trying to phrase my questions in the second person. Like Ayamah, I began to speak to Emmanuel directly.

"He has someone clean it up. They can make a real mess."

"No, I meant for the treatment." Emmanuel relayed the question. Ayamah said that he didn't spend too much time trying to determine what type of insanity a patient suffered from, since he used the same method to treat all of them: he and his assistants tied them up and beat them. Eventually they became docile, and he then stuffed a special blend of herbs up their nose mornings and evenings. "He also maintains a small shrine to commune with his ancestors in the spirit world," Emmanuel explained. "And he might consult the Bible for wisdom."

"The Christian Bible?"

"Well, they translated it into the Bawum dialect," Emmanuel said.

"Yeah, but isn't it sort of a contradiction to commune with one's ancestors and then consult the Bible? You know, one God, above all others?"

Emmanuel translated the question and laughed at Ayamah's response. "He says 'What's the difference?' Jesus is just a really old ancestor of yours. If he wants really old knowledge he talks to Jesus. When he wants to talk to someone more up-to-date he consults his own ancestors."

Emmanuel waited a moment to see if I had any more objections and went on. The only modifications Ayamah made to his treatments were for those who threw their shit. He chained shit-throwers hand and foot. For everyone else, he simply took a log, drilled a hole in it, and after sticking the patient's leg through the hole, nailed in place a second length of wood to close off the hole. Ayamah assured me that it was difficult to get very far dragging a log on one foot.

"Doesn't that bother you?" I asked Emmanuel.

Emmanuel scratched at a five o'clock shadow contemplatively. "I guess it might have, but I grew up in this village. You might say that the sight of madmen in logs was part of my childhood."

Ayamah picked his nose and blew snot on the floor.

"What about Raymond?" I asked. "How come he doesn't have a log on his leg?"

Ayamah chuckled slightly when Emmanuel translated the question. His response had a lot of sound effects. At one point Ayamah acted out hitting something with his walking stick and cried, "Bam-Whacka-Bam!"

Emmanuel turned to me when Ayamah was finished. Again the translation was noticeably shorter than the story. "He said Raymond was a hard case. He never threw his shit, but he made trouble in other ways. He thought he wasn't crazy. They had to beat him to make him understand he was unwell. Once he understood, he was docile."

Joseph, the cook, agreed with all the others. "I was one of the people who brought him back. Some other men had gathered and asked me to help them. I like him. He likes the food I make. I wasn't happy to see him like that."

Whenever I try to explain the worms I saw in Emmanuel's mouth, I get stuck on that exact fact. *I saw them. I saw them come out of his gums.* After a while, I came to the conclusion that I had three ways to explain what I'd seen: I could decide that I had been deceived, I could decide that my eyes had deceived me, or, finally, I could alter my entire world view to encompass the possibility of non-existent worms residing in people's gums.

Unconsciously, I think I explored the first and third options, but consciously, I chose the second. Though the first option was probably preferable, the second option seemed more plausible. My disorientation in Cameroon felt like more than simply the result of culture shock. I had the nagging suspicion that I was experiencing things I wasn't equipped to understand. Which was more probable, I asked myself, that the world was out of whack, or that I was?

I had my erratic behavior as evidence. I acted aggressively. I fought with strangers. I went to the unrestricted pharmacies and invented pill cocktails. I felt unafraid of truculent and dangerous men. For someone who prided himself on having lived alone in foreign countries since he was young—who worked to approach other cultures on their own terms—I was suddenly, disturbingly, patriotic. Cameroon may be a rough and difficult place, but millions of people have no problem catching its rhythm and logic. My experiences elsewhere, or maybe my youth, had made me arrogant. Rather than admit to myself that I had arrived unprepared for certain experiences, I narrated my own explanations to myself. But much like a lie built upon a lie, I found myself unable to revise my stories to fit events without admitting that I knew nothing, and so instead my stories, and therefore understanding of the events around me, grew more and more fantastic.

By the time I met George, I was frequently making up the world as I went along. More to the point, I didn't know when I was doing it, and when I wasn't. Given all this, I was willing to believe that I saw worms come out of Emmanuel's teeth, and I was also willing to believe that worms did not come out of his teeth at all.

On my way home from my interview with Pa Ayamah, I came upon Raymond crouched on a log, reading a pamphlet that outlined how to set up a library in accordance with the Dewey decimal system. "Hey, the missionary!" he called out, grinning. "How's the church work?"

I took a seat next to him. He held the pamphlet up for my inspection. "I'd like to go to a library again. Now I just read about them."

"Did you used to go to libraries?"

Raymond laughed. "I wasn't always like this. I used to study economics at university. I was good at it too."

Like what? I wanted to ask. In my few encounters with him, he struck me as odd, but living in Ayamah's compound would give anyone a few quirks.

"Why did you quit?" I asked.

Raymond waved his hand airily. His wrists were too thick to make the gesture look natural; it came off as studied or affected. "My uncle. He put a curse on me." Once he started talking, the story rolled out of him. I got the sense that no one had ever asked him before; he kept skipping back and forth through his story, trying to construct it in words.

Raymond was the son of a polygamist father who died when he was six or seven. As tradition dictated, Raymond's father's brother took Raymond and his widowed mother to live with him. Raymond's uncle and his jealous wife beat and underfed him. While we talked, Raymond pulled back his lips to show me how hunger had ruined his teeth. "Worst of all," Raymond confided to me, "My uncle was an evil man. He was a member of a secret society. The only thing he was good at was witchcraft."

After finishing *lycee*, both Raymond and his uncle's son were awarded opportunities to study at the University of Buea. "My uncle was furious that I should go to the same university as his son. He kept asking me who I thought I was. But he couldn't stop me and my mother secretly gave me some money." During the school year there was not enough money for Raymond and his cousin to come home, so Raymond stayed at the university studying economics, while his cousin came home during breaks.

"What type of economics did you study?" I asked when he paused to breathe.

He furrowed his brow. "How do you mean?" he replied.

"I mean what exactly did you study economics for?"

Raymond inhaled sharply and shifted his seat next to mine so he could grasp my knee. His face was mottled with little scars, but beneath them the skin was unlined. The whites of his eyes were completely clear, remarkable, given the dust and dirt on the path. "Oh, you know," he said in an off-hand tone. "Lots of different things."

Abruptly, Raymond lifted his head and looked off towards the tops of the trees. "Do you smell something burning?" he asked.

I sniffed the air. "No. I don't smell anything."

Raymond shrugged and continued his story. After months without seeing his family, Raymond's uncle called him home just before exam period. When Raymond left, his uncle gave him ten thousand francs. His uncle had never done anything like that before. Raymond later found significance in the action. "The money was cursed." At this point in his story, Raymond stood and began to wave his hands, acting out his words. His crisp accent contrasted remarkably with his torn blue t-shirt and the caked dirt on his legs and pants.

Raymond returned to school in time to begin cramming for exams. Although he felt he had much work to do, his thoughts kept on focusing on the ten-thousand franc note he had stashed away in his economics textbook. "It was calling to me. Like a beautiful prostitute. Something you know is wrong, but attracts you so much." Twenty or thirty times in a day he would stop what he was doing and check to see if the money was still there.

"It got very bad," Raymond said, his voice almost pleading. "This obsession with the money. I was studying all day for the exams, but I was thinking about the money. The night before the exams, I got sick. It was like a fever, and my chest was tight. I was sweating and moaning and I put the text book with the money in it in my bed."

"The experience you describe kind of sounds like an anxiety attack," I interjected. "Maybe you were stressed over exams."

Raymond rolled his eyes, and dismissed my suggestion. "This," he said slowly, "was not an anxiety attack. I was afraid to trust anyone. It was terrible. I locked myself in my room and held the book with the money in it to my chest. I was like that for twenty-four hours; I missed my exams. Finally it was too much. I took the ten thousand francs and went to the market to buy medicine. But instead of medicine, I asked for poison."

"They sell poison in the markets?" I had never seen any, but then, I hadn't looked.

"For animals. But they wouldn't sell me poison, so I tried to buy Valium to take an overdose, but I was wild and out of control, so they wouldn't sell me any."

"If you could spend the money on Valium, why didn't you just buy a shirt or a radio or something to get rid of it?"

Raymond shook his head impatiently, his wide-set eyes bulging. "Don't you see? They controlled me! I couldn't spend the money on anything but poison! Why of all the ways to kill myself did I try to use the money to buy poison? The money made me do it!"

Raymond noticed he was shouting, lowered his arms slightly, and gave me a weak smile. "Sorry, I forget myself sometimes. Not exactly a smart thing for madman to do."

I shrugged. "Go on."

"I went home in a rage and pulled down the light from the ceiling of my room and tore it open." He forgot his fear of yelling and began to act out tearing apart a light with flailing arm gestures. "And I took it so there were two wires, full of electricity, and I grabbed one with each hand so the electricity could flow through me and cure me of the fever." It was quiet on the path; I could hear the whir of grasshoppers and the gurgle of a nearby stream. Against those noises Raymond's long toenails scraped the bare dirt while he stood in front of me. His arms grasped imaginary wires and his body writhed while muted screams escaped through clenched teeth as he pantomimed his suicide attempt. It lasted long enough for me to grow frightened. Just as I was about to say something, his body dropped motionless on the dirt.

"He was shouting about being on the road." The sun-blackened man whose job seemed to be to remain ever-seated on the lawn chair in front of the tailor's shop agreed with everyone else. "So what? I'm down on the road everyday. It's nothing to get so excited about." He took a pull on his cigarette and nodded sagely at his own words.

By American standards, most foreigners I met who were living in Cameroon behaved bizarrely. Every expat I met had his or her quirks; some of the Peace Corps volunteers were downright zany. A volunteer named John, who had lived in the desert for a year and a half without running water, electricity, or a telephone, had, after a few beers at bar in the Hilton hotel, repeatedly called room service demanding to know why they kept calling him.

In Yaoundé, I met a group of wealthy expatriates who had set up something of a European infrastructure and society nestled subtly within the world of Cameroonians. That wealthy, European bubble was not one that was particularly easy for me to find, and I was happy to have gained their acceptance. They were the twenty-something offspring of diplomats and exporters and they lived a lifestyle that struck me as quite glamorous at the time. Plus, they seemed taken by me; I was new, strange, and for short periods, I had enough money to keep up with them.

It ended when I forgot which person to be with them. One night they took me to a club, some fancy club, where I was ripped off on the entrance fee. Inside, I went to the bar and ordered myself a beer. I asked the barman if he had change for a five thousand. He said he did. He took my money and brought me a tiny beer.

"And my change?" I asked.

There is none.

I decided to be friendly, "Look man, you can keep two thousand of it as a tip if you want, but there is no way a beer is five thousand francs. I pay two hundred at the bar by my house."

"This isn't the bar by your house."

"Just give me the money."

The barman didn't say anything more. He simply nodded to a large Frenchman who had a whore hanging off of each arm. He shrugged off one of the whores and grabbed me by the chin. He yelled something in my ear in slurred French. I told him I didn't understand what he said. I understood him the second time, when he told me to fuck off and slapped my cheek Godfather-style.

I got angry then, and forgot where I was. I forgot that I was a twenty-one-year-old middle-class American boy, who was very far from home. I forgot that a flashy nightclub in an expatriate inter city was not my turf. I forgot that I have not been in a real fight since fourth grade and I forgot that any large Frenchman who has two whores and slaps my cheek like the Godfather is someone not to be fucked with. Instead, I swelled with the sort of self-righteous pride that you find among students at small liberal-arts schools in the United States. Places where things are fair, prices are marked, and some cheesy-looking French Mafioso-wannabe is an abstraction of the movies.

Who the fuck does this mustachioed and obvious low-life exploiter of the African people think he is?

I bitch-slapped him.

The music was loud enough that only a few people heard it. There was a moment where no one moved, not me, not the whores, not the French guy. Then I remembered where I was. With as much dignity as possible I turned my back and walked out of the club. Behind me, the Frenchman was organizing a group of large men. Once outside, I got in the first taxi I saw.

My girlfriend was at the club. She was very confused by my disappearance. I called her on her cell phone and told her what I had done.

She paused a moment, then said, "But a beer here *is* five thousand francs."

Raymond awoke in a hospital, his burned hands fastened to the side of the bed. He had been examined while unconscious. A foreign doctor, an Arab, Raymond thought, had found evidence of possible brain anomalies and ordered a few basic tests to be conducted at the provincial hospital. The doctor concluded, though, that Raymond was most likely suffering from something like anxiety or depression. Raymond felt otherwise. The pieces fit together easily in his mind. His illness was caused by witchcraft on the part of his uncle, most likely with the help of a secret society and most likely with the help of other members of his family. Why else was he suddenly called home? Why else the sudden gift of ten thousand francs, from a man who had never before given him anything? His uncle had given him a gift of bewitched money.

Raymond's conjecture wasn't implausible. Although I found it hard to draw the same initial conclusion as he did, the description of his relationship with his uncle and his uncle's actions follows an almost classic model of bewitchment. Accusations of witchcraft most often occur within families, or at least along some form of kinship lines. Witches and the bewitched nearly always know each other. If Raymond suspected his illness was caused by witchcraft, he would look to the person who hated him most: his uncle. With a little knowledge of witchcraft, the seemingly innocuous gift of money becomes more suspicious as well. While traveling around Cameroon, I found that while I could not leave any of my belongings lying around because they inevitably would be stolen, loose cash left in plain sight was never touched. In the town of Kribi, a group of children went into hysterics when I picked a hundred-franc coin off the beach. The instant I touched the coin, the children screamed "No! Drop it! Drop it! Mami Water, she'll get you! Mami Water! Mami Water!" The youngest of them were nearly in tears. In Kribi, no one touched lost money because of the belief that Mami Water—a mutation of the mermaid myth—used money to entice men into the ocean to drown.

The story varied place to place, but the theme was the same: Don't take money from enemies or strangers. Cash is the perfect medium for sorcery.

Although Raymond remained distrustful of his uncle, he nonetheless left the hospital with him. His uncle remained silent, while his mother pressed his hand and told him that they had borrowed a car and arranged to bring him to Yaoundé where he could be given modern medical treatment. Instead, they drove west, into the grassland regions along the Ring Road. In the village of Bawum, they parked the car on the path that led to Pa Ayamah's compound.

"My uncle got out of the car and walked away. He came back with two men, who opened my car door and pulled me out. I was so shocked I didn't do anything. I fell out of the car and they began to beat me while my uncle and my mother watched. I cried out for my mother to help me, but she kept repeating, 'These men are going to help you.' Then my uncle stood between us. I cried her name many times as they beat me and I began to bleed." Raymond inhaled audibly and pulled at his ear. "My mother began to ask if it wasn't enough, but my uncle pushed her into the car and they drove away."

Almost an hour had passed since I had sat down next to Raymond on the path. We were both sweating in the heat. He lifted the bottom of his t-shirt to wipe his sweat away, leaving trails of dark blue in the light blue fabric.

"They had me chained to a post the first two months," Raymond said, and picked at a stray thread on his shirt. "At first I tried to reason with them. I yelled for days about the rights of man and how it was not right to treat me as they did."

"Were you speaking in English?" I asked.

"Yes, some Pidgin, but mostly English. I don't speak quite the same dialect as they speak here. It's really kind of funny, because I was trying so hard to reason with them, but I was talking about the rights of man, you know, *Liberte, Egalite, and Fraternite*, which must have sounded like complete nonsense. It's no wonder everyone thought I was crazy. A total madman!" Raymond laughed at the memory, but the sound came out dry and mirthless.

By midway through my stay, I had so convinced myself that I was unbalanced, that it took me a while to notice when other people were acting more absurd than I. In a crowded market, I had been pulled out of a taxi by a gendarme with the disgruntled, bovine face of a cop who once had a desk job. He demanded my passport and vaccination records. I produced them and he scowled at the vaccination card. "Your records are not in order," he declared. He blew his whistle and told the taxi driver to move along. The taxi man said he would wait for his fare.

"What is the problem with my records?"

"Are you contradicting me?"

I reviewed what I had just said in my mind, wondering if I had accidentally misused the French words. "No," I said. "I am not contradicting you."

"Good." He squared his shoulders and adjusted his gun belt. Three other gendarmes, brandishing automatic rifles, appeared behind him. They couldn't resist a white kid in a taxi. Tourists hemorrhaged cash at the sight of a couple of Uzis. I sighed and asked what could be done to "remedy" the problem.

"You're missing a vaccination," he said.

"Which one?" I asked.

"You don't have an AIDS vaccine."

"What?"

"You need to have an AIDS vaccine. You don't have an AIDS vaccine."

"There is no AIDS vaccine."

"What?"

"I said, there is no AIDS vaccine."

He blinked and turned to one of the other gendarmes. "This guy, where does he come from? He says there is no AIDS vaccine." He guffawed loudly, the other gendarmes coughed out half-hearted laughs.

I stepped towards him. "Look, I'm telling you there is no AIDS vaccine."

He laughed. "Oh yeah, then how come so many people are sick?"

My words came out soaked in condescension, despite myself. "Well, vaccines cure sicknesses. If there was an AIDS vaccine those people wouldn't be sick. What you have here in Cameroon is an epidemic, something that happens when there is no vaccine."

A small crowd had gathered around as soon as I was pulled out of the taxi. It must have been an interesting scene: an angry white boy who sneered out broken French at four gendarmes who patted their guns like puppies.

The cop tried a new tact. "You think just because there isn't an AIDS vaccine I can't arrest you for not having one?"

I was mad then, and didn't bother to control myself. "What's it going to take for you to leave me alone?"

"You're under arrest."

"For what? Not having an imaginary vaccine?"

The growing crowd cackled with pleasure. A young man made a joke about being framed for a crime against his imaginary friend. "But I swear, I wasn't anywhere near that imaginary car crash!"

One of the other gendarmes told him to shut up, but couldn't totally repress a smile.

The bovine-faced cop was less amused. He put my passport in his pocket and reached for his handcuffs. "You're under arrest."

I pulled out my cell phone and told him I was dialing the embassy. The cop hesitated. The crowd hooted in surprise. It was a new trick for them; they didn't have an embassy to call.

"You lack respect!" the cop screamed.

"On the contrary, I have only used the *vouz* form, where you call me *tu*."

An Anglophone who corrected his French was the final straw. Exasperated, he threw my papers back in my face and told me I was too clever for my own good. This was apparently an insult powerful enough to redeem him. With renewed swagger he turned to berate the assembled crowd.

The taxi-man clapped me on the shoulder as we drove away. "Hey, you argue like a Cameroonian," he said. "I planned to overcharge you, but forget it now."

After months of striving to fit in, I had only to mock a half-witted policeman in order to be accepted.

Raymond squinted at the sun. "I think I will go get a snack."

"What are you having?"

"It's mango season. Mangos."

I walked with Raymond to the center of the compound, where he had left a plastic bag of mangos. The fruit was everywhere; at night the falling fruit thumped in the forest like giant raindrops. We sat against a plank across from a schoolroom chalkboard posted under an overhang.

RULES

1. Take medicine at 9:00 and 5:00.
2. Clean personal space.
3. No fighting.
4. Bathe twice a week.
5. Attend nightly prayers.
6. No crossing the stream.
7. No crossing the road.

The letters were written in a shaky hand, and it looked like there had once been nine rules, but the last two, too low to be shielded from rain by the overhang, had washed away. "Can I take a picture of that?" I asked, pulling a little point-and-click from my pocket.

Raymond looked eagerly at the camera. "I've never taken a picture before."

I gave the camera to him and showed him how to zoom in and out. "Can you take a picture of those rules?" He stood up and carefully lined up the shot, trying different angles. Behind him, a large man carrying a load of wood walked around the corner. His hair was cut in a flat-top, and his t-shirt sleeves had been torn off to reveal arms that looked like they had been drawn by a comic book artist. In a single fluid motion, he dropped the firewood, caught one of the falling sticks and flung it at Raymond. The stick flashed past Raymond's ear as the shutter clicked. With a roar the man was upon us, towering over me and dwarfing Raymond. Raymond smiled benignly and lowered the camera. There was a quick exchange in Pidgin and Raymond handed me back the camera. The man fixed me in a hard squint, and I, in an attempt to look away, ended up reading his t-shirt, which advertised a music festival. "That is a madman!" he growled. "You don't give him your things." I didn't say anything. He backed away with a menacing finger pointed at Raymond and I stayed quiet while he gathered his firewood and stalked past us.

Raymond switched back to English and said in a steady voice. "He is one of the men whose task is to beat and control us. He doesn't want me talking to you."

"Why not?"

"Because I am a madman, of course. Just as he said." Raymond picked at the gaps between his teeth during the silence that followed. I couldn't tell if he was serious. He may have been a bit odd, and perhaps he talked in church and wouldn't explain what he knew of economics—but in the time I knew him, he was always lucid. In fact, he was the most friendly, forthcoming, and sensible person I had met in days.

"Okay," I said finally. "But you don't really seem like a madman. Forgive me for saying so, but mostly you just seem unlucky."

Raymond held out an empty hand and a sour look crossed his face. "As I told you, I am a simple man. It was my uncle's witchcraft that drove me insane. The madness is there, even if it doesn't show. Not to you. Not to me. But it is there."

I put the camera back in my pocket. "People write books about that, you know. The insane are insane because they don't know that they are insane. By that logic, I would say your belief in your own madness proves you are fine."

Raymond sighed and spat on the ground. In the sunlight, his scalp shone through his hair. "That's a fun word game," he said at last. "But some of us in places like this require more than that. We must prove our insanity to ourselves."

"How could you possibly have done that?" I cut in.

Raymond pointed at the chalkboard. "Do you see rule number 7?"

"Yeah. Don't cross the road."

Raymond turned and pointed in the direction of the road. "You might think that Pa Ayamah has that rule to keep us from wandering through town. That's not it. Pa Ayamah says that this area is protected. Out on the road, we are exposed once more to the demons that cause our madness. If we cross the road, we go mad again."

Raymond tapped his head. "A few days before you arrived, I went and tested his rules. I'm a madman all right."

After the AIDS vaccine incident, I wrote an e-mail that described the event to my professors in the United States. It was meant to be humorous, but apparently taunting armed police just doesn't strike the same funny chord in the States. I got a call from my Journalism professor shortly afterwards. Rather than saying outright that he felt worried, he told me about two psychological syndromes.

The first was the Florence Syndrome. It is a condition that affects young people—usually artists—when they travel to Florence, Italy. Suddenly they find themselves inside a world that they had only seen in books. All their lives, they studied art printed on a page or projected from a slide. But in Florence, there is no book to close, no switch to kill the projector. They overdose on art. Their brains overload and they lose perspective. The art becomes an obsession, an addiction, as crippling as any drug, and the importance of their lives before Florence slowly fades.

The Jerusalem Syndrome is more serious, and religious, rather than artistic, in nature. People from a culture like America's—only two hundred years old—go to Jerusalem and find themselves inside of *history*. Scraps of the Bible, or the Torah, or the Koran, are made tangible before their eyes. They have no chance to close the Bible and decompress, instead the Bible is all around them, they are inside the Bible. A man with the Jerusalem Syndrome finds himself at the end of the long road of religious history, the course of which traces its path all the way to *him*. And what must it mean that all that is holy and recorded leads to the moment of his arrival in Jerusalem? Simple, he is the Messiah.

While my professor talked, I thought of the spring leaves outside his office in Massachusetts and contrasted it with the bare dirt and open sewers I saw from the balcony. Was he really paying five dollars a minute to tell me these stories?

"Let's talk about this other pattern I've noticed," he continued. "Lots of young people go to Africa. But they all go through programs and organizations. They have a safety net, Peace Corps, NGOs . . . but when they cut themselves loose, they change. They become disillusioned, they get mad, they take on Africa single-handedly." My professor paused; I heard static. "They pick fights with men carrying guns. Any of this sound familiar?"

"I see what you're getting at," I said into the mouthpiece, "but tell me, does this particular syndrome have a name?"

His laugh sounded dry across the line. "Not that I know of. But in your honor, we'll just call it the Yaoundé Syndrome. Take care."

"A moth that tastes like copper?" The eminent biologist frowned.

"That's what he told me."

"I really don't know about that. But hey, maybe he was he having a seizure when he ate it. Epileptics taste copper and smell burning rubber before seizures. The Epileptic Aura." The eminent biologist's belly shook with a chuckle.

Raymond stood on the far side of the road and waited to go insane. Nothing happened, and it wasn't long before it was clear that nothing was going to happen. It was all bullshit, the rules weren't worth anything. He was fine.

"Please," Raymond shouted to the empty road, "I have crossed the road and nothing happened. What's more, I will cross it again!" He was almost hysterical with laughter as he sprinted back across the road. Three months of beatings had almost convinced him. He remembered how seriously he had begun to take Ayamah's mumbo jumbo and hooted at the thought.

"I felt like celebrating. It felt wonderful to be so free," he told me later. "It was a wonderful celebration. I knew at that moment that I was cured. Probably there was nothing wrong with me in the first place."

Four times he crossed the road. Each time he proclaimed his accomplishment to the uncaring trees and dusty rocks. Then it was ten times. His voice was hoarse with laughter and he barely had enough breath to keep it coming. Standing in the middle of the road, he raised his hands heavenwards and shouted, "I am free to cross the road. Free to cross the road!"

Just beyond the far side of the road, a stream ran fast and clear over brown pebbles. A young girl had been wading in the water, her red dress turned dark at the hem. Frightened by the shouting, she ran to the nearby cooking shack where her mother was pounding huckleberries. The mother wiped her hands on a rag blackened by kitchen smoke and told her daughter to go inside. Outside, the sound of shouting carried across tree tops. On top of a bridge made of split logs, a group of villagers all faced the same direction. The mother followed their gaze. A young man skipped and laughed as he crossed and re-crossed the road, proclaiming his accomplishment each time. The women clucked their tongues in dismay, while the men discussed how to subdue him. How sad that so promising a youth could be so hopelessly and so obviously insane.

FROM THE AUTHOR

"The Bamenda Syndrome" began as a ten-page essay in which I simply re-counted my meeting with Raymond and the story he told me. Other than interspersing a few details about Bawum, I wrote an essay that was chrono-logical, straightforward, and clinical. Yet I have never used any of those adjectives to describe my experiences conducting research in Bawum. In-stead I have used words like disorienting, uncomfortable, and faux pas-inducing.

The first version of that essay presented incidents that I had barely grasped as correct and complete. To avoid over-reaching, I had pared down my writing to simple descriptions of events and people. But even that skeletal version read as somewhat false—as though I were some de-tached journalist with complete faith in his own ability to collect the who, what, when, where, and why with calm professionalism.

The falseness lay in how the narrator presented himself: he seemed totally reliable. Whereas an accurate depiction of my experiences in Bawum would show how unreliable my take on those events might have been. Un-fortunately, that proposition raised a second, more technical problem: How, in nonfiction, do you deploy an unreliable "narrator," while still main-taining some level of credibility for the "author"?

Shortly after writing that first draft, a professor pointed me towards the work of James Clifford, a historian who roiled the field of cultural anthro-pology when he began to criticize ethnographies in the same manner as scholars had traditionally criticized literature. When anthropology was read as literature, the biases and subjective opinions of the narrators be-came obvious. In the same way that Humbert Humbert betrays himself through his language in *Lolita*, Clifford found that anthropologists tended to disclose their opinions and positions even as they attempted to record dispassionate works of social science.

In response, the field of anthropology went through a period of soul-searching. A number of anthropologists wrote reflexive ethnographies in which they made clear, up front, how confused and lonely they felt among cultural norms and practices alien to them; how their own prejudices and subjective notions frequently kept them from grasping motivations or rea-sons for what was going on around them; and finally, how, rather than pre-tending to be emotionless recorders, they often best connected with their informants through empathy, care, and love.

After some initial resistance, peer-reviewed anthropology journals began publishing ethnographies replete with doubt. But the authors' doubts did not diminish them as scholars or as experts. Instead, careful proclamations of doubt and emotion became standardized within the field. Anthropologists accepted reflexivity as a methodology and incorporated it as a necessary part of fieldwork.

That's the kind of doubt I wanted in my essay: incisive, specific, and involved. But when I tried to insert my doubts into my essay according to an ethnographic method, the story grew leaden and lethargic.

At the same time that I was reading anthropological texts, a professor in a nonfiction class had us read the introduction to John McPhee's first collection. In that introduction, and in a series of subsequent *New Yorker* articles, McPhee famously detailed his system for structuring nonfiction. He wrote short scenes and bits of research on notecards. Afterwards, he tagged the notecards according to themes and characters and began to arrange them until he found a narrative structure that he could stitch together with minimal transitions.

Inspired by this, I printed out my Raymond essay, physically scissored it into short scenes, and color-coded it according to themes and ideas, using a set of Crayola markers borrowed from my neighbor's daughter. With the essay shredded into little bits, I found it easy to detect its themes: insanity, youth, religion, sickness, cultural relativism, collective consciousness, and money. I then went back to my notes and research, and pulled out observations and moments that seemed to fit the themes I had highlighted. I unearthed a treasure trove buried among my past e-mails, missives in which I'd written of doubts and mishaps to friends and family much more honestly than in my notes, where I still played the part of journalist, even for myself.

I printed the e-mails too, cut them up, and colored them with Crayola. Paying attention to the colors, rather than the text, I began to arrange them visually, and suddenly certain resonances between me and Raymond resolved themselves. The empathy I had wanted on an anthropological level took shape on a structural level, as I arranged the slips of paper so that Raymond's mishaps mirrored my own. For instance, just after Emmanuel announces that Raymond is a reluctant patient at Pa Ayamah's, I cut to a scene of myself as a reluctant patient of George Fanka's. I recklessly slap a French man, and Raymond awakes in a hospital. In other places, where the oscillating transitions between me and Raymond didn't occur so neatly, I could insert other voices, or moments of exposition that had previously seemed out of place in the narrative. Even better, the more intricate structuring gave the impression that, while the narrator might appear unreliable, the intentions of the author were not—a distinction that solved my technical dilemma.

I awoke the morning after that Crayola frenzy with the realization that the essay that had stymied me for more than a year—two, if you include re-search—had actually all been written months before. Just out of order and across multiple texts. But that morning, it hung in more or less its finished sequence, tacked to my wall on scribbled-upon colored slips.

Over the following week, I smoothed out the e-mails and notes so that they read as scenes, and wrote a few transitions. Then I waited six years for someone to want to publish it—probably the most crazy-making part of it all.

High Maintenance

JOHN T. PRICE (1997)

(Originally published in *Orion*, reprinted in
Man Killed by Pheasant and Other Kinships)

I encountered the first illegal pet during a routine visit to fix a dripping faucet. Of course, this being my first plumbing job as maintenance man for OK Apartments, it was anything but routine. The owners of the animal, college students like myself, had called that morning to report the leak and I'd spent the entire day preparing. I took notes from my five recently acquired fix-it books, bought additional tools, and chewed my fingernails into haggard, bloody nubs. It wasn't enough. When the fluffy blond tabby sauntered into their bathroom, I'd been working on the sink for over two hours, its grimy black parts scattered on the linoleum. To make matters worse, in order to disassemble this one faucet I'd had to cut off the water supply to half the complex. Unable to take a shower for their Friday dates or even flush their toilets, tenants were angrily calling Steph, who kept coming over to ask when I might be finished. On her fourth visit I was seriously tempted (for the first and only time in our marriage) to tell her to shut up and get me a beer.

After another half hour of futility, I stomped into the living room and called the previous maintenance man, Ted, on his cell phone. He said he'd be there in an hour. I broke the news of the delay to the tenants—two huge, football-player types wearing soaked Hawkeye muscle shirts, one gold, the other gray. They'd just returned from the gym, sweat trickling off their prominent biceps and foreheads, and were probably desperate for a shower. I expected to get punched. Instead, they offered me the much-desired beer. As I took a long swig, they looked at each other, then lowered their heads.

"Are you going to tell the landlord about Ditka?" Gold finally asked, pointing at the cat rubbing against my ankles. He appeared to be on the verge of tears. "We don't have anywhere else to take him, except back to the shelter."

I should've seen it coming. During my interview for this job, Jerry, the co-owner of the apartment complex, had explained that my responsibilities included keeping an eye out for pets, a violation of the lease agreement. I was an unlikely candidate for any job that required fixing things—I'd only recently learned that cars require regular oil changes—but I'd been desperate. Steph and I were about to be married and we'd spent months trying to find an affordable apartment. Luckily, Jerry—an attractive man in his fifties, very white teeth—didn't test my mechanical knowledge. Instead, he asked me about my parents (he knew people in Fort Dodge, Iowa) and was especially interested in our latest family dog, a Brittany spaniel. Jerry had a couple of Brittanys himself, he said. At the end of our conversation, to my surprise, he handed me the contract. For half off our rent, I would handle all maintenance duties for the twenty-four units in the complex. He added that if I needed any help, I could call Ted, my predecessor. Ted had resigned to dedicate more time to his mobile engine repair business, "Doctor Highway," but would still be living in the complex with his wife, Janet, who collected the rent, and their teenage daughter. Jerry emphasized, however, that I was to report all major maintenance issues, as well as any illegal pets, directly to him. We shook hands on it.

Now here I was, newly married and three hours into my first plumbing job, waiting for Ted to come to the rescue and being asked to decide the fate of someone's cat. I looked at the yellow beast, still rubbing against my shoe. I wasn't a fan of cats—I'd been bitten by one as a child—but at the moment, Ditka was probably the only resident of the complex that didn't want to kill me.

"No, I won't tell the landlord. Just try to keep him out of sight."

"Oh!" they exclaimed, massive shoulders slumping. *"Thank you."*

Actually, the hulks in Apartment 12 weren't the only tenants harboring an illegal pet. We had an eastern box turtle named Methuselah whom Steph had purchased when she first moved to Iowa, claiming she needed another boyfriend in case it didn't work out with me. We refused to give him away when we moved to OK Apartments after our wedding—we'd miss his pulsating throat, his affectionate hiss, his ancient soul. We adored him. Plus his behavior wasn't likely to betray us to the authorities. Inside the apartment, he'd disappear for days and then, like a good fugitive, sneak out from beneath the couch or refrigerator to demand we hand-feed him smoked turkey, meal worms, and grapes.

Methuselah might have been my role model during my early weeks as maintenance man, as I tried to hide from the other tenants. I lived in fear of the next knock on the door, the next invitation to fail to fix something, the next chance to provoke the wrath of the community. Sometimes, when the phone rang in the early morning, I'd pull the covers over my head and stay there for hours.

It may have been under those covers that I began to recall the happier times I'd spent at Deluca Dwellings, a dumpy foursquare where I'd rented a room starting in my junior year and on into graduate school. It was owned and operated by Clarence C. Deluca, a bald, elderly man who always dressed in the same olive coveralls, zipped too tight at the crotch. During my initial week as a resident of Deluca Dwellings, I received the first of many news-letters Clarence would deliver to me and the other twelve people living in the house. "To the New Lessee," it began, "I say: Welcome to your New Home-Away-From-Home."

If you are a fan of Astrology, you may take pleasure in the fact that I am a typical Arien. Also, it will not be difficult for you to believe that I will be energetic, enthusiastic and steadfast in my pursuit to be your ideal land-lord: not easily discouraged by temporary setbacks; enjoy the challenges of over coming obstacles; like things to be done quickly; whole approach to life is youthful and optimistic; generally gets along with all kinds of people.

YOU, and each of you, are a select person in the strictest meaning of the word. The Landlord is very proud of you and have literally set you upon a pedestal! Therefore, the landlord expects you to be exemplary as tenant in compliance with Agreements including a Clean Dwelling AND the main-tenance of your Good Reputation. Enjoy Your Home-Away-From-Home To The Maximum; However, In This Pursuit, Remember That Your Liberty Ex-tends To The Point Of Non-Infringement Upon The Rights Of Others.

QUOTES OF THE MONTH:

Douglas Jerrold: The character that needs law to mend it, is hardly worth the tinkering.

Samuel Smiles: To be worth anything, character must be capable of standing firm upon its feet in the world of daily work, temptation, and trial; and able to bear the wear and tear of actual life. Cloistered virtues do not count for much.

Clarence C. Deluca: Be mindful of other people; and the purity of ones character will manifest itself generously, if one is truly well-meaning.

At first, I found Mr. Deluca's high-minded enthusiasm to be infectious. I was in the process of switching from Pre-Medicine to a Religion major, and was in a high-minded mood myself. In addition, the other occupants of the house were the kind of people who, like me, had moved there out of a hard-earned desire for privacy—mostly humanities majors, foreign students, and ex-cons. They made very few social demands, so there was plenty of time to maintain my dwelling and my good reputation. This was publicly acknowledged in Deluca Dwellings Newsletter, Volume 8, No.4, Sept. 1, 1986:

UP-AND-COMING-STAR: John Price (3–2)—He has demonstrated himself Worthy of his High Character Recommendations and the Trust and Pride of your Landlord by applying a brand new coat of paint to his room and by producing a sparkling Bathroom during his first few months as a resident. Keep Up The Good Work!

QUOTE OF THE MONTH:

Colton: No man can purchase his virtue too dear, for it is the only thing whose value must ever increase with the price it has cost us. Our integrity is never worth so much as when we have parted with our all to keep it.

Then I got a pet mouse. I can't recall why I purchased him—pets were strictly forbidden at Deluca's. Perhaps it was because my girlfriend had just dumped me or because the consequences of giving up a medical career (again, the girlfriend) had begun to finally hit home. Or perhaps it was the way he appeared at the pet store, the only black mouse crowded in with dozens of whites and browns, all waiting to serve as lunch for someone's boa constrictor.

Whatever the reasons, I brought him home and named him Ernest T. Bass after the mischievous hillbilly on *The Andy Griffith Show*. During the first week, Ernest repeatedly escaped from his cage and, like his TV namesake, thwarted all efforts to contain him. I finally bought him one of those plastic free-rolling hamster spheres, but then, one evening, he rolled out my door and bounced down two flights of stairs. I caught up in time to see him roll into Kurt's room. I stood in the doorway, panicked that this stranger would report my pet to Clarence. Kurt picked the sphere off the floor and grinned at Ernest, who stared back, apparently unfazed by the strange face or the two flights of stairs. During the ensuing conversation, I learned that Kurt was a graduate student in the creative writing program. He was the first serious writer I'd ever met, and the close friendship that developed was one of the reasons I would become a writer myself. All because of a wayward mouse.

Ernest soon became the house mascot, roaming the halls in his sphere, entering other rooms, and introducing me to more people than I would ever have approached on my own. As a vibrant, sometimes rowdy social life blossomed at Deluca Dwellings, we had less time for maintaining the bathroom on our floor, and its condition rapidly declined. We weren't the only ones who noticed. Despite Clarence's Arien optimism, his newsletters became increasingly despondent, culminating in Volume 8, No.9, April 2, 1987:

EXPOSE!

Landlord Denounces And Labels Four Residents As Bad Tenants: Namely:

JANE PILLHOUSE JOHN PRICE TRAVIS KING AND LING YEOK CHONG

By definition, bad means: failing to reach an acceptable standard. FACT: The Bad Tenants named above failed to meet the Clean Bathroom standard during the "Mandatory Clean Bathroom Days" of March 15th and 29th, 1987.

Disclaimer: The intent of the Expose is not to slander the persons named (for by definition, the truth and slander are incongruent), but to use a reasonable means, namely: Embarrassment (a state of self-conscious distress), within the limited confines of this Dwelling Family, in an attempt to correct a Health Hazard.

The Landlord hopes that this "public" revelation has done its intended job well; that a wise attitude of course of action subsequently will reflect intelligence commensurate with their chronological age and apparent educational status; that the 4-Bad Tenants are not incorrigible and will recall and heed the good home training taught by their parents; that the Characteristic which carries the label "BAD" shall be discarded for the label "GOOD".

Two adages are worth repeating here: "Character Will Out" AND "Time Will Tell."

The Landlord hereby makes apology to all except the 4-Bad Tenants for terminating the letter at this point. The frustration and depression which has resulted in the writing of this report consumed all the energy and enthusiasm which is usually devoted to an "up-beat" communication . . .

QUOTE OF THE MONTH:

Aeschines: He who acts wickedly in private life, can never be expected to show himself noble in public conduct; he that is base at home will not acquit himself with honor abroad; for it is not the man, but only the place that is changed.

In addition to being distributed to every resident of the house, the letter was sent to parents and to those who'd written recommendations, among them our bosses, professors, and spiritual mentors.

"He sent this to Reverend Hearn, for godssakes!" my mother shouted into the phone. "He makes it sound like you all crap in the bathtub— *What's going on over there?*"

In response to this humiliation, my floormates and I cranked our favorite Smiths song—"Sweet and Tender Hooligan"—and spent the afternoon scrubbing porcelain, pausing only to drink more beer or pay homage to Ernest, who directed us from his cage on the back of the toilet. In a generous spirit, we even cleaned the bathrooms on the other floors, helping Kurt overcome his orange-streaked, mildewy shower stall. A month later, to my mother's relief, we were publicly exonerated in the *Deluca Dwelling Newsletter*:

YES, a single happening! And that's all it takes sometimes to make or break one for life: remember Wallace?, Agnue?, Nixon? And Hart? This single accomplishment (Bathroom Cleaning) may be construed "virtuous" (demonstrating "a commendable quality" and "conformity to a standard of what is right and good"). For anyone who may be struggling and are now vindicated, your Landlord suggests that you "exercise" your integrity (however small and weak). Consequently, if you are truly one of goodwill (predisposed to conform to sanctioned codes or accepted notions of right and wrong,) your Character shall "grow" and become "strong".

My floormates and I celebrated by filling the bathtub with ice, purchasing a pony keg, and throwing a house party. All night, amidst the revelry and dancing legs, the guest of honor rolled in his plastic sphere.

Ernest lived another year or so before dying peacefully in his sleep. When I told my neighbors, there was general sadness—we had lost one of our own. At a sunset funeral in the front yard, Kurt read a poem while others tossed violets and small bundles of seed into the grave. I remained close to several of them, including Kurt, who took off for Los Angeles to become a screenwriter. A few years later, he was murdered in an attempt to steal his car. The last time I saw him, during one of his brief visits from

California, we sat in our favorite bar reminiscing about Deluca Dwellings and about Ernest. We lifted our glasses to the memory of a lost friend.

Recollections of Kurt and Ernest and the fellowship enjoyed at Deluca Dwellings only amplified my misery at OK Apartments. I tried to convince myself that our social isolation was due to the layout of the buildings: Each unit looked out on the dirty concrete of the parking lot. This place lacked the character and intimacy of Mr. Deluca's old house. A more likely reason, which I'm sure Steph suspected, was my disastrous skills as a handyman. After several more half days without water, people became openly hostile toward me: sour looks, prank calls, screaming. One person scooped the feces out of his unflushable toilet and dumped them on our doorstep.

The only friend I really had there was Ted. He was always pleasant, even when I called him after midnight to help with a plumbing emergency, but his wife Janet was a hard knot of repressed anger, lashing out at tenants (and me) for the smallest infractions. Unlike the other tenant complaints, Janet's criticism barely registered: I felt too sorry for her, for both of them. Ted once told me that he and Janet had enjoyed a passionate affair when they were our age and, following a hasty wedding, were full of big plans: She would be a photojournalist and he a structural engineer for sports coliseums. Now they were in their forties, had a teenage daughter, and lived in a small apartment surrounded by college students, most of whom drove better cars than they did. Whenever I visited their place, the claustrophobia was as thick as the smell of shaving cream and hamburger grease that seemed to be always hovering in the air. Three bicycles hung from the ceiling above their couch, next to plywood wall shelves overflowing with family photos, knickknacks, and golf videos. To their credit, Ted and Janet had carved out a pink refuge in the second bedroom for their daughter, Eveline. Their bedroom was a blizzard of discarded clothes that often hung, dripping, from the unused Stairmaster doubling as a night stand and plant holder.

This was a version of the future Steph and I didn't need to see. We were only just discovering that being married involves the art of having simultaneous emotional breakdowns in the same room. Steph was finding the experience of student teaching to be something akin to exorcism, while I was beginning to question seriously my decision to pursue a doctoral degree in English. Things culminated, for me, during comprehensive exams—a brutal experience after which I purchased a bottle of gin, collapsed in front of the TV, and watched, over and over again, the *Hallmark Hall of Fame*'s presentation of *O Pioneers!* Late at night, Steph and I often talked about relinquishing the traditional life and moving to a small town in Idaho or Oregon, where she'd open a bead shop and I'd write best-selling novels. We'd wake up groggy with hope, until one of us bumped into Ted or Janet and was reminded of what happens when risky dreams go bad. Lying on our couch, we could almost see the bicycles swinging, like pendulums, above our necks.

In December, Jerry called to announce they'd experienced the biggest mid-year flight of tenants in memory, and asked if I knew why. I expressed surprise, but suspected it might have something to do with the combination of my poor plumbing skills and Janet's poor attitude. A week later, Jerry called to tell me that they were flooded with new applications. Once again, he asked if I knew why. I didn't, but eventually discovered that the tenants in 12—Ditka's boys—had spread word around our university town that OK Apartments was pet-friendly. I was soon introduced to Paula the parakeet and Fernando the ferret and Satan the albino boa constrictor, as well as a number of other new tenants who had rushed to our complex as if it were the ark.

At first, the dramatic increase in illegal pets made me even more anxious, but those feelings soon became lost in the newly elevated spirit at OK. Suddenly, it was a much friendlier place—people dropped by to say hello or to invite us to dinner or keg parties. Some even volunteered to help with small fix-it jobs. Over the next few months many of us became friends. And as our affection grew for each other, so did our affection for each other's pets. The women in 18 made a weekly habit of dropping off organic greens from the co-op for Methuselah, while I became especially attached to a pair of mice—AC and DC—owned by the heavy-metal guys in 21, even giving them Ernest's old traveling sphere. All this without any noticeable change in my skills as a handyman. What had changed was the community itself—now largely composed of people willing to go without water for a few hours every week if it meant they wouldn't have to go without the animals they loved.

For a while, we were able to keep our little ecosystem secret. Janet, unlike me, had to give twenty-four-hour notice before entering an apartment, so tenants had plenty of time to hide their pets with neighbors. But then one morning Janet spotted Ditka grooming himself in the window and immediately alerted Kenneth, Jerry's usually silent business partner. Kenneth gave the tenants the opportunity to give up their cat, but they refused. He promptly evicted them, minus their damage deposit. I watched in sadness as they loaded up their rusted Escort and drove away, Ditka perched in the rear window. I had to admire them: Instead of giving Ditka to the shelter, they'd given up their own shelter—no easy thing in winter, in the middle of a semester.

A few minutes later, Janet knocked on the door.

"I just talked to Jerry," she said. "He's very upset that Kenneth had to deal with this mess. *Very* upset. He said you had strict instructions to report any animal activity to him. And by the way, how exactly did you miss seeing that cat? You've been over there a thousand times fixing your mistakes."

I gave her some lame excuse, but she was clearly suspicious.

"You'd better be careful," she warned, "or you'll lose your job."

This time, Janet's threat hit the mark. From under the covers, I considered the fact that if I lost this job, we wouldn't be able to pay the rent. Like Ditka's owners, we'd be cast out into the dismal winter where, the price of virtue aside, finding an affordable place would be nearly impossible. There's no question who our families would blame; I could already hear Steph's father: *First year of marriage and he has them living in the streets!*

Later that week, I got a call from the women in 19, who said their toilet had been running all night. I grudgingly gathered my tools and, after knocking repeatedly on their door, let myself in. Inside the bathroom, I spotted Chowder, their rabbit. Chowder was brown and huge—the biggest rabbit I'd ever seen—and his flabby bulk was stretched out between the base of the toilet and the wall. "Hi guy," I said in an overly friendly tone that, in retrospect, I probably hadn't earned. When I reached down near his belly for the water shutoff valve, Chowder let out a horrifying screech and attacked my forearm with his sharp claws and teeth. I fell backwards onto the floor, kicking at my surprisingly animated assailant until, still screeching, he retreated to the bedroom.

While washing my wounds in the sink, I resolved to tell Jerry about Chowder. There were several good reasons. First, the fat freak had attacked me. Second, his owners were the kind of women—tall, beautiful, and aloof—who tapped into several of my residual teenage resentments. Third, and most importantly, by betraying this bad animal I might not only save my job, but I might also protect the other, good animals in the complex. Jerry's trust would be restored, so he wouldn't go snooping around the apartments. The individual would be sacrificed, but, as Aldo Leopold directed, the general health of the biotic community would be maintained.

When I announced my plan to Steph, I became the victim of another unexpected attack. She questioned, loudly, how I could ever think of doing such a thing. She recalled some of the animals I'd cared about in my life, including Ernest. "Imagine what Mr. Deluca would've done to that mouse!"

she said. "It's an evil plan, John. Even if you do get caught, we'll find another place. We'll live."

"Yeah, but where?" I replied, and stomped out of the apartment.

In the dim cave of the laundry room, I paced a row of yawning dryers
and tried to convince myself that Steph had no right to say those things
to me. Conjuring up old Clarence had been a particularly low blow—I did
know what he would've done had he caught Ernest. I recalled a conversation we had during my final week at Deluca Dwellings. Clarence sat in my
red corduroy recliner, having just finished the final bathroom inspection,
scolding me for another poor score (things had gone downhill after Ernest
passed away). He wondered aloud what my family would think of my behavior, which prompted me to wonder what Mr. Deluca's family thought of
his. Actually, I didn't know if he had any living family. I'd guessed from a
few short visits to his house—a small, cluttered ranch near a strip mall—
that he lived alone. No pictures stuck to the refrigerator, no birthdays
scribbled on the wall calendar, no dog toys or cat litter on the floor. After
all those years, the man was still a blank to me.

"You're a student of the Bible, aren't you, John?" he asked, though he'd
once congratulated me for being named the Religion Department's "Outstanding Student of Judaica." He'd even introduced me—a Congregation-
alist—to a prospective Jewish tenant as having won the award for "Top Jew
at the University of Iowa." This had been one sign among many that it was
time to leave.

"Yes, I'm a student of the Bible."

"Well, you'd never know it. I've been re-reading the book of Amos, which
I strongly suggest you review. In that book, God destroys all the cities that
displease Him. Contrary to several so-called theological opinions, I have
no disagreement with God's harsh treatment. He warned his people, he
was merciful, but they continued to break his laws. It's as if you made some
human or animal figures out of putty, but they didn't meet your standards.
What do you do with them? Well, you *smash* them and start over!" He drove
his fist into his palm, probably to illustrate what he was about to do to
my damage deposit. But years later, pacing the laundry room at OK Apartments, what I pictured was the jellied body of Ernest running between his
fingers.

I was still unsure what to do—I was no longer a boy living on my own.
I stared into one of the chicken wire storage units at a tattered corduroy
recliner. It was similar to the one Clarence had sat in to deliver that final
sermon. Years before, my friend Kurt had sat in the same recliner on the
eve of departing for LA. Earlier that day, I'd helped Kurt move his furniture

into the basement of his family's home in Dubuque. I'd asked him about the people pictured on the living-room wall, his parents, his brother, about whom he told several affectionate stories. Upon returning to Deluca's, Kurt sat in my recliner and confessed he'd been thinking of calling the whole move off. He said that in all the excitement of leaving Iowa, he hadn't anticipated feeling so attached to friends and family. He got quiet for a while, stood up, embraced me, and left.

That's when I knew: I wouldn't betray Chowder and his owners. I wouldn't betray any of them. They had a right, those people and those animals, to live together and be happy. They had a right, quite simply, to live.

The rest of the semester went surprisingly well; no one was caught harboring illegal animals. On the personal front, Steph landed a teaching job near the small town of Belle Plaine, about an hour away, and I was awarded a small dissertation scholarship. We'd be moving to the countryside, just the way we'd dreamed.

Things weren't going as well for Ted and Janet. On our last day they were hosting a high school graduation party for their daughter, and it was raining heavily, as it would most of that summer. Earlier in the week, I'd treated Ted to lunch to thank him for all his help. He surprised me by revealing that he and Janet were going to file for divorce as soon as Eveline left for college. They'd kept it together for her sake, he said, but there was no longer love there, not even much friendship. He invited us to attend Eveline's party, but now, watching their silent guests eat sloppy joes on the wet balcony above the Dumpsters, we decided to keep packing.

While Steph was off gathering boxes, someone knocked on the door. It was Jerry, holding a paper plate with a soggy, half-eaten slice of cake on it. He said he'd decided to drop by to return our damage deposit and to ask a favor. It was time to renew leases, he said, and though Janet was supposed to make the final inspections of the apartments, she was busy with the party. He wondered if I would mind doing a quick run-through on my own. I'd completely forgotten about the final inspection, which might've spelled disaster for us all. This fortunate visit from Jerry, along with the fact that I'd convinced him to hire a friend of mine—another animal lover—to be the next maintenance man, suggested the purity of my character was, as Mr. Deluca had promised, manifesting itself generously.

"I'm happy to do it."

"Thanks," he said, stepping inside. "If you don't mind, I'll just park myself here until you get back. I have some deposit checks to write."

Although school was out, there were quite a few people in the complex, and this gave me a chance to say goodbye to them and their pets. I even said goodbye to Chowder, with whom I'd long been reconciled. At last count, there were five cats, four hamsters, three parakeets, two rabbits, two ferrets, two mice, a green water dragon, a snake, and numerous fish (which weren't technically illegal, though I took moral credit for them anyway). Ascending the stairs to our apartment, I carried the satisfaction that this little community, this dwelling family, had become more diverse, more integral, than when we'd arrived—a collective strength of character that, to recall another favorite quote of Mr. Deluca's, should require no law to mend.

When I stepped through the doorway, Jerry was sitting on our couch reading the paper.

"How'd it go?" he asked, without looking up.

"Fine," I replied, then saw something move in the background. Methuselah, probably disturbed by our packing, had decided to emerge from his hiding place and was now in the middle of the floor. Jerry put the paper down, stretched, and stood up.

"Thanks again for all your help," he said, walking past me through the doorway. He stopped and turned. "Oh, yeah. Did you find any animals?"

"No," I said. Methuselah's claws scraped loudly against the kitchen linoleum. Jerry's eyes shifted over my shoulder, into the apartment. At that moment, despite my earlier conviction, despite everything, I was ready to confess, ready to turn us all over to his mercy. Before I could speak, Jerry handed me the check for our damage deposit. The amount in full.

"Well," he said, smiling, "that's a relief."

FROM THE AUTHOR

"High Maintenance" began as a portraiture piece in a 1990 graduate nonfiction workshop with Carl Klaus, who was then directing the NWP. The title was "Landlord" and the focus was on the eccentricities of Clarence C. Deluca (not his real name). It included all the quotes from the newsletters, as well as our collective response, as housemates, to his public scolding over the poor condition of our bathroom. I was still living in Deluca Dwellings at the time, so the essay was about contemporary events and people—including my friend Kurt, who read an early draft and offered suggestions, though he had already moved to LA by that time. This first version was a fairly straightforward, humorous piece that I considered submitting to a local magazine. Carl, however, encouraged me to wait and see if something larger, and more universal, emerged in subsequent drafts. What that larger something might be, he couldn't say and neither could I, but this is a mystery I've since confronted many times as a writer and a teacher: essays, like people, sometimes need time to grow and mature, to experience a fuller range of emotion and thinking, some of it painful, before they truly come home to themselves.

Back then, though, I was reluctant to follow Carl's advice—I was eager to publish, since I could already feel the pressure of the looming academic job market. But after receiving similar responses from my writing group, self-named "The Sacrificial Bunnies"—which included Hope Edelman, Dale Rigby, Kristen Gandrow, Rochelle Nameroff, and Robin Bourjaily, who hosted us at her family's farm house—I decided to set it aside for a while. A while turned out to be fourteen years. In the meantime, several major events occurred that changed my thinking about those years at Deluca Dwellings. The first was my marriage to Stephanie in 1992, and then beginning my job as maintenance man at OK Apartments, where I soon began confronting all those illegal pets. Then there was Kurt's murder, a devastating event which occurred the same month we moved into the apartment complex. These experiences—all of them raising questions about our responsibility to others—began to inform one another, leading to my decision not to report the pet owners, with whom I'd since become friends.

Other than sketching out some of those key events in a journal, I didn't write about them for another dozen years. 1992 was such a difficult year for Stephanie and me that I think, once we moved away, I just wanted to forget about it. I believe that part of the writer's job, however, is to return to those uncomfortable, tangled places and unearth something meaningful and useful for ourselves and, more importantly, for others. My unexpected return to that time period began as a simple assignment—"Write about your first years of marriage"—meant to fill in a chronological gap in an autobiographical book I was drafting. I reviewed the relevant journal entries and began free-writing. Most of the raw material for the final essay emerged from those early sessions, including the key link between my friendship with Kurt, his death, and the ethical decisions I was facing not only as a maintenance man but as someone who had just entered into the most significant commitment of his life to date. The context of my time at Deluca Dwellings, where I first became friends with Kurt, became relevant, and I re-read the old "Landlord" piece, searching for details. Suddenly all of Clarence's pontificating about "being mindful of others" took on new depth in the context of that year at OK, and I began integrating it into the draft. In addition, the humorous tone of the earlier essay infected subsequent drafts of the new piece, now entitled "High Maintenance." Humor is my natural way of dealing with things, but it felt especially appropriate for this piece, since humor (at least the kind of humor modeled by Mark Twain, whose nonfiction I studied at Iowa) is ultimately about recognizing our shared vulnerability and fallibility as human beings—and then, perhaps, embracing it. This is also known in some spiritual circles as *grace*. And grace was what all of us at OK Apartments, human and animal alike, were in desperate need of that year.

The essay was first published in 2006, after I had just emerged from what I considered an extended period of failure, having spent several years completing an unpublished memoir, as well as some initial chapters of a novel that would (thankfully) never see the light of day. I had, however, been regularly publishing nature essays, and at some point I gathered them together to see if they might become a book. I submitted "High Maintenance" to my editor at *Orion*, Aina Barton, but worried it wasn't environmental enough for that magazine. As it turned out, they were putting together an edition focusing, in part, on Hurricane Katrina, which included all those lost pets and the owners who desperately searched for them in the flood waters, defying laws and risking their own lives. Even though my piece had nothing to do with Katrina, Aina felt it spoke to the deep bond between people and animals—as deep, for some, as any human relationship. Perhaps bringing these two seemingly disparate ethical contexts together (something I'd seen modeled in essays by E. B. White, Virginia Woolf, James Baldwin, Loren Eisely, and others) would contribute to some larger understanding. I don't know if that was the case, but I do know that the essay helped rescue me as a writer. My future editor at Da Capo, Merloyd Lawrence, read the piece in *Orion*, contacted me, and about a year later, in 2008, my book *Man Killed by Pheasant and Other Kinships* was published.

Slaughter

A Meditation
Wherein
the Narrator Explores Death and the Afterlife
as Her Spiritual Beliefs Evolve

BONNIE ROUGH (2005)

(Originally published in *Bellingham Review*,
recipient of the Annie Dillard Award for Creative Nonfiction)

Part I
The Narrator, Crushed by an Evergreen Fallen
onto the Cabin Roof, Goes to Heaven

In junior high the girls took me to church camp. It was winter. They said, "Ask Jesus into your heart." In the cabin on the second night it was dark but I could have sworn there was an iridescent blue haze over the ceiling just for me while everyone else was breathing deeply, dreaming heavenly dreams. They wanted to save me because I was doomed. They wanted to help me because I was Catholic. Maybe they didn't want to help me. Maybe they were afraid because if that girl was Catholic and she looked all right, then what could that mean? The blue haze stayed as long as I didn't blink. Then it slowly built up again. I visualized my heart. It was dim with red fleshy walls and it had a wooden door cracked open. Light came from inside the door. Outside it was dark. I said to myself, Jesus, come in! My heart is nice. Maybe you are already here. But I don't want to take any chances. What about my mother and father? What about my sister and brother? Can I ask you into their hearts too? Let me be a messenger. What about my cat? What about her kittens? Let me stroke you into their fur.

But there would be no chance for that.

The blue hazed away; my eyes readjusted. I could see the creosote-covered beams in the ceiling and I could see snowy evergreen boughs outside the window. Something too big struggled inside my chest, pushing tears from my eyes.

Earlier we had played capture the flag. Two huge teams all snow-bundled and whispery, carrying flashlights and sneaking in the dark. I turned my flashlight off. The flag nestled across a snowy field somewhere in the next stand of trees. Someone else could get it. I crouched next to a Douglas fir, my back on its bumpy bark. Something let me breathe out deeply then. My eyes closed. I felt the tree and I felt the snow and away in the distance a cabin light cast soft amber into the brush, and I wanted to be blind. I wanted to be deaf. I wanted no taste or feel or smell. Something else was there, something sixth, and it wanted to be the only thing I felt. I wanted to let it take me over. I wondered how. Someone called my name. I remembered the flag. I remembered Jesus. I ran.

That night the wind picked up. The evergreen boughs bounced and shed their snow. Tiny crystals fell, spittering against the cabin windows. The wind blew harder. The girls woke up and some began crying. Something cracked. Not like a piece of kindling but resonant and huge, filling every molecule with sound. We went silent. We listened to the walls pushing back against the wind. The crack came again, popping.

That is all I know, except there might have been a moment when the roof was gone and it felt like I was outside except I was not cold. I might have seen the stars. I might have seen tree branches criss-crossing the moon.

Nothing happened next except something in my feet was different and I could stand on a carpet of clouds. The fence was white and it went as far as I could see in either direction, disappearing at each end into sun-bright fog. Behind me in line and before me in line were middle-aged men, like my father, with tired sad eyes and gently bulging bellies. It seemed I was the only girl, the only child. The white man with a white beard and a white robe had a leather book with infinite pages and he raised his quill and looked at me with one eyebrow cocked.

"Saint Peter," I whispered.

That was all I needed to know. He let me in. And when I was there I could see God if I wanted to. Jesus would be sitting in his right hand. His right hand would never get tired of holding Jesus. But what I really wanted was my gift. All my life I had known I would get a gift when I went to heaven. The gift would be called my I-Wonder List. It would hold the answers to everything I had ever wondered about. I could be in the second-grade bathroom thinking about my stuffed animals at home and softly say, "I wonder what my room looks like right now" and know that I would see an image of the room when I died. I could see a sad boy and say, "I wonder about his life." And I would have a long view of his life, like a video with every minute, except maybe bathroom time. Sometimes I asked about myself: "I wonder if I have done something beautiful." I hoped that sorting through these images of earth would keep me busy for eternity.

Part II
The Narrator Feels Small in the Universe and, Struck and Killed by a Dark Car, Becomes a Star

In a college science class I stared at the back of a boy's head. He had been talking to me for a few days, and he wanted to hold me. He did not go to church and he was the most peaceful person I had ever met. He was Dan. In the Bible, God judges Rachel worthy and gives her a son. She calls him Dan. It means "he judged."

I worried.

I worried because the professor said that many of the stars you see are not stars at all but other galaxies full of stars, and that glimmers within those galaxies are more galaxies still; and that our sun is more than a hundred earth-widths across, yet it is a small sun, much too insignificant to appear on a map of the universe unrolled over a whole city block. I worried, because if nothing was significant, what were Dan and I to make of our discovery that years before we met, when we were schoolchildren living hundreds of miles apart, we had eaten cotton candy and touched rough-skinned elephants at the Moscow Circus in Seattle, beneath the same tent, on the same Christmas Day?

When the moon waxed full, we stood on the roof of the science building with the telescopes. We were to find valleys and craters. I was careless with the telescopes, and Dan said so. Dan was always honest. I thought I was crying because he said I was careless. But really I was crying because he was always honest, and this stunned me with possibility. Bundled against the cold autumn, I walked home alone when we finished our work. My stocking cap low, my eyes still full of quiet tears. The car did not use head-lights and no one ever figured out why because all the old man driver told police was that his wife was gone and left knitting needles knitting needles knitting needles and nothing else for him to hold onto. He had been a farmer and a husband and a father and now he became nothing but the old widower who hit that girl walking home from astronomy.

But I don't learn any of this. There is a sipping sound in my mind and I watch as my bones accelerate to the speed of light. They melt into a liquid line, a stretching string of pearls. I become a star. Maybe I want to be a red giant but instead I become something small and yellow and stable like our own sun. Stars are innumerable. I am tremendous, but I feel smaller than a human being. I suddenly remember that stars die. I wait, burning slowly.

Part III
The Narrator, Consumed by Food Poisoning, is Reincarnated as a Housefly

Before we married, Dan's mother asked us one day, for fun, what drove us nuts about one another. She asked this on a day like all of our days: a day when we walked to the park on the bluff and watched the stocking-capped children swinging and the mountains slow-inching beyond the icy sound. A day when he told me stories about throwing blueberries as a boy. A day when I cut his hair. When he took my picture. When we biked to town, counting the mailmen. When we grocery shopped together and waited for each other at the end of every aisle.

The answer to his mother's question was easy for me. I said, I wish he'd wash his hands more.

There were times when we were safe in bed and ready to sleep and I felt his hands and some little stickiness on them and I made a fuss big enough to send him out of bed and downstairs to the bathroom sink. Once, in Munich, we navigated subway stations and town squares and public restrooms all day. At night he held me in our hostel bed. I had a head cold. I felt his hands, grimy, and said, "You're disgusting." I blamed him for my virus. He rolled away from me. I still protested. He got up, angrier than I had seen him before, and put on his jeans before opening the door, pounding down the hall to the shared bathroom, slamming the faucet on and off. He came back and did not speak.

But it didn't take many months more. His honest logic wouldn't let him argue with the idea that germs live on tennis balls and toilet seats and running shoes. He began to wash voluntarily.

We moved to the Midwest. We loved the storms. We kept busy and had friends. I was getting ready to have supper with the women one night, parking the Honda outside the diner. A black carpenter ant scuttled over the floor in front of the passenger seat. Using two fingers, I flicked his back straight into the floor. But I didn't crush him nearly hard enough. He writhed and something told me that I could not look away. I couldn't touch him again with my bare fingers. I had to wait there until he died. I had started this little misery, after all. He struggled on and I began to feel sick. I rustled around the car looking for something to shield my fingers as I finished him. I found a three-by-five note card and I slid his body onto the paper and made a crease and crushed him in the fold with one hard squeeze. But by that time—it had been minutes—it seemed to be over anyway.

In the restaurant I forgot about the carpenter ant, trundling on his way to work, minding his business, following his program. I ordered a hamburger with no bun and ate the meat and fake orange cheese doused in ketchup. I smiled with the girls but it was hard to focus away from my husband. Eating a meal apart from him felt off-track; how could fifty or sixty years together be enough? Each day at breakfast I began yearning for the next bedtime, the way our shapes molded together in the dark.

I wiped the ketchup from my lips, paid my bill, and left.

The next day, something clamped down. My intestines twisted like a pair of double-dutch ropes. I was hot and cold. I filled the toilet with blood. Dan took me somewhere. I remember sweat and that high-ringing TV-screen sound. I remember the phone, Dan on the phone with other people. I remember him. I remember him crying when we were alone. He said there is nothing that drives him nuts about me. He said things to me that I cannot say here, things too bare.

But also I don't remember. Some part of me slipped into wings.

Flying! I can see the rooms of the Midwest home I shared with my husband. I can see him with his books, with his head in his hands. I want to touch his hands. If only there were a little watermelon juice or barbecue grease on his fingers, a little dirt under his nails, I could land on his skin to feed. I could feel him again. But his hands are just-soaped, so I must stay here on the crusty windowsill where there is tiny carrion for me to eat and if I'm lucky Dan won't take the cat litter out too soon and I can lay these terrible eggs there. Some stranger's terrible eggs. If I'm lucky Dan won't remember how often I asked him to get rid of the bugs so I could sleep. If I'm lucky Dan won't remember what I would have liked, and in that way he will let me live.

Part IV
The Narrator Dies in Childbirth and
is Reborn as Her Own Second Son

Childbirth comes as a shock to me. And the fact that here is a son. This son is in first grade and his teacher laughs with me because we are amazed at how much they have to learn: she says Put your name at the top of your paper, but they are too young; they don't know where the top of their paper is. They pee their pants in class and they say Miss G, I peed my pants. They are not embarrassed and the other children do not giggle. This is life, they seem to know.

This son wants to make me food when his brother is growing in my belly. He wants to bring me oatmeal but he doesn't know what oatmeal is or how it starts. Dan helps him to pour the oats and pour the water and push the microwave buttons. This son loves his dad and Dan, oh, who is this man I married? He is richer now in everything. His eyes are more soulful and his touch is softer and his honesty has never gone away. This son is just like his father: black hair with a blue sheen in the summer-squash morning, a few freckles on the tops of his cheeks, big straight white teeth, a laugh to charm swifts out of the sunset. His little brother will look like me: sandy brown hair, olive skin, green eyes stark in winter like a beggar's, strange in summer like a painter's. His little brother will look like me, but I don't know this.

Please, I cry to no one, to the blackness, to my womb, *please*. It's all I can say. I have no other words. Soon, I can't even say please. I cannot speak at all. I cannot walk. I cannot lift my head. All I can do is cry. I scream. I am hungry. I am cold. I scream. I am angry. I am cold. I scream.

My father is angry too. I feel it when he holds me. He holds me away from his body and looks at me. He shifts me to his shoulder and looks away. He won't put me to his chest and tip his chin down and stare at my little hairs, hairs the color of my mother's. My mother is many floors down. She is under a sheet, and there is my milk. I will see her stone on my birthdays and sometimes on other days. I don't remember the first time I saw it. It started before I could remember. There is a rough-barked tree next to her stone. Before I'm old enough to wonder such things, I wonder where the tree's roots go. I wonder if they will topple my mother's stone. I remember the last time I saw it. The last time I saw her stone, my father cried and said forgive me forgive me. We did not go back. They said I would have no trouble with the new wife but my big brother might, since he could remember. But I surprised them all.

Part V
The Narrator Writes to Her Sons,
then Suffocates Herself with Flame

You boys are in Portugal and West Africa. My candle is here. Your father is gone. Your father is gone. I can say your father is gone because fathers are meant to go. But lovers cannot go. Lovers cannot. My candle is here and it is single, it is white and flickering and I hear the thunder and I wonder about his eyes. His soft eyes. Did they leave the eyes beneath the lids? I never know how these things work, yet I can never ask. You have to know boys: When we were young, when we first met in college, we walked in the fall. We walked to the cemetery where the October sun was still shining and the leaves had gone to orange but mostly still held on. That day I had mailed a gift to a New Zealand man I'd met that summer. When I taped up the package in my dorm room, I thought I loved the New Zealand man. Your father had a car. He drove me to the post office. He waited outside. By the time I pushed the package across the post office counter, I knew I loved your father. Then we walked in the cemetery. We read the tombstones. We looked for people who had died at our ages: eighteen, twenty-one. We stood silently over tiny graves for infants. We read riddles etched in stone. We compared statues: geometric shapes, angels with unchanging faces. Dan said, Do you want to be buried or cremated? I said, Buried. He said, Right. Me too. He showed me a bench, a monument over the shared grave of a husband and wife: a place to sit and remember them. Dan said, This is the right idea, don't you think?

But now it is raining so hard and the thunder seems to vibrate this candle's flame and that is a phenomenon I have never noticed before. What else could I notice if I live on? How much of the obvious have I missed? This house is full of shadows and wind. It is raining and cold outside and I think of your father's eyes, if they are still there. If they are there, are they wet? Are they cold? Have they any color left? Wouldn't it be better if they were no longer in the world, so I could stop wondering every time it rains? Wouldn't it be better if I could pour his ashes over my pillow and make myself sleep, breathing him with my mouth open, breathing him as he tenderly suffocates me? I am looking for ashes. I am looking for a pillow. I am looking for sleep.

FROM THE AUTHOR

I was a newlywed when I returned to campus in fall 2003 for my third semester in the NWP. Even though Dan and I had been dating for years, our marriage was just a few weeks old, and the shift in my identity gave me the need for self-examination. Who was I becoming, in my life, in my work? My poor freshman Rhetoric students, as always, would suffer my brooding through the assignments I gave them. That fall, I stopped requiring academic papers on social issues and asked instead for the personal, reasoning that self-knowledge is the first essential to good criticism. How could I ask my students to write *Here's what I think* before asking them *Who is this "I"?* How could I go on writing essays of my own without working harder to answer that question for myself? "I will never," I told my students on the first day of that semester, "ask you to do something I wouldn't do." And a week later, I handed them their first assignment. *This assignment asks you to exit your comfort zone, and by doing so, to learn about what defines you,* I had typed, making myself increasingly nervous. *The key is to be sure you're out of your everyday space and vulnerable—susceptible to emotional experiences, which can lead to learning.* To start, we opened our notebooks and silently brainstormed lists of everything we never wanted to do. Then we circled the scariest things of all and went home to face our fears.

That afternoon, sun poured like honey into the little Sears bungalow where I lived with Dan. He was just home from his classes in the School of Business, quietly reading to himself in the room next to mine. We each had our own space to study and write, plus a kitchen to share, a dining table where we came together for meals, a bed where we came together at night. And still we never seemed to tire of one another's company. In my writing room, two open windows let in the light and the breeze. I sat in my slip-covered secondhand chair in the corner of that sweetest room with warm harvest air sifting in. I wondered if I'd ever been happier. Then I imagined it all gone. With my computer on my lap, I wrote and cried, wrote and cried, wrote and cried.

The next week, with the weather still warm, my students insisted we move class outdoors. So we sat in the prickly dry grass outside the English-Philosophy Building. When I asked my students how they had exited their comfort zones, they had to raise their voices—really to shout—to be heard over the traffic on Iowa Avenue. "I talked to old people." "I went to a gay bar." Energy gathered with each declaration: "I talked about my actual feelings." "I went to a play by myself." The recitation picked up speed. "I went to church!" "I re-tried all the foods I hate!" "I visited my dad in the hospital!" "I asked a girl out—sober!"

A few months later, in a workshop led by then-visiting writer John D'Agata, several people—myself included—objected to "Slaughter." It was fuzzy in genre and purpose. We circled like vultures, stuck, waiting, until John picked up his copy and held it toward the trash can by the wall. "Are you saying she should just stop working on this piece?" he asked. And with that, a quick wind changed the question from whether such a thing ought to exist to how it might. Then my classmate M. M. C. Nussbaum said,

"What about stage directions? Just a little more, to help the reader know how to move through the piece?"

With such fine advice, I kept working on the strange thing I had written. Eventually, "Slaughter" won the 2005 Annie Dillard Award for Creative Nonfiction from the *Bellingham Review*. But before that happened, back in my newlywed year, my assignment eliminated a student.

One day, Kayte didn't come to class. She sent me a long email in place of her essay: she had dropped out of the university. *I asked myself what was keeping me here*, she wrote. *I don't want to let everyone down.* Her boyfriend back home, her family, the doctors and nurses she'd worked for—all of them wanted Kayte's dreams of becoming a physician to come true. But instead of fueling her studies, all of that love from her hometown just made her wonder why she'd left. So without telling anyone, she packed up and went home. *When I got there, I walked up to Josh as he was faced away from me in mid-sentence. I kicked the back of his shoe. He kind of hesitated, but turned around when everyone in front of him started to smile at me. When he realized it was me he dropped his drink, then tried to catch it in midair, spilling all over the place. It almost looked like he got hit by a water balloon. After a nice long hello kiss, I took him upstairs and told him I wanted to give him his Valentine's Day present. I confessed to him everything about school, and where I see myself years from now. I gave him a little white box with a navy blue ribbon on it. As he opened the box I told him that I see him in my future more clearly than anything else, and I asked him to marry me. He said yes.*

Sobered, I saw my lesson: To trust other people when they trust themselves. Maybe that would make me a better critic, a better teacher, a better writer. I kept asking my students to exit their comfort zones, and they kept surprising me. But I struggled—and still do—to keep visiting those most vulnerable places. Anything can happen.

Things I Will Want to Tell You on Our First Date but Won't

RYAN VAN METER (2008)

(Originally published in *Gulf Coast*)

That I've had a crush on you for a long time. That besides your name, I don't actually know you. That the first time I saw you I didn't think you were as cute as I think you are now, and this is a good sign. That the first time I saw you, I just thought you looked nice, and I thought if we went on a date, we'd probably have a nice time. That I also thought, He could be one who gets me over my ex. That I even thought, He could be *the* one, but not like the other one, my ex, who I used to think was *the* one—until he broke up with me, and then became just the last one. That I don't understand how you can think you're with *the* one only to find out later you are not. That I've Googled you.

That, like a sixth-grade girl with a pink notebook, I've thought about how our names go together. That, unlike the girl with the notebook, I've never written our names next to each other to see how they look, though I've considered it. That I am thankful your name isn't the same as mine, which is probably the biggest disadvantage gay people have in dating—the chance of dating someone who has your name. That I could never, never date someone with my name. That I think this is so creepy, I can't think of a man perfect enough to be the exception to this rule. That I'm also thankful my name isn't Michael or something as hopelessly common because then my already shallow dating pool would be suddenly drained. That in high school when I was obsessed with 1960s Warren Beatty movies, I wanted to change my name to Warren, which is embarrassing to admit but would have helped with this no-same-name policy because I've never actually met a Warren.

That our first date will be my first date in eight years, and counting. That our first date will be my first first date since my first date with my ex. That I don't know what to do on first dates. That my first date with my ex is a blur because I was thinking, This is my first date with this guy I like so much! It's happening right now! the whole time so I won't have much to compare our date to. That I didn't date much before my ex and then when he came along, we were together for eight years. That other than a two-week thing with this too-beautiful and too-young guy whose idea of dating was to stop by my house whenever he wanted to make out with me on my sofa and then leave about an hour later, I haven't dated since my ex and I broke up a year ago.

That for a long time after my ex broke up with me, I thought I was fine because I always think I'm fine. That I'd pretended I was fine all of spring and summer until one afternoon I was talking to him on the phone. He and I are trying to be friends, which is sometimes hard because when I first saw him, I didn't want to be his friend, I wanted to be his boyfriend. That I don't want to be his boyfriend anymore, though this hasn't always been true since the break-up. That when we were talking on the phone and he finally told me the name of his new boyfriend, even though I already knew he was dating someone else and thought it was way too soon for him to be doing so, it was hearing the man's name. That we talked a bit more and then he had to go and it wasn't until I tried to aim my fingertip at the END on my cell phone that I noticed my hands were shaking. That his new boyfriend's name is not Warren or Michael or the same as mine.

That I wasn't fine. That I had been ignoring how non-fine I was. For example, I had chosen not to notice the fact that I hadn't really slept since he broke up with me. And if I ever slept, I'd wake in the dark as if out of a nightmare, breathless, my heart knocking hard like an angry landlord. And my hands didn't only vibrate after hearing the names of new boyfriends—they shook all the time. My stomach was stuck on simmer, and all I ever ate were spoonfuls of peanut butter *and* jelly straight out of the jar. That I was usually wearing only underwear when I ate these spoonfuls, and afterwards, I'd lie down in the middle of the afternoon and take long naps on the hardwood floor and wake up sweating. That I hated turning so easily into the jilted sad-sack cliché. That I finally understood the point of clichés—they feel comfortable.

That I should have known something was wrong because I was writing a lot of break-up poetry. That when I searched for "gay break-up" books at Amazon.com, the first result was *Cowboys: Erotic Tales*.

That I saw a therapist, another cliché, which felt comfortable. That when my therapist said, "Why don't you start at the beginning?" before I could make the first syllable of the first word, which was going to be something simple like, "Okay," my voice came undone, and I started crying. That I hate crying in front of people, especially men. That crying in front of him felt embarrassing but also oddly consoling *because* he was a man. That once I started, I couldn't stop talking and crying, and telling the whole story from the beginning while my therapist took notes on a clipboard. That once I stopped, he looked at his scribbles and said, "I'm just doing the math here, but was this your first boyfriend, your first significant relationship?" and I said, "Yes." That my therapist leaned deep in his chair as his eyes turned to the ceiling and his head tilted back, and he said, with a big open mouth, "Ah."

That I hate when I tell people we were together for eight years and now we're not, and they put their hand on my shoulder and say, "Oh I'm so sorry," as if somebody died. That sometimes it feels like somebody died. That even my therapist said, "What you need to do is mourn the loss, to give yourself permission to grieve for the relationship." That months later, I was teaching a poem about death and grief to a room full of nineteen year olds, and I asked, "So how do we bring an end to mourning?" and one of my students said, "Eat lunch." That I think this kid should be my therapist. That I never say the word, "dumped." That I always say it was my ex's decision.

That if he hadn't broken up with me, I would have stayed with him forever.

That when I see you, I don't know what to do with my body. That when I see you, my eyes just want to stay there looking at your face. That whenever you see me looking at you, I have to look away because of the not knowing what to do with my body. That I don't know how to walk across rooms and talk to strangers, especially male strangers who are cute, and who have seen me look at them and then look away, even if I think they want me to. That I also don't know how to arrange my body to look like someone who wants the cute male stranger across the room to walk over. That the first time I crossed the room to talk to a cute stranger, and tried to hand him a small square of paper on which I'd written my phone number, he didn't want it and said so in a nice enough way, but I still walked off vowing never to do that again. That I have never done that again. That I will never do that again.

That I realized my ex breaking up with me changed the way I thought about my body, which is why I don't know what to do with it when you look. That I once imagined what I must look like to you, and from this point-of-view, I understood I needed new jeans and to start doing sit-ups. Also, a haircut. That I stood on tiptoes in front of my medicine cabinet mirror, shirt off, and actually said to the dog, "I *really* have to start doing sit-ups," and when she didn't know what I meant, I realized how much I talk to the dog. That she used to be our dog and now she's just my dog.

That my body actually feels different now, maybe even unfamiliar, as though it was gone eight years and suddenly returned, like when a friend borrows a book for so long that when you finally get it back, you forgot you ever owned it. That it's because he knew my body better than any other man, and he told me he loved it while overlooking its certain flaws, and now that he's left, I feel as though I don't only have to meet a whole new man but I also have to convince him to think the same way about my body. And on top of it, I should probably like him back. That one of the first things I said to my ex when he broke up with me was, "I can't believe you're making me have to date again."

That other than the too-young and too-beautiful two-week guy, and a stranger who grabbed me from behind in a public restroom, no man has touched me since my ex.

That I think you know you have a crush when the man you already think is cute is always cuter than you remembered each time you come across him in your day, and it's something about seeing him move around in the world which makes him cuter, not just his face. That sometimes I imagine what we'll do on a quiet Saturday afternoon, like get to-go cups of tea and take the dog to the forest preserve and hook our index fingers together and walk the trails swinging arms, half-mocking couples that walk swinging arms and half-enjoying the swinging of arms. Or even if the sun is out and shining, we can lie on the bed, each of us reading separate books while sharing a bag of candy and not caring that we're wasting good weather because we'll both agree that books are better than anything. That small thoughts of you—even though I don't know you—sometimes interrupt what I'm doing; like if I'm stirring a pot of soup, I'll wonder if you love tomatoes as much as me. Little things like that. That I try to assume this is what everyone does when they think about a crush though I've never confirmed this. That I do not want to confirm this.

That part of the weirdness I feel when you look at me is the sensation of having a crush, and it's because I haven't been on a first date in so long that I've forgotten this feeling. That I wonder if you can keep having a crush on a man you know and love.

That the truth is, even though I thought my ex and I were mostly happy, or happy enough, I could still always imagine loving another man one day. Not any man in particular, and I don't mean a UPS man sex fantasy either, but some other future love that wasn't him. Even when we were together. That sometimes I believe in *the* one, and sometimes I don't, though most of the time when I believe in *the* one I think we've never been guaranteed we'll actually meet this person, or if we do meet, that it can work out—maybe you're moving in two months, already have a boyfriend or wife, are named what I'm named, or maybe I'm just too heartbroken to pay attention to the fact that the guy standing in front of me is you, my one. That, at some point, I realized my imagining another man as a possible future partner, even when I was satisfied with the one I had, meant I was going to be ok. That, at some point, I also realized most of the time when I thought I was talking to the dog, I wasn't really talking to the dog.

That the absolute truth then is there isn't even just one of you. There's a whole crew of possible you's—faces I see around and glance at and act anxious in front of. You are the one with the adorable ears who seems even more nervous than me. You are the one who sings when he dances, who might look a little too much like my ex. You are the one who is so tall and with such wide shoulders that the gentleness of your smile surprises. You are the one with the dark beard, and the laugh that makes your whole serious face break open.

That for a long time, I thought it wasn't possible for two men to love and be happy together forever. That later, I started believing in this kind of love again, even though I'm still not sure it's possible. That I want it to be this way, or else I don't want it.

That on our first date we shouldn't go out for Indian food because it gives me the flu. That we shouldn't go out for sushi either because I tend to dislike people who like sushi. That I will wear my striped shirt because it makes me feel taller. That I may stare into your face from time to time and think, This is happening! That it would be nice if we could laugh often, and at some point, if you think we're having a good time, it would also be nice for you to smile and tell me so, and then I'll say something like, "We should do this again," and then, at the end of the date, we won't have to wonder what the other one is thinking. That I will want to hear your boyfriend history but will not ask, and this I promise. That sudden silence doesn't always mean awkwardness, sometimes it means ease. That we should split the bill. That you will have to lean in first to kiss me. That if you lean in first to kiss me, I will kiss you back.

FROM THE AUTHOR

I know I want to write an essay when I recognize a contradiction within myself, usually within a personal experience I want to figure out—an event, more or less, with a beginning, middle and end. In the case of this essay, I wanted to write about a contradiction of desires: newly single for the first time in eight years, I wanted to go on a date but didn't want to have to ask someone to go on that date. I wanted to start a new relationship but didn't want to have to tell the story of my previous relationship—the eight-year one. I wanted to be able to tell this story but didn't want to have to tell it on a first date, even if that's the moment when it would be most helpful—to the guy on the date with me.

An initial challenge in writing this essay was recognizing that it wasn't about an event with a beginning, middle, or end. There were events in it, but it was about that contradiction of desires, as well as about loss, grief, confusion, doubt, and healing. It was about a whole long list of ideas and feelings.

I first tried the essay as a monologue—as opposed to a soliloquy—very chatty and performative, delivered hypothetically to a guy I used to stare at in the Java House on Washington Street. Then I tried it as an open letter to the same guy—a private correspondence published publicly, such as in a newspaper. It never felt exactly right in either form, but I turned the open letter version in to Susan Lohafer, whose workshop I was taking that semester. In her comments back to me, she didn't think I was using the open letter form to its fullest potential. She suggested that if I was going to borrow a form, I needed to really *use* it.

Writing "Things I Will Want . . ." (and its initial failed versions) was the first time I really grappled with the relationship between an essay's subject and its form. Until this essay, taking an experience (by which I mean an event) that already had a beginning, middle, and end and transcribing it into an essay that also had a beginning, middle, and end wasn't ever easy, but it was a process that I understood, though only instinctually. But the content of an essay, I came to understand, should justify its use of a form and that form—whether borrowed, "conventional," or "experimental"—shouldn't be used *only* as a container. Susan helped me recognize that the open letter form was containing my material, but it wasn't helping me to realize it. An essay's form should do more than hold.

Later on, after I put those failed versions away, I read an essay by a classmate of mine, T. Fleischmann, which was in the form of a list, and I also read *The Pillow Book* by Sei Shonagon, which contains many lists, including "Rare Things," "Alarming-Looking Things," "Things That Fall," and "Things That Look Lovely But Are Horrible Inside." I liked the flexibility of these lists, especially how the "things" in each Shonagon title was obnoxiously and playfully imprecise, inviting a different kind of tension and surprise than offered by the beginning, middle, and end structure. But I thought most about how a list allows other kinds of order. On a grocery list, "carrots" aren't necessarily more important than "milk," even if they appear first. Carrots might simply appear on a list first because walking in the store, you walk through the produce stand before you walk by the dairy case. Because the subject of my essay already felt like a whole list of ideas and feelings, fitting them into a form that was also a list felt right, instinctually.

I presented this essay in workshop the following semester. In class, there was much discussion about the repetition of "that"; it began all of the sentences in the essay except two, and such insistence divided the room pretty evenly, love vs. hate. I had pictured this narrator counting off on his fingers a few things he would want to say if he were ever on a date, and then not being able to stop counting, and each "that" represented another finger. I also wanted each sentence to respond in its own way to "Things" in the title, and so each sentence needed its own "that" as a kind of verbal bullet point. There was as much disagreement about the turn near the end when the narrator reveals that the hypothetical listener isn't only one man but is actually several. Some of my classmates felt such a turn broke the rules of the essay because the narrator has more possibilities than he acknowledges at the beginning. Others felt, perhaps rightly, that it was gimmicky. But our workshop leader, Mary Ruefle, the visiting writer that year, shook her head. "It makes it lonelier," she said, and I trusted the ache I heard inside of that.

But the comment from that workshop conversation that I am most thankful for was the one suggesting I streamline my original title: "Things I Will Want to Tell You on Our First Date but Know That I Shouldn't."

What I notice now about my search for the right form is there was always something seductive to me about presenting this material as a second-person, direct address, as much as everything else lurched about. I believe that this is the most vulnerable narrator I've written, and part of what invited that vulnerability was the inexpressibility built into the essay—the "But Won't" of the title. He allows himself to articulate exactly what he wants to say because he knows he'll never actually say it.

The Last Days
of the Baldock

INARA VERZEMNIEKS (2013)

(Originally printed in *Tin House*)

In summer months, the residents of the Baldock threw open the doors to their homes and wheeled coolers out to those picnic tables that had not yet surrendered to rot. They sat, cans clutched in cracked hands, as the dogs whipped circles around the trunks of the Douglas firs where they were chained. And for a moment, it was possible to pretend that all of them had merely stopped here briefly on a long road trip, like the men and women with sunglasses perched on the tops of their heads who trooped in and out of the nearby restrooms, rumpled and squinting.

Sometimes they walked over to the information kiosk and collected travel brochures, so they could rustle the pages and pretend to plan journeys to state attractions they knew they would never reach. *Crater Lake is the deepest lake in the United States . . . Shop Woodburn Company Stores!* Later, when it grew dark, they crumpled the sun-warmed paper in their fists and used it to start fires in the barbeque pits. When the flames finally died, they tossed whatever leftovers they had to the dogs, their eyes spectral in the dark, and left them thrashing beneath the trees. Then they climbed inside their cars, stuffed blankets in the window jambs, released the seats to reclining, and slept.

It would never be entirely clear who first settled the rest stop. Without any kind of written record or historical archive to consult, the collective memory of the community extended only as far back as its oldest resident, a vast, coverall-clad man who claimed to have arrived in 1991, after years of wandering the bosky wilds along the interstate with his pet cat. Together they set up house in one of the rest stop's secluded back lots in a ragged van that remained more or less parked in the same place for the next eighteen years. In that time, dozens more joined the man and his cat, drawn not by any map, or formal settlement plan, but by stories that had begun to circulate among those versed in a certain kind of desperation, how there was a place off Interstate 5, about fifteen miles outside Portland, Oregon, where someone with nothing left but car or a camper and a tank of gas could stay indefinitely. Just past milepost 281, the blue signs signaled the way: REST AREA NEXT RIGHT. There, in the farthest corner of the rest stop named for Robert "Sam" Baldock, "father of Oregon's modern highway system" and "honor roll member of the Asphalt Institute," in a lot marked overflow parking, battered rigs creaked to a stop and never left.

Screened by thick stands of evergreens planted under Lady Bird Johnson's Highway Beautification Act, this back lot settlement grew in relative isolation, its residents largely invisible to the outside world as they pursued the dystopian task of making a life in a place where no one was ever meant to stay. They were a population of fifty, give or take, although no formal census was ever attempted on their part, or deemed necessary for that matter, since they all knew perfectly well who they were and the myriad ways in which they spent their days. Seniors waited on social security checks. Shift workers slept. Alcoholics drank. A single mother knocked on truck cabs. A one-eyed pot dealer trolled for customers. Others sat locked in their compacts fingering sobriety tokens.

They even had a name for the state in which they found themselves. "We call each other Baldockians," said a woman named Jolee, who had spent the last three years residing in a rusting van that now only occasionally ran and which periodically needed pushing across the parking lot to a new stall in order to appear in compliance with the rest stop's posted rule that a vehicle remain parked on the premises for only twelve hours at a stretch.

The orientation of new arrivals was typically left to a man everyone called The Mayor. It could never be precisely ascertained just what he had done to earn this title, whether it was down to a general sense of grudging respect for the fact he had once let a gangrenous toe rot in his boot because he was too cussed to see a doctor, or the rumors that he kept a pistol in his RV. Either way, The Mayor took it as one of his principal duties to greet all incoming residents: "I don't have money, booze or cigarettes to give you, and don't give me any shit. But I always have food to share. Ain't no one out here gonna starve."

Rest stop etiquette discouraged questions, and this allowed most people to maintain a presence as blurred and unfixed as the reflections cast by the bathroom's unbreakable mirrors. No one asked about the swastika tattoo that crept just above a collar's edge. Or why a police scanner rested in the pocket of a driver's side door where insurance papers were normally kept. In his own more talkative moments, The Mayor liked to remind anyone who cared to listen that "you meet all kinds here, the bad and the good. Mostly good. Still, best advice I can give is to look out for yourself. Don't trust anyone." What he meant was that everyone at the rest stop, himself included, had versions of the truth they preferred to keep to themselves, maybe even from themselves.

The owner of a 1970s Dodge motor home known as the Vaquero was a perfect example of this: Ray, of ashen face and hair, who smoked away his days beneath a sign that warned oxygen tanks were in use. Nearby, a small fawn colored dog named Sweatpea nipped the air, trying to catch circling flies with her teeth.

For as long as any one at the Baldock could remember, Ray had been saying he had six months to live. He also said that he had been born in Kentucky, but moved to Oregon when he was 15 or 16, and over the years had felled trees and labored as an auto mechanic. Somewhere along the way he had done irreparable damage to his lungs and now had emphysema. "All that asbestos in those brake pads," he figured.

Sometimes he would bring up wives, children. "Buried," he said, in a voice pumiced by all the years of smoking. But it was never clear what he meant by this, whether he meant them or his memories of them.

He told some people he was 70, others that he was 68. Sometimes he said he had fought in Vietnam. Others times he said he'd never been. He had been at the Baldock for going on 15 years. Twelve. Thirteen. Maybe he didn't know himself anymore, one day so much like all the rest, mornings with the paper, coffee on the hotplate, and then when the shakes set in, a nip or two, on through the day, until his voice feathered at the edges and his eyes bobbed and pitched behind his glasses.

"It's not that we want to be here," he said. "It's just we can't get out of here. I'm 68 years old. I get $667 a month in social security and some food stamps. That's all I've got except for what I can make panhandling or rolling cans. Everyone here's the same, figuring out how to get by on less than nothing. But I'll tell you, I don't know how much longer I can make it. Last winter was a bearcat. It was hot dogs on Christmas. I was snowed in for three days. Icicles from top to bottom." It was his habit to pull out a pouch of tobacco and some papers and roll a cigarette with yellowed fingers as he talked. "I'm too damn old for this anymore. I don't like being here. But this is all I have left, just me and my dog and this damned old rig. You live in an old RV cooped up for days on end. It's a helluva thing to keep your sanity."

Lately, he'd had a mind to light out for the coast. He was sure he could get a job as a park host somewhere. He was rationing gas, trying to hold back some cash. He'd even picked a day for his escape: "First of the month, I'm fixing to be gone."

He said this in October 2009. He said it again in November and in December and in January and in March and in April.

He was, in fact, among the last to leave the Baldock.

Jack was among the last to arrive, driving in the night after the Fourth of July, his gas gauge near empty, the trunk of his little white Ford four-door loaded down with what he had managed to take while everyone was gone, like his wife had asked him to, so the kids wouldn't see: a Route 66 suitcase packed with clothing, including his good church suit; an old camping cooler; a pile of books; a sleeping bag; a tent; and a scrapbook his wife had made that contained the boys' baby pictures and photos from the barbecue they threw in the backyard the day he got his union card.

He'd told himself he'd leave the rest stop come morning, but the truth was he had nowhere else to stay, not on $206 a week in unemployment, not with his wife and kids needing money whether he lived with them anymore or not and the debt collectors lining up. None of his family would take him in, and for a long time, he felt it was no less than what he deserved for what a fool he'd been. He'd known, after all, as someone who'd been raised in a strict family of Jehovah's Witnesses, and who had married a committed convert, that secret strip club visits and hours of adult moves streamed over the internet and the TV ranked up there on the list of the faith's most grievous sins, right along with lying about it all, repeatedly. Not to mention the fact that it seriously ticked off his wife. Still, he couldn't stop. According to the church elders, who referee such matters, excommunication was the only fit punishment. Disfellowshipping, they called it. And while a part of Jack wanted to believe that maybe this was all a bit out of proportion to the offense, he did, as he put it in his more contrite moments, "regret the crap I put my wife through, and I really did put her through crap—it's not as if I was an angel, and then got kicked out." And so he accepted the elders' pronouncement of his exile, if only because he did not know of any other way to appropriately express his sense of humiliation, other than to make himself disappear.

At first, he had pitched a tent at the state campground, but at $15 a day, the campsite fee added up quickly and he was left with less than $100 a week. It was there, in passing, that another man mentioned the Baldock.

He resisted the idea initially, but then, one day, driving along Interstate-5 on his way to a job interview, he decided to pull off at the rest stop exit.

At first, he told himself he was only stopping to use the bathroom. But when he still had some time to kill before his appointment, he found himself following the man's directions, guiding his car past the rows of mud-spattered semis and the volunteers dispensing Styrofoam cups of grainy drip coffee, until he reached the invisible line separating those who were simply passing through from those who had nowhere else to stay. He sat for a few minutes and watched through the windshield, his engine ticking. He watched the dogs, running and rucking the earth beneath the trees to which they were roped. He watched the groups hunched around the picnic tables, sunburned and knotty-limbed. Their laughter, loud and muculent, beat against the sealed windows like birds' wings.

It took three more days for his resolve to build, then take. He parked that first night as far as he could from all the other cars, which were gathered close, fin-to-fin, as if in a shoal. For much of the night, Jack sat bolt upright, certain he could hear voices, the jangle of dog collars outside his door. But in the morning, he couldn't think of anywhere else to go and he wanted to conserve what little gas he had left. And so he'd remained there, just sitting in his car, although the heat was oppressive, and he'd tried hard to look like he wasn't looking. He could sense everyone else was looking at him, too, though not in an unfriendly way. Sometimes someone would wave. Or nod at him, like an unspoken acknowledgement of something shared. It made him uncomfortable, the way they seemed to recognize something in him before he saw it in himself. At the time, Jack didn't yet feel he had anything in common with anyone at the rest stop; he still believed he was only meant to remain there temporarily.

No one else thought he'd be long for the Baldock, either. He worked hard at cultivating the appearance of normalcy, or what passed for it in the world beyond the rest stop, anyway. His clothes looked freshly pressed, though he had no iron. "If you take them out of the dryer and fold them just the right way while they're still warm, you can make it look like you've creased them," he explained. He spit-shined his shoes. Although he had only a high school equivalency degree, he regularly worked through stacks of books and in careful handwriting filled pages of a journal.

He had grown up in rural Clackamas County, province of swayback mares grazing in pastures beneath power lines, blankets over windows, wood smoke in the winter, but also, here and there, scattered starter mansions with river views and streets named for song birds and mountain glens where garages sat full of ATVs and boats and tools bought on credit. The childhood Jack described, when asked about it, sounded isolated with few friends and life largely revolving around the family's faith. At some point though, he had become possessed of the idea that he would like to live in a world that offered experiences more expansive than those he'd known. After years of working variously as a pizza delivery man and a swing shift worker at the local dairy, he had decided it might be wise to learn a trade, like carpentry, and had been fortunate enough to apprentice out just as a condo-building boom swept through Portland, industrial wasteland giving way to *planned urban communities*. Suddenly, he was framing walls in million dollar penthouses with Mt. Hood views.

Once, during that time, he recalled how he had taken his wife to a restaurant near the development in downtown Portland that he had been helping to build from the inside. Up until then, he and his wife had only gone out to places like Applebee's and months later, Jack could still recall the white tablecloths, the white flowers, the way the food came out on white plates, "like paintings." They'd sat by a fire pit, and looking back, he realized it was the first moment he had allowed himself to think he might be different, that all along he had been living the wrong life, and he had imagined they might return, maybe for an anniversary, but then work started slowing. And then the housing bubble collapsed completely, and the condos men like Jack had been working on were left to stand empty, their interiors an expanse of white.

The layoff came not long after they bought their first house. At the time, Jack had thought it made sense to enroll in school again, learn another trade, like driving truck, so he'd have something else to fall back on. The school told him he could take out loans, and he figured if he found work quickly he could pay it back before long. He graduated with his CDL just in time for gas prices to spike, and companies to start slashing fleets. He'd added another $5,000 in debt to his name. It wasn't long before they had to let the house go, the minivan, too.

Now, at the rest stop, he often read Dave Ramsey's book, *Total Money Makeover*, by flashlight at night, marking passages that seemed particularly relevant, such as Ramsey's "7 Baby Steps to Financial Success." On Ramsey's advice he had started to portion his unemployment money into envelopes which he marked, "bills," "gas," "savings," "fun," and "allowance" for his two boys, even if it was just a couple of singles. Later, he would add "child support." At this point, he had had been out of work for six months. He was 36.

He carried copies of his resume in the front seat of his car, in case an opportunity arose to hand them out. Once he had flagged down a maintenance crew working at the rest stop and pushed a sheet in their hands, but that had so far failed to yield any leads, as had any of the applications he had filled out through the unemployment office. He did not have a criminal record or a problem with drugs or alcohol, though he had joined a 12-step group, hoping it could help him fix whatever it was that was broken in him, as he put it. He'd even tried to keep going to services at the Jehovah's Witness Kingdom Hall in the nearby town of Aurora, although, in keeping with the expectations of the excommunicated, he sat in the back, and did not try to speak to anyone.

In the context of the rest stop—where a convicted pedophile with a habit of luring little boys into his vehicle, driving them to out-of-the-way places, then forcing them to have sex at knife point, happily lived out his last days in a Baldock parking stall; where, a few years ago, the decomposing body of a 56-year-old man believed to have been murdered was found in the underbrush not far from where vehicles parked; and where, more than once, the grip of a pistol could be glimpsed peeping out from under a seat—Jack, with his resumes and scrapbooks and savings envelopes seemed remarkably naïve, impossibly good, even. "Just a baby," said Ray.

Of course it all depended on your perspective. Jack knew his parents and his in-laws, and most importantly his wife had plenty to say on the subject. Or not say, as was the case when they hung up on him. And he couldn't disagree. He was all those things. He was nothing. He had tried to come up with a list of good things about himself in his journal. He wanted to be honest.

Finally, he wrote, "I am alive."

They had their own ways of measuring time. One month had passed when the medical delivery truck arrived to drop off a new set of oxygen tanks at Ray's Vaquero. It was fall when the school buses came to fetch the children. Saturday when the church group came round, offering pancakes and prayers. Thursday, when the bus from St. Vincent DePaul pulled in with its on-board kitchen and cafeteria tables where the seats should have been, a place out of the cold where they could eat plates of fettuccini and turkey melts. Night when the jacked-up pickup came through the lot, its driver tapping his brake lights, waiting for one of the semis to wink its high beams back, the signal that he should park and climb inside to name his price.

They marked the persistence of loneliness by the frequency with which a knackered blue van appeared, groaning its way through the parking lot, the driver waving gently like a beauty queen on a float. It was the man and his cat. A local social service agency had managed to get them both into a low-income apartment complex, before they had to face a 19th winter at the Baldock. Still, the van coasted past nearly every day. "Too quiet in my new place," was all he'd say, before launching into his latest theories about the causes of unemployment and homelessness to anyone who stood outside his window long enough to listen—NAFTA, globalization, illegal immigration. He never required any kind of acknowledgment, except to be heard, engine idling, cat perched unblinking on the passenger seat.

Soon, they felt the weather turn, winds wailing cold out of the Gorge and turning the condensation that accumulated inside their windshields while they slept into streaks of ice. Mornings, they followed each other's footprints through the frosted grass to the restrooms where they washed and shaved beneath the industrial lights. They smoked to feel their fingers again.

One night, after most of the other residents had retreated to their cars, Jolee stood by the picnic tables with an insulated coffee cup in her hands, watching the receding taillights of cars bound for the freeway onramp. "All any of us want is to get back over there one day," she said, her eyes tracing each exit. "We want to be over there with them, doing normal things. Like paying taxes. I'm serious. Don't laugh. The day I pay taxes is the day I know I've made it back to the mainstream. That's what I want, to feel normal again."

Less than a month later, she was gone. She gathered her things from the floor of the van and stuffed them in a backpack, then walked over to Jack's car to borrow his cell phone, which she pressed against her bruising cheek. "I'm sick—I need to go somewhere to get better," she said. Her boyfriend watched silently from the open door of the van with the dogs, his own face welted and swollen. Eventually, Jolee's father's pickup appeared and she climbed inside the cab. When the car carrying her had disappeared onto the freeway, her boyfriend got up and walked over to a sign directing patrons to the rest rooms, and he drove his fist into the metal as hard as he could. Finally he spoke. "Time to go to the store," he said. "Who's going to give me a ride?"

He went on a bender that lasted days, stumbled around in a fog. He accidently locked one of the dogs inside the van, the pit-bull mix who'd so loved Jolee, and by the time he remembered and opened the door, the dog had torn the stuffing from the two front seats, shredded all the clothing strewn about, then snapped at the boyfriend's reaching hand. No one knew what to say, and one of the cardinal rules of the rest stop was that no one was in a position to judge, so they all kept quiet, and let him go on saying that the tears he wiped from his red eyes were down to the dog.

Jack for his part had given up his silent visits to the Kingdom Hall and had stopped talking about one day reconciling with his wife. He felt embarrassed when he thought about his uneasiness that first night at the rest stop, how he had imagined he could somehow hold himself apart. He'd seen enough now of "what people do to survive" to realize that he had been deeply misguided to ever presume he'd known what it was to endure. Like the woman who often left her 10-year-old son alone in their motor home while she visited the rows of parked semis—and even the rigs of her neighbors—creeping back hours later, sometimes with what looked like bite marks on her chest. Or the people who stood by the low wall near the rest stop bathrooms, which they called just that, The Wall, flashing signs made from the cardboard backs of empty half-racks at all the weary travelers emerging from the cocoons of their cars, road-tired and bladder-full, hoping to part them from some change. They organized their panhandling in shifts in an attempt to maintain some kind of order and equity, but there were often fights when they tried to chase off anyone who didn't live at the rest stop, the tweakers who had homes or hotel rooms, but who would parachute in just long enough to beg money off tourists for a hit. In the hierarchy of the rest stop they were openly disdained, cursed as cheats and liars, not because of their habits, but because they presented themselves as homeless when they had somewhere else to go.

As a rule, the police tended not to bother the rest stop residents, unless someone called in a specific complaint. Although officials had long been aware of the community living there, and the local District Attorney's office certainly made its position on the matter clear when it began referring to the Baldock as "Sodom and Gomorrah," the unspoken policy, at least on the ground, appeared to be one of benign neglect, so long as the residents kept themselves out of the run sheets.

But then, one day, a particularly ambitious state trooper came through and red-tagged a number of vehicles for lapsed tabs, and rather than watch their homes disappear on the back of tow trucks, those residents had quickly disappeared. The whole scene had struck Jack as unbearably unfair, and he couldn't stop thinking about it, like a pawl clicking over and over again into the grooves of a gear. He sat at one of the picnic tables for hours, trying to organize his thoughts. Finally, he had gotten in his car and driven to the local community center. There, in front of the pubic computer, he began to type.

Rest stop residents often spoke of how much they feared breakdown— as in, "My car's broken down on me twice now and I don't what I'll do if it happens again"—but the community counted among its members enough mechanically minded tinkerers and auto parts pack rats to stoke even the faintest hopes of a vehicle's possible resurrection. Once, the head of the local faith-based community center came to see the reality of life at the rest stop for herself. She had hoped to remain inconspicuous, but one of the residents immediately spotted that her car's bumper was close to falling off. Before she could say anything, he had thrown a blanket down onto the pavement, and begun to poke around the car's underside. He quickly diagnosed the problem, dug up the necessary parts, fired up a soldering iron, and within a few minutes, was waving her back on the freeway. Impounds were an altogether different matter, however, and represented perhaps the most frightening possibility of all for someone whose car was their final vulnerability, the one thing left tethering them to any illusions of stability. Losing a car to impound almost certainly meant losing that car for good. Or as Jack wrote at the computer that day: *How can we afford to get them out? . . . (W)e cannot pay for towing or impound lot fees. Even if we pull all our money together, this is an expense we cannot afford . . .*

He typed: *We have a very difficult time paying auto insurance, gas and food. Many of us are looking for work, and have to travel long distances in search of employment. Gas prices are high and food stamps are good but not enough people receive them. None of us can afford a home, an apartment, hotel or even campgrounds . . .*

He typed: *We are homeless!*

And he typed: *All we seek is a safe place to live, until we find better options. The rest areas provide us a place to sleep, help each other out and have access to the rest rooms 24 hours a day . . .*

He kept going until he'd filled the whole page. He imagined it could be a letter of grievance, written on behalf of the entire community. He ended with the line, *Thank you for your support.* Later, Ray read a copy at his dinette, holding it close to his glasses. "Boy can write!" he said, speaking as if Jack was not standing next to him. "Fancy. There's even semi-colons!"

For Jack, the biggest declaration in the whole letter had come down to a single word.

We, he had written.

It was a word drawn from the nights they made communal meals, pooling their ingredients to stretch emergency food boxes and food stamp allocations. And someone would fix up plates for those who slept during the day and did shift work at night, balancing leftovers and thermoses of coffee on the hoods of cars for the drivers to find when they woke. When they bought each other presents from the Dollar Store, socks and singing cards (Wild Thing, You Make My Heart Sing). When they climbed on Ray's roof to fix the leaks that soaked his bedding, or when they helped Jack change his oil, or lent one another cooler space or propane. But also: the moments when the dogs wouldn't stop barking, and someone was screaming for them to shut the fuck up, and the trash cans were overflowing, and someone else was asking yet again if they could get a ride to the Plaid for more beer and smokes, but offering only pocket change to cover the gas it took, and the old timers would grouse about how the young had no work ethic, just wanted to smoke dope and have everything handed to them, and then they'd ask if they could take a shift at The Wall. It was Ray, pawing women's asses, braying and frothing at The Mayor that he was nothing more than an imposter, that he, Ray, had more right to appoint himself sovereign of the Baldock. And the boy who spent his nights alone in the motor home, waiting for the sound of his mother at the door—he did not go to school, but no one said anything, just as no one said anything about the abrasions on his mother's chest that turned purple, then green.

In a single word, Jack had written himself into the Baldock, and he meant it unequivocally—the whole kind, desperate, resourceful, ugly truth of it—without denial or defense.

Later, after the exodus, but before the vanishing, sometimes the memories would still surface. What it smelled like: cedar boughs and boggy earth; urinal cakes; the fug of wet fur and hunger breath; moldering floor mats; wet socks against the heating vents. And what it sounded like: the snick of rain on the car roof; the bronchial, hawking churnings of the semi engines; the rest room air dryer, screaming against their cold-burned scalps and faces; the way the freeway never stopped squalling, like the sea.

Thanksgiving marked the turning, the point at which time and memory began to pull away from them, though no one recognized it at the time. They were all too preoccupied with the planning of a Baldock-wide turkey feast, and a list had been drawn up of ingredients to procure, and while everyone seemed to agree on mashed potatoes and gravy, some people disagreed over the value of stuffing and yams.

Given the local inclination toward fabulation—"Don't trust anyone," The Mayor had said—it made sense, in retrospect, that people were more inclined to favor holiday preparations over a disconcerting little story that was knifing its way through the populace. Apparently, a few days before Thanksgiving, one of the cleaners told someone who told someone else that as of the first of the month, the rest stop would have a new landlord, and this one was not likely to be predisposed to the current laissez faire living arrangements. Rumor had it there were all sorts of plans to spruce the place up—artist demonstrations, fancy coffee, solar panels, nature trails (Ray had harrumphed over this one: "Nature trails my ass; if there was any nature to find here, we'd have killed it, gutted it and eaten it by now, had a big old barbecue").

But disbelief gradually gave way to paranoia. Whether it was the maintenance worker cum informant who was the first to mention the possibility of police sweeps, mass roustings, or it was the result of the residents' own grim future-casting, soon the rest stop was frantic with speculation of an impending eviction. And so it came to pass that the inhabitants of the Baldock found themselves in a curious and unexpected position: after telling themselves for as long as they could remember that they couldn't wait to leave this place, they now realized they wanted nothing more than to stay.

They tried to talk about other things. On Thanksgiving morning, the early risers crammed into Ray's motor home, downing cups of coffee and taking turns putting the soles of their shoes on the propane heater until they could smell the scorched plastic, savoring the burn of their numb toes. "You know what I love most about Thanksgiving?" Jack said. "Football. It's been months since I've actually seen a game on a TV, not just listened to it on the radio." Everyone nodded and they talked about how luxurious it would be to sit on a sofa again, stupid with turkey, tasked with no other concern but whether to flick between the college or pro games. It struck them all as the height of decadence, of insanely good fortune.

And then the man who looked like a gnome and hardly ever socialized had knocked on the motor home window, faced flushed. "Did you hear they're going to kick us out?" he shouted.

"You're late to the party," Ray barked through the window. "We've been hearing that days now. All bullshit. Just scare tactics. They want to make the panhandling stop. I've been here for thirteen years and this one always makes the rounds, but it's all show. Look at me, I'm still here. Haven't run me off yet."

He raised his cup of coffee to his lips, but his hand was trembling.

"Anyway, I'm leaving. Come the first of the month, I'm outta here. I'm sick of all the drama. The doctor tells me I got six months to live and goddamned if I'm gonna die at the Baldock. I should drive this heap to Mexico, drink beer morning to night and ask pretty senoritas to sit on my lap for the rest of my days. I won't let them kick me out. I'll be long gone before that happens."

His face was red and the cords of his neck had stretched taut, and no one spoke for fear of winding him up even more. He reached down, took a beer from the case he kept under the motor home's dinette, and poured some into his coffee as though it were cream.

And at this, the day began its slow slide into drunkenness, everyone except Jack who agreed without complaint to make a run to the convenience store when provisions ran low, and came back with $5 worth of Powerball tickets, bought from the "fun" envelope. The jackpot had reached $183 million. "I figured if we won, we could all buy houses, maybe even the rest stop," he said.

Eventually, the main rest area, which had been heaving with holiday travelers, slowed to a few scattered cars. Afternoon tipped toward evening. The food remained uncooked, the air inside the motor home brackish with smoke. Ray, who had been brooding over his mug for some time, finally spoke. "Some people would say they wouldn't be caught dead living like this, in this nasty old RV," he said. "But you know what, I consider myself so fortunate to have this. Because when you've had nothing—and I've been there—living like a no-good dirty bum, low as you can go, in the streets, and people won't even look you in the face, like you're an animal or something and you don't have shit. You're thankful for whatever you can get. Let me tell you, I've never been so thankful."

He jabbed his face with his fists, trying to hide the tears.

"I don't know what I'll do if I lose this. I can't live like that again."

No one spoke.

Abruptly, Ray collected himself, and motioned for another beer. "You know, when I leave here on the first, I won't miss a single one of you fools, stuck in this place. Now if you excuse me, I need the pisser."

The dreaded December 1st arrived without incident. Outwardly, at least, each day resembled the next. Ray's Vaquero did not budge. The blue van traced its lonely revolutions. Jack dropped money into his envelopes. Finally, he had found a job, working the graveyard shift at a manufacturing plant for $9.30 an hour, making "plastic injection molded components." And while at first he was relieved to be receiving a paycheck again, he had been doing the math and it had dawned on him that it would never add up to the kind of money he needed to move into even a modest apartment, first, last and a deposit. He'd toured a complex in Wilsonville—"They had microwaves built into the cabinets, it was beautiful; I'd give anything to live in a place that nice"—but they wanted to see proof of income of at least $1400 a month. He made just under that. "It's like a merry-go-round you can't get off," he said. "I don't know how I'm going to get out of this."

So he continued to sleep in his car at the rest stop, and hoped each day that it would not be his last. Everyone did. Some people urged a discussion of contingencies, the way some families spoke of fire escape plans or des-

ignated meeting places following natural disasters. What about forest service land? Was there a remote wooded space where they could all caravan?
Too cold this time of year, the pessimists argued. Think of all the food and
propane and water you would need to stockpile.

For those who did not possess a high tolerance for ambiguity, the public computer at the community center had yielded some valuable recon-
naissance. And while it did not net answers specific to their fate, a cursory
Google search had at least given them a more solid idea of where to project their fears. For example, they now knew the name of the new landlord: Oregon Travel Experience, a "semi-independent state agency," which
had been granted the go-ahead by the legislature to take over operations
of five rest areas that had previously fallen under the purview of the department of transportation. None of what they could find was written in
what one would call plain, unadorned speech, but one phrase in particular, about helping the rest stops achieve their "full economic development
potential," seemed to them to translate as having something to do with
money—be that making money or saving it. Either way, it was not a concept that tended to live comfortably alongside homelessness. Intuition told
them that much.

Then one day, a woman appeared in the back lot and by the pristine
condition of her vehicle, they immediately rejected her as a new arrival.
Later, as they dissected the encounter, they hoped that it had not been
held against them that the first person from the Baldock to greet her had
been one of the community's most dedicated drinkers, and she was not
at her most sober or her most modulated. As it turned out, their visitor
was the new landlord, head of the OTE. Her name was Cheryl, she said,
and she'd stopped by because she wanted to personally reassure everyone that they were not just going to kick people out of the rest stop, but
they should know things were going to change at the Baldock, and those
changes would affect them in ways they were probably not going to like.
Also, they were not going to tolerate any more panhandling. She had been
talking to people from the community center where many of them received
assistance, and she hoped that over the next few weeks they all might be
able to work together to find a way to help everyone move on from here to
something more stable.

"We're not stupid," Ray said later, after she had left. "It was just a different way to say the same thing: you're out of here."

Jack, for his part, was not ready to embrace Ray's cynicism. He wanted
to believe that the promise made to them had been sincere, that no one
would be kicked out of the rest stop until they had somewhere else to go.

But where would that be? Whenever he tried to trace a clear path out of the Baldock for any of them, it always came out confused, occluded, unmappable. No sooner had he considered a possible exit route, than his mind would throw up a fact that directly contradicted this option, and so it went, fact upon fact, one after another, like a thicket of construction barricades choking all conceivable ways forward.

Fact: There's not a single homeless shelter in this particular county.

Fact: What if you have a criminal record, or are living with someone with a criminal record? What if you have an eviction in your past? No one rents to you.

Fact: Most RV parks won't rent a spot to rigs ten years or older, yet that's what most people here own.

Fact: Most one-bedroom apartments in the area rent for $750 a month.

Fact: You are losing sleep, Jack.

Indeed, it had reached the point where he was reporting for his graveyard shift bleary, his thoughts smudged, sluggish. He blocked his car windows with sunshades to keep out the daylight, but still he winced and churned at the sounds of his neighbors, who seemed to be tuning their voices to a pitch that matched the collective anxiety level.

They were all growing irritated with each other. It was easier to cloak fear with anger. Ray, for one, erupted that his motor home was henceforth off limits to any more coffee klatches. He locked himself inside and did not speak to anyone, though they could see him, lowering at them all through the blinds. He should have been happy. The Mayor had abdicated, putting the Baldock in his rearview mirror. As it turned out, he was not homeless, merely restless, prone to long cooling off periods when confrontations arose at home. After carefully considering his options, he'd apparently found the idea of returning to the missus preferable to gutting out another day in the uncertain climate of the Baldock.

In this way, they welcomed spring, agitated and aggrieved. Finally, a meeting was called at a local church. Cheryl from the OTE promised to be there, along with the man she had recently appointed the rest stop's new manager, as well as local politicians, a deputy district attorney, a trooper from the state patrol. A good number of people from the rest stop showed up, even a few people who no longer lived there, including Jolee, and the man with the cat. Ray had said he would boycott it.

"Ornery old fart," Jolee said, and called him on his cell phone until finally he relented and showed up late, smelling of drink, his face gray. Jolee pressed a mint on him.

They sat at tables set with tablecloths and formal place settings for lunch and bouquets of lilacs and bulb-flowers and bowls of pastel wrapped candy. Someone had set up a white board at the front of the room. The Canby Center, the social service agency that had worked most closely with the residents over the years, had organized the event, and the center's director at the time, a woman named Ronelle, the one whose car had been fixed by a rest stop resident, spoke first.

"We're here so that you can have a chance to speak," she said. "Please be frank about the obstacles and the barriers you face so that the people here can understand what you are up against, and what might help you. "

But how to make it all fit on a whiteboard?

They each tried to tell a corner of the story, but it came out fractured, a chorus of elisions:

"A lot of places won't let you have animals and animals are part of our sanity."

"I had to sell my house and move into my motor coach."

"Your *motor coach*?"

"SHH!"

"You have no idea how scary it is trying to imagine where to go to next."

"I never thought in my life I would panhandle, but I've flown a sign to raise money for my tags, my insurance."

"A lot of us have jobs, but they aren't very stable or we don't have enough hours to make what it takes to get back in a place. I make just above minimum wage, and I have child support to pay too. "

"Some of us just slipped through the cracks. We don't have alcohol problems, medical problems, or a mental illness. There seems to be no help for us."

"I've had times where I've worked double shifts, and then I need to catch up on my sleep all at once. I might sleep twelve hours straight in my car. I need a place where I can do that, so I can keep my job."

They tried defiance:

"You know, if you move us, you aren't going to get rid of us. We just go hide."

They tried humor:

"How long have you been at the rest stop?"

"A long time, kiddo."

They even tried nostalgia, as if summoning lost time could alter the future: "We used to have movie nights in the summer. Jack had this portable DVD player and he'd set it on one of the picnic tables, and we'd all pretend like we were at a drive in . . ." But on this day, in this context, the suits, the flowers, the hushed and shrouded tables, it came out more like a eulogy.

Ray said nothing.

Finally, the director of the OTE rose and spoke. "We understand you're a community, a neighborhood." She respected that very much. She knew they were afraid, but she wanted to reassure them a "transition plan" was being developed. "We promise to keep you informed every step of the way."

So much talking, and yet, in the end, it would be silence that told them the most, the phrase that went unspoken—*you can stay*—only the scrape of chairs all around, the rustle of skirts and suits departing.

It was time to go, but they dawdled. The man with the cat shook the remainder of candy into the front pocket of his overalls. Jolee went with her boyfriend off to a quiet corner to talk, their heads close together. And Jack stood off to one side, rehearsing one last speech: "What if I did some maintenance work for you, strictly volunteer. Could you let me sleep there during the day?"

Maybe, in those last days, if they had been different people, more like the people they saw on the other side of the rest stop, those so seemingly certain in their slacks and sedans, counting down the miles to home, maybe then they might have known what say to each other that sounded reassuring, how this was a good thing, a fortunate thing, to be given the chance to leave this place and pretend as if it never existed, wasn't that what they had wished for all along. As it was, they hid their faces under propped hoods, screwdrivers clenched between their teeth, cussing recalcitrant old engines into cooperating for the drive ahead.

Proffers had been extended to each resident, elaborate relocation plans crafted by a committee of representatives from the county and state, police officers and social workers and housing specialists, assembled at the request of Oregon Travel Experience.

For Jack, and seven others, immediate slots in a six-week class offered through the county that would help him land low-incoming housing. For the more complicated cases which eluded immediate solutions, pre-paid spots in campgrounds and motels. For one man, detox. For others, help navigating social security applications and untangling veteran's benefits.

For Ray, a stall had been secured in an RV park willing to allow his old motor home, but he wasn't having it. "It's nothing but a drug den. Place is full of methheads and thieves. Sweatpea and I won't go. No sir." He was convinced that everyone who agreed to leave the Baldock was just being set up for a fall. "Once they get you alone," he said, "you just become a number. We should hunker down, like a family."

He was still refusing to budge, right up until the last day in April when everyone was asked to caravan to Champoeg State Park, where a block of adjoining campsites had been booked for the weekend, after which everyone would head on to whatever was next. True to its word, Oregon Travel Experience had not kicked anyone out, but now that all the residents had been offered someplace else to stay, that promise was no longer in effect. From this day forward, anyone who remained at the rest stop, or who returned, was subject to trespassing charges should they violate the twelve-hour rule. Or as Ray, put it, "Once you leave, you leave. They've got you."

As the others made their last minute preparations, packing and replacing flat tires and loading squirming dogs into cargo holds, Ray hunkered down in his Vaquero. "This is gonna get nasty," he promised through the blinds.

His standoff lasted less than two hours. By late afternoon, he'd pulled into one of the empty berths at the state park, next to Jack, who stood shrouded in tent fabric. "Can someone please help me with the poles?" he called. This was the campground where Jack had first stayed when his wife had kicked him out. It also marked the first time in nine months he did not have to sleep in the seat of a car.

The sun warmed the leaves of the ash trees, and together, they sat at one of the communal picnic tables, shouting at the dogs as they skittered through the underbrush—"Sweetpea! Sweetpea! Come back here! Listen to Daddy!"—and admiring the trailers of their new, if temporary neighbors. "See that pop-up camper over there, that's probably only a year or two old. Lots of room. What would you think something like that costs?" It was a nice campground, everyone agreed, though they would never venture further than their assigned row. They would not go where there were birding trails and pet-friendly yurts, or to the field reserved for disc golf.

Once, long ago, this had been a pioneer settlement, the last stop for those who had set off across the plains, drifting west until they couldn't drift any more. Now, on special occasions, volunteers in period garb demonstrated for park visitors the difficulty of life for those who had once tried to settle on the frontier's edge. Once a year, in "a celebration of Oregon's rugged pioneer roots," the curious and the masochistic could attempt the skills once required for daily survival, such as wheat-threshing, butter-churning or wool-carding. This particular weekend, however, happened to mark the occasion of Founder's Day, when, one hundred and sixty-six years ago, the settlers had gathered here and voted to establish a provisional government. The land where the park now sat was to have been its capital. Already, in preparation for the festivities, men in boots and braces were rigging draught horses to plow furrows in the earth, as minivans puttered past.

Such re-creation was all that was left of what had once transpired here. Eighteen years after the historic vote, the nearby river tongued its banks, then surged. The settlement vanished beneath seven feet of water, and the pioneers scattered. They never rebuilt.

Twelve miles away, for the first night in more than a decade, the back lot of the Baldock stood empty, like a stretch of backshore licked clean by the tide.

Ray disappeared first, pulling out of the campground in the middle of the night. No one heard from him for months, and everyone started to wonder if he might really be dead.

The rest of them tried to forget the Baldock, as they moved into rent-assisted apartments and bought plants and hand towels, and carefully positioned throws on the backs of donated sofas, where they sat, absorbing the quiet. Some of them found jobs, and some of them lost those jobs when they failed the drug tests. Those who had not been visited by their children in their car days practiced unfolding hide-a-beds, stored plastic cartoon cereal bowls in the cupboards.

They called each other, until they didn't.

Months passed.

They did not see the workers bent over the long-neglected flowerbeds of the Baldock, planting local bulbs of peony and iris.

Then Ray finally surfaced, alive, but rigless and grieving. "I did a dumb thing," is how he says it. "Had some drinks with a friend, drove off, cops stopped me. I'm not gonna lie, I had beer on my breath, so they gave me a DUI, took the motor home and I couldn't get it back."

How he hated to beg, but he needed a place where he and Sweetpea could stay, and for a while the joke was it looked like a Baldock reunion, because it was Jolee who offered to help. She had a couch of her own now— she'd managed to get a little rent controlled apartment in Oregon City that she shared with her boyfriend, though since he'd left the rest stop, he was no longer a boyfriend but a fiancé—and she told Ray he was welcome to the living room. Just like old times, they'd said, and crammed into the little apartment. And it was true, that it was just like old times, but that wasn't always good. Ray grew restless—"can't stand being cooped up"—and took to walking Sweetpea around and around the apartment by himself, until one day he slipped on a patch of ice and shattered his hip — "broke the socket clean through" — sentencing himself to forty-five days in a hospital bed.

"I've got nothing," he said upon his release. "I'm 70 years old and not a damn thing to my name." He'd left Sweetpea with Jolee and he hoped to buy a van "come the first of the month, something less than $750, if I can find it." But even if he found a new vehicle, he had no idea where to go anymore. He insisted he had no desire to return to the Baldock. "That's all in the past. Gone now. Buried." But the way he said it sounded like he wished that wasn't true.

Jack was the one who went back.

"Yes," he'd said, and then he'd hung up the phone and set it on the coffee table of his apartment where he now kept his journals and scrapbooks in a neat, angled stack. Then he'd picked it up again to quit his job at the manufacturing plant.

On his last shift, his colleagues presented him with a sheet cake. They had scribbled a message onto the chocolate frosting. "Good luck Jackass!"

He pulled back into the parking lot of the Baldock on New Year's Day.

It was January 1, 2011, and he had stayed away from the rest stop for a total of six months.

They set him to work mowing the grass and emptying trash and erasing graffiti that erupted in the bathrooms. He pruned the trees where the dogs once howled and paced. He made it his special project to tame the overgrown spinneys that romped the edges of property, only to unearth in his sculptings a decade's worth of discarded liquor bottles, tattered condoms, needles, all carted away like evidence of an obscene archeological dig. He worked until no signs of the old settlement remained.

Also among his duties was to tend to travelers who might be stranded, who needed a jump or a tire changed or some gas. Sometimes, he gave directions. For all this he made $10 an hour, and received benefits better than those he had known when he was with the union. It was the happiest he'd felt in a long time, but also strangely the loneliest.

For company, he sought the continued counsel of Dave Ramsey, who strongly advised a second job if one hoped to shed debt more quickly. And so, on his days off, Jack returned to the manufacturing plant and his cake-giving colleagues of the graveyard shift.

The borders of his life had now contracted to a simple triangulate: work, his boys, and the garden apartment where he hung his sons' framed school photos on the wall and taped a flier for a one-bedroom house for sale at the end of the road with an asking price of $129,000 to the refrigerator. He had been adding figures endlessly in his head, and although he was so tired he sometimes found his mouth refusing to form whole sentences, he was certain, if he could keep this up, and his car did not break down on him, he would be debt free within the year, maybe even build up an emergency fund.

Sometimes rumors reached him about his former neighbors at the Baldock. Ray had disappeared again and no one knew where he had drifted to this time. Jolee had lost her apartment and was last sighted living with her fiancé in the bushes at the confluence of the Willamette and Clackamette Rivers, where, according to the local Parks and Recreation Department, "the beaches attract both the sun worshipper and the nature lover with sun, water, nature paths and wildlife!" A notice in the classified section of the local newspaper had recently announced the auction of all the possessions in her storage unit for lack of payment.

Mostly though, Jack lived in silence, quietly and deliberately tracing the same route each day, from rest stop to apartment, and at the end of it, the sound of his key in the door; then, dinner at a small pine table with a single place setting, and his manager's first review of his work at the rest stop which he re-read as he ate: "Keep up your consistently good attitude and strong work ethic and you'll do fine."

You'll do fine, he tells himself. And most days he believes it, but still, at work sometimes, he'll see a car in one of the rest stop parking stalls, belongings strewn in the back, and in a glance he knows.

FROM THE AUTHOR

Out in the field, I tend to be very quiet. Intense, but quiet. It turns out I'm pretty good at sitting in silence in truck cabs next to someone for hours as the rain beats down and an old wet dog gums a bone at our feet. I like to wait and see what unfolds, rather than jumping in and trying to shape a situation to my expectations. The downside of this approach is that it requires a tremendous amount of patience—constantly talking yourself down from the ledge: what am I doing, what does any of this mean, where is it headed, how will it fit together? It also demands a significant investment of time—being willing to stick around even when nothing is happening. The word I use to describe this is inhabitation, sitting still with something long enough that I'm no longer registering only its loudest, most extreme details. Instead, I'm becoming familiar enough with the physical and psychological landscape to start perceiving the silent, day-to-day rhythms, the small, but significant moments that make up a life but so often go unwitnessed. With this particular essay, many months would pass before I could see the arc of it with any real clarity, before I started to grasp its deeper and more significant implication—what would happen to the residents of the Baldock once they lost the only community many of them had known.

When I arrived at the NWP in the fall of 2009, I had logged close to a year on the ground with the residents of the rest stop, and I wanted very badly to start writing. I remember turning in a draft my first semester that focused on the point of view of just one resident—in response to a workshop prompt to write an biographical essay—and my professor at the time, Susan Lohafer, said in her comments something to the effect of, interesting, but you seem to be skating past the complexities. *Write to the paradox.*

That's the line that cracked everything open for me. I should get somebody to put that line on a sampler that I can frame, or better yet, turn it into a tattoo, because I still think about it and find it helpful, even now.

And so I kept re-shaping the essay with Susan's advice in mind, while continuing to report on how the lives of the rest stop's former residents were unfolding now that they had scattered. But as I shared drafts in workshop, one question that emerged, and which would ultimately set off a deep internal struggle for me, was the degree to which I should be present as a narrator. Back in my newspaper days, I'd often been called out by editors for being too present in my stories, for using the "I" too freely. I was reluctant to claim complete omniscience, to wash away any sense of the consciousness—however flawed, however fragile, however human—through which my accounts were filtered. But with this particular essay, my gut instinct was to keep my presence in the narrative as spare as possible. It felt wrong somehow, when writing about a group of people who had for so long felt invisible, unheard, to suggest that this could also be about my experience. But now, in workshop, I was hearing people say, where are you?

I certainly admired other nonfiction writers who had grappled with this question, perhaps none more achingly or intensely than James Agee in *Let Us Now Praise Famous Men,* his account of the lives of three Alabama sharecroppers and their families. As much as Agee saw it as his responsibility to document the unfolding present in which he was embedded, he also saw it as his responsibility to document his own emotional responses to the very intimate and ultimately fraught task of trying to tell the story of another's life.

And yet when I attempted a draft in which I appeared more heavily, it felt clumsy, awkward, distracting. The other option, as I saw it, was writing from the omniscient third-person point of view, as journalists like

Katherine Boo have done to moving effect, giving readers the sense of total immersion in the lives of people whose struggles are often the subject of intense legislation and debate and yet whose day-to-day experiences frequently go undocumented. So I wrote a version in which I completely banished the "I," kept the self telling the story at a remove, but that also felt stilted, the seamlessness off-putting. I went on like this for some time, debating with myself, writing, deleting. Nothing felt right. Then another NWP professor, Robin Hemley, helped snap me out of my paralysis with a simple question: Why are you framing this as a question of all or nothing, one or the other?

Not that I would ever wish the frustrated, stuck and fretful part of my experience on anyone, but I can see now how useful it was to have flailed about for a bit, how much it helped me to have wrestled with two possible approaches, and to feel stuck because I found both equally compelling. When I was a reporter, there was rarely time for radical revisions—your first draft was more often than not your only draft—so I'd never had practice at imagining all the alternate realities that could exist for a single story. I suspect that's why my first impulse was to define my choices in the narrowest terms possible—the "I" visible in every frame vs. complete detachment—when, in fact, I would come to see there was much more room for nuance and complexity in how to signal my presence within the narrative. In the end, it was not unlike like the process that I had learned to trust out in the field reporting: a willingness to sit with what is not immediately understood and to wait, to resist easy answers, to realize how valuable a sustained period of uncertainty can be.

Desperate for the Story

GEORGE YATCHISIN (1988)

(Originally published in *Quarter After Eight*)

My life doesn't have order unless I'm reading a novel.

Right now my life is messy inside and out. My cat's often flecked with fuzz and dust. Foods mutate on plates waiting to be washed in the kitchen. My desk piles up with unwritten letters, unfilled forms asking an airline, my academic department, and the government for money. Each afternoon I'm eager to nap, while enjoying seven hours of sleep anyway.

I am not reading a novel now.

Many people (myself included) like to blame the decline of the world on television. This notion is too easy. Perhaps the novel is the problem. The novel offers us a neat procession of event to event. A friend once joked that in Dickens, if an old man sat down next to the hero in a hallway, you knew the man would become important a few chapters along. It would be comforting to be in such a world. Loose ends would be tied, questions answered. We would all understand the old man in the hall.

Alone, no one makes sense in our lives, but we can weigh them up against a Heep or Micawber and something is bound to turn up. To get to C from A you'll visit B. It's easy, isn't it?

The third Saturday of every month I drive to Mechanicsville to hold a poster in front of a GWEN tower. GWEN stands for Ground Wave Emergency Network. Strategic Air Command built these $1.4 million installations in case an electromagnetic pulse destroys all normal forms of communication, threatening to divide the United States into cut-off localities. The towers really mean people are planning to fight and win a nuclear war. Bombs will be dropped, and GWEN's purpose will be to keep the missiles coming. It's for people who think an individual payload has a meaning, like a bullet with a name on it.

The dictionary is the novel of the English language. The story's still going; it's run of the mouth. Like our lives, our stories, we can't be sure of the end. So the dictionary stands between life and the novel. They are frightening books, even abridged, for they contain all life's mysteries.

A "spider diver" is a "dabchick" is a "European little grebe." That's just one stupid bird. Knowing about it is worthless. I cannot even attempt to picture a dabchick, wouldn't be able to point one out if a hundred birds waddled into this room. Yet the word itself is currency, diffusing the dictionary, somewhat.

I am desperate for the story.

"When the show ended, someone asked about the plot to kill Hitler. The discussion moved to plots in general. I found myself saying to the assembled heads, 'All plots tend to move deathwards. This is the nature of plots. Political plots, terrorist plots, lovers' plots, narrative plots, plots that are part of children's games. We edge nearer death every time we plot. It is like a contract we must sign, the plotters as well as those who are the targets of the plot.'

Is this true? Why did I say it? What does it mean?"

–Don DeLillo, *White Noise* (a novel)

Novels lie. Life doesn't fit Freytag's Pyramid. I am young, so I can imagine I'm still in rising action. When things go right — they must in my novel — I'll be at the climax. Then there's the long slide with the mellifluous French name, denouement. That's old age, senility, death. Part of me looks forward to this pattern, knowing all the twists and turns that can occur. All my life I've been in school, reading, knowing how much I still have to read, but getting suckered in every minute.

Days spill into days. I can't tell you what I did January 23, 1988 or 1986 or 1984. Maybe if I did some research, hunted up a syllabus. There might be a novel half-opened somewhere for each of these days, quietly leading me on.

I wonder if the people who do film continuity, who make sure the angles of tea cup handles don't alter from take to take, I wonder if they have more ordered lives. Can their awareness of the minute, can it be a grace? My guess is they burn out faster than air traffic controllers.

Jean-Luc Godard made their lives much easier with *Breathless*. With the jumpcut he took continuity away, characters could now begin and end sentences in two very different places, rooms, worlds apart. Godard kept moving. For a while turned political. Recently he's said, "I'm not interested in politics, I'm interested in women's panties." Even his ability to find pretty French women and undress them doesn't keep me interested in recent, disjointed films, too much. I keep looking for the meaning.

I must admit that I don't make it out to the GWEN tower every month. Sleep is one excuse, uselessness another. Often I go for the people. Bob Lamb, protest leader, got famous holding up a box of Cornflakes on Donahue. A year or so ago, Donahue covered the farm crisis from Cedar Rapids, and Bob raised his box and said, "It costs three times as much to pay for this box than it does to pay for the corn that goes inside it."

John Tinker, home-made bumper sticker maker, won a U.S. Supreme Court case. John, when in high school, wore a black armband to protest the Vietnam War. The Court said his school had no right to suspend him.

When I tell people about GWEN, I tell them these stories. It's all I have to tell.

A metaphor will do. Perhaps a jigsaw puzzle, and it's not merely the middle that's the problem. All I can find is edge. Each piece extends on, every few connect, but they all possess one smooth side. Eventually three sides of the rectangle come clear. I'm persistent and sweating: I'm not sure how far this puzzle might extend.

I could be Susan Alexander Kane in the unfinished Xanadu. Swallowed by that fireplace, she looks like a log waiting to burn. Susan puts puzzle after puzzle away, but the house is never finished. Welles had to have it that way, or the sets would have run up too much cost. He couldn't have afforded to shoot a magnificent mansion, tapestry draped, furniture full. But jigsaws come cheap and easy, with time. She'll walk away to belt-out her life in some Atlantic City dive. Notorious enough to still be found by the press, she's a swizzle stick stirring on its own. Puzzle for puzzle.

This essay isn't possible without films and books. This life. Fiction shouldn't be Robbe-Grillet's attention spent on a man riding an escalator. He cannot be forgiven. I'm hungry for Dickens, page after page of coincidence reconciled. If a novel would let me in, I'd jump, willing to wallow in its fiction, its lies. I would ride the tide content, forgetting a life where I might fall into a Big Boy for a thrill some Saturday, not hungry, not hungry for food at all.

FROM THE AUTHOR

The essay has its roots in the commonplace book—not that I'm sure I knew what that one was when I wrote this one. I came to the essay academically late, with much reading to do, after years as a poet (Iowa MFA 1984) who also wrote journalism because it at least nominally paid and I was/am an opinionated cuss about films and music. The Nonfiction Writing Program was a wonderful place to learn about how the essay was related to assay, a way to weigh things out, and as someone digressive to a fault, to me it seemed like home. I'm far too fascinated with coincidence over cause, confusion over motivation, mixed metaphor and genre deconstruction over the through line, true and tried. "Desperate for the Story," then, gets to be a sort of confession and dismissal. Originally written for Carl Klaus' Essay Writing Workshop in 1985, it was my attempt to have the traditional and fracture it, too. Build a shape with words and the meaning will come.

As for commonplace books, think of them as verbal scrapbooks, the place you store ideas, lines, words, titles that catch your fancy. Bacon, Milton, Emerson, Thoreau, they all kept them (as if they knew generations of scholars would need sources to pore over later). I love that one Renaissance Italian named Giovanni Rucellai kept one and referred to it as a "salad of many herbs."

"Desperate for the Story" is just that, an attempt to build up enough sections that a greater story could be told. It's also a place to keep a host of things I liked, from an excerpt from *White Noise* (I remember Klaus asking if others had read it and then he said, "Someone gave it to me when I was in the hospital recovering from my heart attack and it almost gave me another one") to protesters devoted to a cause in an era when the Cold War hadn't quite finished thawing (it amazes me we're now in an age where you need to explain a fear of atomic annihilation to people). I love Dickens and the dictionary, roadside food and randy auteurs, and I wanted them all in one place, somehow. (As a side note, many of my essays were film besotted as I also had the amazing luck to be co-director of the University of Iowa Bijou, a student-run film series that screened more than fifty films a semester. My MA/W thesis was about films.)

So the trick became how to bring it all together and have it not be a trick.

To do that, I worked hard on having each section sing a bit on its own—I figured if each chunk worked as a kind of mini-essay, that might help build up the power of the entire piece. I also knew I needed to keep it short, as no reader would have the patience for a work with twenty of these "essayettes." Numerous sections got started and perhaps began to get some polish but were abandoned. The piece actually got longer after it was workshopped, thanks to helpful comments. I needed to bring it together even more, as it originally was too fractured and centrifugal. That's when Susan Alexander Kane dropped in, working on those puzzles in Xanadu, an image, a symbol, someone I'm still writing about, having penned a poem about her just this year. So, yes, writing is one way we work our obsessions out.

In fact the essay kept growing, sort of becoming a commonplace book all its own. A few sections got longer; I had to learn to trust finding the right closing beat for each one, to avoid the temptation to over explain. I realized while writing "Desperate for the Story" that much of what happens happens in the pauses, when the reader makes connections (you would hope you've led them to)—for instance writing, "Novels lie," right after quoting from one. There's even a years-later version that tried to graft a whole 'nother essay into it; that turned out to be a sum much less than its parts.

And then the essay ended much more definitively in yet another draft, with this:

> Blundering endward, of all things. How about this: I don't welcome the old man in the hall with open arms—he might be me. The hall might be long. It's dark (such hallways always are), painted black, scratched and chalked with letters I sense spell. So I walk and read in the dark. Is a sense of ends enough for an end to come to? It's enough to make me cry: the last page of my novel is held just out of my eyesight.

Even today I like that last line, but again, writers often have to kill the lines they love if they don't work in the work at hand. Of course those lines can then go into the commonplace book and rise, as every orphan eventually deserves a home.

Acknowledgments

The editors of this volume would like to extend their deepest gratitude to the Founders of the Nonfiction Writing Program, those who have taught in it, and the students over the years who have benefited from one another as well as their mentors. Particular thanks to Carl Klaus, David Hamilton, and Susan Lohafer for their early assistance, and Joe Mackall and Ned Stuckey-French for valuable feedback at the end. Most of all, we would like to thank Mary Laur at the University of Chicago Press, who was an unflagging supporter and whose wise guidance made this book possible.

From *Man Killed By Pheasant*, "High Maintenance," by John T. Price, copyright © 2008. Reprinted by permission of Da Capo Press, a member of The Perseus Books Group.

Ryan Van Meter, "Things I Will Want to Tell You on Our First Date But Won't," from *If You Knew Then What I Know Now*. Originally in *Gulf Coast* (Summer/Fall 2009). Copyright © 2009, 2011 by Ryan van Meter. Reprinted with the permission of The Permissions Company, Inc., on behalf of Sarabande Books, www.sarabandebooks.org.

Editors and Contributors

HOPE EDELMAN graduated from the NWP in 1992. While still a student, she sold the proposal for her first nonfiction book, *Motherless Daughters*, which was based on an essay she began in Mary Swander's portraiture class in 1991. *Motherless Daughters* became an international bestseller and has since been published in seventeen countries and thirteen foreign languages. Five subsequent books include the bestsellers *Motherless Mothers* and *The Possibility of Everything*. Her work has been widely anthologized in such collections as *The Bitch in the House*, *Behind the Bedroom Door*, and *Goodbye to All That*. She has taught at the Ohio State University, University of North Carolina at Wilmington, the University of Iowa, and Antioch University-LA, and frequently speaks about nonfiction at events that have included the LA Times Festival of Books and multiple AWP and NonfictioNOW conferences. Every summer she returns to Iowa City to teach in the Iowa Summer Writing Festival. In 2012 she was inducted into the Medill Hall of Achievement at Northwestern University, where she received her undergraduate journalism degree, and in 2014 she was honored as an Alumni Fellow at the University of Iowa.

ROBIN HEMLEY is the author of eleven books of nonfiction and fiction and has won numerous awards for his writing, including a Guggenheim Fellowship; three Pushcart Prizes in both fiction and nonfiction; The Independent Press Book Award; an Editors' Choice Award from The American Library Association; State Arts Council grants from Washington, North Carolina, and Illinois; The Ohioana Library Association Award; and fellowships from the Fine Arts Work Center in Provincetown, The MacDowell Colony, and many others. His work has been published in the United States, Great Britain, Canada, Australia, Japan, Germany, the Philippines, Singapore, and elsewhere. Among his works are two popular craft books, *Turning Life into Fiction*, now in its fifth edition, and *A Field Guide for Immersion Writing*. He has also written two memoirs, *Do-Over* and *Nola: A Memoir of Faith, Art, and Madness*; four collections of short stories; a novel; and a book of investigative journalism, *Invented Eden: The Elusive, Disputed History of the Tasaday*, which centers on a purported anthropological hoax in the Philippines. *Invented Eden* is currently in development with the BBC for a feature length film. With Michael Martone, he coedited the groundbreaking literary anthology *Extreme Fiction: Fabulists and Formalists*. A graduate of the Iowa Writers Workshop, he returned to Iowa to direct the Nonfiction Writing Program for nine years before moving to Singapore to direct the writing program at Yale-NUS College and also serves as writer-in-residence there. He has recently completed a film with Erik Sather, *Jewish Caviar*, which is an official selection of several prominent film festivals. He is also the founder and co-organizer of NonfictioNOW, a biennial literary conference exploring the myriad forms of nonfiction. He has recently completed his second novel, which is set in the contemporary Philippines.

ROBERT ATWAN is the series editor of *The Best American Essays*, which he founded in 1986. He has published on a wide variety of subjects, from American advertising and early photography to divination in the ancient world and Shakespearean drama. His criticism, reviews, essays, humor, poetry, and fiction have appeared in numerous periodicals nationwide. He lives in New York City.

MARILYN ABILDSKOV is the author of *The Men in My Country*, a memoir set in Japan. Recent essays and short stories have appeared in *The Pinch*, *The Sun*, *AGNI*, and the *Laurel Review*. A recipient of a Rona Jaffe Writers' Award, she lives in the Bay Area and teaches in the MFA program at Saint Mary's College of California.

FAITH ADIELE'S NWP thesis, *Meeting Faith*, about becoming Thailand's first Black Buddhist nun, was published by W. W. Norton and won the PEN Beyond Margins Award for Memoir. She is also writer/subject/narrator of *My Journey Home*, a PBS documentary based on her Nigerian/Nordic/American heritage, and coeditor of *Coming of Age Around the World: A Multicultural Anthology*. Winner of the Millennium Award from *Creative Nonfiction*, Adiele was named "One of Five Women to Learn From" by *Marie Claire* magazine and teaches in the Bay Area, at VONA: Summer Workshops for Writers of Color and in the MFA Program at California College of the Arts. "Black Men," short-listed for *Best American Essays 2005*, was the first essay she wrote at Iowa.

JON ANDERSON, a former staff writer for the *Chicago Tribune*, *Chicago Sun-Times*, and *TIME* and *Life* magazines, lived in the Edgewater neighborhood of Chicago and was married to Pamela Sherrod Anderson, a writer and documentary filmmaker. He was the author of *City Watch: Discovering the Uncommon Chicago*. A devoted friend of the NWP and its graduates, Jon passed away in January 2014.

JO ANN BEARD is the author of a collection of autobiographical essays, *The Boys of My Youth*, and the novel *In Zanesville*. She has received a Whiting Foundation Award and a Guggenheim fellowship in nonfiction, and teaches in the MFA program at Sarah Lawrence College.

JOE BLAIR is a refrigeration mechanic and writer who lives in Iowa with his wife and four children. He is the author of the memoir *By the Iowa Sea*. His essays have appeared in the *New York Times*, Salon.com, the *Iowa Review*, and the *Christian Science Monitor*.

ASHLEY BUTLER is the author of the essay collection *Dear Sound of Footstep*. Her work has appeared in *Ninth Letter, jubilat, Gulf Coast, Creative Nonfiction, POOL*, and *The Believer*. She lives in Austin, Texas.

JOHN D'AGATA is the author of the collection *Halls of Fame* and the book-length essay *About a Mountain* and the coauthor of *The Lifespan of a Fact*. He has edited *The Next American Essay* and *The Lost Origins of the Essay*. Currently he is serving as director of the Iowa Nonfiction Writing Program in Iowa City, where he lives.

WILL JENNINGS'S work has appeared in the *Wapsipinicon Almanac, ICON, Fugue, Water˜Stone Review, River Teeth* and the *Southern Humanities Review*. His work has been nominated numerous times for The Pushcart Prize and was awarded the Brenda Ueland Prose Prize. He teaches at the University of Iowa where he lives with his wife, Susan Futrell. He still aspires to play centerfield for the Chicago White Sox.

TOM MONTGOMERY FATE is the author of five books of nonfiction, including *Beyond the White Noise*, a collection of essays, *Steady and Trembling*, a spiritual memoir, and *Cabin Fever*, a nature memoir. His essays have appeared in the *Chicago Tribune*, the *Boston Globe*, the *Baltimore Sun*, *Orion*, the *Iowa Review*, *Fourth Genre*, *River Teeth*, and many other journals and anthologies, and they often air on National Public Radio and Chicago Public Radio. He teaches creative writing at College of DuPage in suburban Chicago.

MICHELE MORANO is the author of *Grammar Lessons: Translating a Life in Spain*, published by the University of Iowa Press. Her work has appeared in journals and anthologies such as *Best American Essays 2006*, *Georgia Review*, *Missouri Review*, and *Fourth Genre*, and she has received honors and awards from the Rona Jaffe Foundation, the American Association of University Women, the Illinois Arts Council, and the MacDowell Colony, among others. She teaches creative writing at DePaul University in Chicago.

ELENA PASSARELLO is on the MFA faculty at Oregon State University. Her book on the human voice, *Let Me Clear My Throat*, was a finalist for the 2014 Oregon Book Award and received the gold medal for nonfiction at the 2013 Independent Publisher Awards. An actor and voiceover artist, she has written essays on music, performance and the natural world that have appeared in *Oxford American*, *Slate*, *Creative Nonfiction*, the *Normal School*, and the *Iowa Review*, as well as the anthologies *Pop When the World Falls Apart* and *After Montaigne*. She is currently writing a book about animals in popular culture.

DAVID TORREY PETERS has had short stories and essays published in *Prairie Schooner*, *Epoch*, *Shenandoah*, *Indiana Review*, *Fourth Genre*, *The Pinch*, Gawker.com, and *Best Travel Writing 2009 and 2010*. He has worked for PBS's *News Hour with Jim Lehrer* and as an editor for the *Kampala Dispatch*, a Ugandan newsmagazine.

JOHN T. PRICE is the author of three memoirs, *Man Killed by Pheasant and Other Kinships*; *Not Just Any Land: A Personal and Literary Journey into the American Grasslands*; and *Daddy Long Legs: The Natural Education of a Father*. A recipient of a nonfiction fellowship from the National Endowment for the Arts, his essays have appeared in *Orion*, *Creative Nonfiction*, the *Christian Science Monitor*, *In Brief*, and *Best Spiritual Writing*. He teaches nonfiction writing at the University of Nebraska at Omaha.

BONNIE J. ROUGH is the author of the 2011 Minnesota Book Award-winning memoir *Carrier: Untangling the Danger in My DNA*. Her essays have appeared in numerous periodicals including the *New York Times*, the *Sun* magazine, *Florida Review*, the *Iowa Review*, *Ninth Letter*, *Defunct*, and *Brevity*, as well as anthologies including *The Best Creative Nonfiction*, *The Best American Science and Nature Writing*, and *Modern Love*. She teaches in the Ashland University low-residency MFA program in creative writing, and she is a prose editor for *Versal*, an award-winning international journal of literature and art based in Amsterdam. She lives with her family in Seattle.

RYAN VAN METER is an assistant professor of nonfiction writing at the University of San Francisco. His work has been published in *River Teeth*, the *Gettysburg Review*, the *Iowa Review* and others, and has been selected for *Best American Essays* and *Touchstone Anthology of Contemporary Creative Nonfiction: Work from 1970 to the Present*. He also holds a Master of Arts degree in creative writing from DePaul University in Chicago.

INARA VERZEMNIEKS worked as a reporter for thirteen years at the *Oregonian*, where she was a finalist for the Pulitzer Prize in feature writing. Her writing has appeared in the *New York Times Magazine*, *Tin House*, *Creative Nonfiction*, and *Southern Humanities Review*. In 2012 she received a Rona Jaffe Foundation Writers' Award for nonfiction as well as a Richard J. Margolis Award of Blue Mountain Center. Her first book is being published by W. W. Norton.

GEORGE YATCHISIN is the Communications Coordinator for the Gevirtz Graduate School of Education at UC Santa Barbara and a freelance food and wine journalist. He taught writing at UC Santa Barbara and Penn State University for thirteen years and is coauthor of *Writing for the Visual Arts*. In addition to his NWP degree he has an MFA in poetry from Iowa and a MA from the Writing Seminars at Johns Hopkins.